Harriette M. Forbes

The Diary of Rev. Ebenezer Parkman, of Westborough, Mass

For the Months of February, March, April, October, and November, 1737

Harriette M. Forbes

The Diary of Rev. Ebenezer Parkman, of Westborough, Mass
For the Months of February, March, April, October, and November, 1737

ISBN/EAN: 9783337116408

Printed in Europe, USA, Canada, Australia, Japan

Cover: Foto ©ninafisch / pixelio.de

More available books at **www.hansebooks.com**

THE DIARY

OF

Rev. EBENEZER PARKMAN,

OF WESTBOROUGH, MASS.,

For the months of February, March, April, October and November, 1737, November and December of 1778, and the years of 1779 and 1780.

His motto was:—"*Sinceritas in Cordo est dulcis Natricula senectutis.*"
"Thy Heart is not right with God. Let me bear this saying in mind that I may keep clear of such a charge upon me!"

EDITED BY

HARRIETTE M. FORBES.

PUBLISHED BY
THE WESTBOROUGH HISTORICAL SOCIETY.
1899.

PREFACE.

In giving a part of Mr. Parkman's Journal to the public, the Westborough Historical Society feel that they are making a valuable contribution to local New England History. It is not only a vivid picture of their own town during the last century, but a type of all New England towns,—the petty cares and economies, the small jealousies and quarrels, and back of it all and broader than all, the earnest, honest, God-fearing lives of those only a few generations before us.

We especially feel indebted to Mrs. Edward Tuckerman, of Amherst, who lent us most willingly and kindly the manuscript Journal. Miss Eliza S. Parkman, of Boston, has given us help repeatedly in too many ways to be separately enumerated. Miss Alice B. Gould, of Boston, lent the picture of Edmund Quincy— Mrs. George Sumner, of Worcester, those of Rev. Mr. Sumner, of Shrewsbury, and his house—Mr. Bradford Kingman, of Brookline, the two blocks taken from Barbour's Collections, Harvard College and Eli Whitney's house—Mr. Arthur B. Denny, of Chestnut Hill, made the copies of Madam Parkman and of the Parkman Coat-of-Arms—the latter from a water-color illumination which formerly adorned the walls of the Westborough parsonage.

The extracts from the Natalitia are published through the courtesy of the American Antiquarian Society.

The drawing of Mr. Parkman on the cover is the only picture of him known to be in existence. It was a memory sketch, done with pen and ink.

The photograph of the handsome old table which Elias brought up from Cambridge is taken from the original now owned by Mr. Parkman T. Denny, of Leicester, and coveted by all of the old minister's descendants. The slate top has been replaced by a board.

PREFACE.

but the handsome carving and beautiful wood might well excite the enthusiasm of a greater connoisseur in antique furniture than Elias Parkman.

The Journal has been carefully copied, but for the sake of clearness most of the abbreviations have been written out. Mr. Parkman usually wrote they, y*y*—them, y*m*—their, y*cir*, and abbreviated many other common words. The italicized words have been retained, except in the case of proper names—which he always underscores. In a very few cases where the words were illegible or blotted, an interrogation mark indicates the uncertainty.

The notes have been written mostly from town records or authentic history, tradition very rarely being allowed a voice.

HARRIETTE M. FORBES.

WORCESTER, MASS., May 29, 1899.

INTRODUCTION.

The following pages are part of the Journal of Rev. Ebenezer Parkman. It is probable that he kept it for the whole period of his long pastorate in Westborough. Much of it has been lost—that for many years burned.—a few volumes are in the Library of the Antiquarian Society in Worcester,—one at least in that of the Massachusetts Historical Society of Boston. This volume, which the Westborough Historical Society is enabled to print through the kindness of Mrs. Edward Tuckerman, of Amherst, is owned by her. It is all in one book, sewed together probably long after Rev. Ebenezer's death. Mrs. Tuckerman writes: "The book came to me directly from my aunt, Mrs. Asa Rand, an older sister of my father's who received it from her mother Sarah, daughter of Rev. Ebenezer. My good old aunt had more of her grandfather's diary, but in some of her movings (she was a minister's wife), it got left behind in a box of papers, on a closet shelf, she told me, and she could not recover it, probably destroyed as waste paper."

Ebenezer Parkman was born in Boston, Sept. 5, 1703. His father was Wm. Parkman, who in 1680 married Elizabeth Adams, also of Boston. She is buried on Copp's Hill—dying on the 13th of April, 1746. Wm. Parkman had died sixteen years earlier, Nov. 30, 1730. He was born in Salem, where his father Elias had settled, in 1658. This Elias, born in 1635, was also the son of Elias Parkman, who had come among the earliest settlers to New England, and grandson of Thomas Parkman, of Sidmouth, Devon, England.

Ebenezer Parkman was admitted to Harvard College in 1717, when he was fourteen years old, and graduated in 1721. The next year he taught school in Newton, living with the brother Elias, whom he mentions in the first part of the Journal. This brother was a mastmaker, and in 1728 an advertisement appears in a local paper:—

"April 1. Mr. Henry Richards wants to sell a parcel of likely negro boys and one negro girl, arrived from Nevis, and were brought from Guinea. To be seen at the house of Mr. Elias Parkman, mastmaker, at the North End."

As the Rev. Ebenezer purchased a slave boy, Maro, in August of that year, it is very possible that he was one of this "parcel." Maro lived only a little more than a year at the Westborough parsonage, and Mr. Parkman writes under date of Dec. 6, 1728: "Dark as it has been with us, it became much Darker ab^t ye Sun Setting. The Sun of Maro's life Sat. The first Death in my Family! God, enable me to see thy Sovereign mind and comport with his holy Will."

This brother Elias and his wife are both buried on Copp's Hill, dying in 1741 and 1746.

Mr. Parkman's son Elias was undoubtedly named for this favorite brother, and indeed most of his children bore the names of his brothers and sisters—Mary, Elizabeth, William, Sarah, Susannah. Alexander, Samuel, John, and Elias being names common to each.

In 1723, Mr. Parkman commenced to preach, and twice during that summer occupied the Westborough pulpit. In 1724, he and the Rev. Jacob Eliot, of Boston, were nominated in a Town Meeting as candidates for the position of Town Minister in Westborough, and he, proving the successful candidate, was installed nine months later, over the little church organized just before.

Those nine months had been very busy ones to the young man. Only a month had passed since he had become twenty-one years of age. He had built himself a house on the bleak hill-top where the Lyman School now stands, and he had married a wife in July—Mary Champney, of Cambridge.

The Church was organized in this new house of Mr. Parkman's—with twelve members besides the pastor. They were: Thomas Forbush, John Pratt, Edmund Rice, Isaac Tomlin, John Fay, David Maynard, Thomas Newton, James Bradish, David Brigham, Joseph Wheeler, James Ball and Isaac Tomlin, Jr. It was five years before the little church near the parsonage was finished.

INTRODUCTION. vii

"In the year 1729"—so says the Book of Church Records, "A Flaggon was sent the Church from a Friend of its Welfare at Boston. See Zechariah 6, 14, latter part.

"In the year 1735, 10 sh. was given ye Church towards a Baptism Bason, afterwards another 10 sh. was given by the same person, who also bought ye Bason Dec., 1739, and devoted it to ye Chh's use. N. B. A Frame for ye Bason with its shaft and Screws, etc., price 20s., was given and Devoted by ye Same."

The flagon and basin have been guarded from the destruction which has overtaken nearly everything else connected with the little church on the hill, and have found their way through the kindness of Mr. John A. Fayerweather, into the collection of the Historical Society. They are both of pewter, and bring before our eyes more vividly than any words could do, the simplicity and poverty and sincerity of these first members of the Westborough Church.

BAPTISM FLAGGON AND BASON.

INTRODUCTION.

In February, 1737, when we begin in the middle of an entry in the minister's Journal, he was living in his house on the Lyman School Hill. His wife had died January 29, 1735. They had the following children :—

Mary, born September 14, 1725.
Ebenezer, born August 20, 1727—buried by his father's side in Memorial Cemetery.
Lydia, born September 20, 1731, and died June 21, 1733.
Thomas, born July 3, 1729.
Lucy, born September 23, 1734.

Mr. Parkman married again, Hannah Breck, September 11, 1737; and their children were :—

Elizabeth, born December 25, 1738—died January 14, 1739.
William, born February 19, 1741.
Sarah, born March 20, 1742.
Susannah, born March 13, 1744.
Alexander, born February 17, 1746.
Breck, born January 27, 1748.
Samuel, born August 22, 1751.
John, born July 21, 1753.
Anna Sophia, born October 18, 1755.
Hannah, born February 9, 1758—died in 1777—and buried in Memorial Cemetery.
Elias, born January 6, 1761.

Sixteen children in all, of whom only two died in infancy.

FEBRUARY, 1737.

by ye means thereof. That we may be *awares* & have our Eyes open our minds *apprehensive now*, and not have ye first thorow sense of those Things in ye midst of ye unhappy Experience of y^m.

14. I put off my Journey by means y^t it was Town Meeting.

15. I rode to Concord. Mr. Flagg of Grafton my Company, from Biglo's in Marlboro. Mr. Whiting[1] and his wife had rid out. Capt. Joseph Buckley Spent the evening with us. I had conversation an hour or two with Mrs. Israel Whiting, lodged there.

16. Lieut. Trowbridge came to Mr. Whiting's & was my Company to Watertown. Lodged at Father Champney's[2] at Cambridge.

[1] Rev. John Whiting, of Concord, died May 4, 1752, aged 71. He was pastor of the church for 26 years, "a man of wealth, learning, influence and talents"—"a gentleman of singular hospitality and generosity." His second wife, whom he married in 1731, was the widow of Dr. Jonathan Prescott. He was the grandson of Hon. Thos. Danforth, deputy-governor.

[2] "Father Champney" was Samuel Champney, of Cambridge, born March 8, 1666-7 and died in March 1745-6. Mr. Parkman's first wife was his daughter Mary, who was baptized May 21, 1699, married July 7, 1724, and died Jan'y 29, 1735-6.

"Sister Hicks" and "Sister Lydia," often mentioned in the Journal, were two younger sisters of the first Mrs. Parkman. Rebecca, born in 1703, married John Hicks, while Lydia, born in 1705, was unmarried and seems to have made her home part of the time in the minister's family.

17. Rode to Boston. My mother[1] still in a measure of Comfort thro' the Blessing of God. I could not be seasonable for lecture. N. B. At Mr. Increase Sumner's[2] in ye morning. N. B. Capt. Foot & Sister Elizabeth & Mrs. Mary Tilestone took a ride with me in a double Slay at evening to Capt. Robert Sharp's[3] at Brookline, and Br^r Elias came to us upon my Horse, after supper there. At 10 o'clock they returned in ye Slay but I tarried. N. B. The discovery of my Inclinations to Capt. Sharp and to Mm. By y^eir urgent Persuasions I tarried and lodged there. N. B. Mrs. Susanna Sharp.

18. I rode to Father Champney's and thence to West-

---

[1] Among the Epitaphs on Copp's Hill is the following: " Here lyes buried the body of Mrs. Elizabeth Parkman, the virtuous and pious consort of Mr. William Parkman, aged 85 years and 7 months, Apr. ye 13th, 1746."

[2] Mr. Increase Sumner was a son-in-law of Capt. Robert Sharpe, having married his daughter Sarah, a year or less before this date. She, as well as " Mistress Susanna," was a cousin of Susannah Boylston, the mother of Pres. John Adams.

Their son Increase, born in 1746, was Governor Increase Sumner of Massachusetts.

[3] Capt. Robert Sharpe was a prominent citizen of Brookline. He owned all the land from the corner of School and Washington streets on the north side to a line above Park Street extending across Harvard Street to the Longwood Marshes, above the Aspinwall lands and below the present Stearns lands. His house was standing until about thirty years ago, never painted except the window frames, which were white. He was a man of wealth.

Mistress Susanna was born May 29, 1716,—so, was a maid of twenty-one summers at this time. She afterwards married Thomas Snow, of Boston.

borough. N. B. Mr. Tilestone & Capt. Wm. Roby of Boston my Company from Watertown to Sudbury.

19. Engaged in my preparations. N. B. I cast a handful or two of Salt into my Pump.

20. On Luke 16 23 P. M. repeated Sermon on Heb. 12.1. At evening visited Mr. Stephen Fay who was very low, &c.

21. The small matter of Salt which I cast into my Pump on ye 19th wonderfully loosened the Spire though it had been hard frozen for a long time (See Downs') and to our Joy and Pleasure had the use of ye Pump again. Very pleasant weather.

22. A number of Hands came to get wood. Mr. Grout with his Team, Mr. Tainter[1] with his and Mr. Harrington

---

[1] Simon Tainter, and his son Simon, Jr., were always good friends of Mr. Parkman. The father in his will styles himself "gentleman" and bequeaths his "silver cup," valued in the inventory at £1, 6s. 8d., to his grandson Simon. He died in 1763 and Mr. Parkman writes in his journal under date of April 2: "My dear friend and brother, Deacon Simon Tainter Dyd! He expired about 11 A. M. May God Sanctify this death in a peculiar manner to me and mine. Tho my good deacon is gone, yet God who is All-Sufficient lives and is unchangeable." And April 5 he writes: "I read Isac. 51. Preached A. M., on the occasion of the Sorrowful Death on 1 Thess. 4-18, read also 14, but could not handle that."

"His Duty," says the Boston Evening Post—in a piece probably written by Mr. Parkman, "was manifested by his high regard to the house of God, his constant attendance there, his esteem of the ordinance and ministers thereof.

"His deeds of *Charity* were unstinted, his heart and hands being ever open, to relieve and help, and to supply the necessitous, who now deplore the loss of such a friend and father."

Simon, Jr., was born in 1715.

with his, Mr. Grow, Daniel Hardy, Dan. Forbush, Elias

DEA. TAINTER'S HOUSE.

Mr. Parkman's later Journals are full of instances of Dea. Tainter's kindness to him—breaking in an unruly mare, killing, with his son's help, cattle or hogs, inviting him and his wife to dinner, when "they had dressed a very large Pigg to entertain us," sending him fresh meat and wood, a bottle of Madeira, or a few oysters from Boston, selling divers sorts of edibles for Mrs. Parkman in the Boston markets, ploughing, sowing and reaping, and helping him in a thousand ways, and the pastor writes: "I hope he does all sincerely and as to the Lord, for I am utterly unworthy, but this conduct must quicken me to endeavor to deserve it. May God reward him with Abundant Special Blessings."

He lived on Mt. Pleasant Street, in the house now known as the Wadsworth house.

Rice, Noah Rice, James Fay, James Bowman, Zebulon Rice, Solomon Rice, John Rogers, Tim. Warren, Jon{{n}}. Forbush jun., Thomas Winchester, David Baverick, Eben' Nurse, Simon Tainter jun., and Samuel Bumpso.

23. Very stormy. Rain and Wind, especially very Windy in y{{e}} Night. N. B. Sister Hicks another son, born a little before night.

24. Had sent to Mr. Prentice of Grafton [1] and very much depended upon him to preach my Lecture, but he

[1] Rev. Solomon Prentice—ordained as minister of the Grafton Church in 1731. "He became," says Rev. Peter Whitney, "what was called in that day a zealous new light, or more properly, a raving enthusiast." He died in 1773, leaving a will in which he provided that his wife Sarah, is to live in his house, and have all his household goods and furniture and indore movables; his riding chair and horse which is to be well kept for her, summer and winter, and replaced if he fails; her firewood cut at her door; as much cider as she shall have occasion to use in the house; full and free liberty to put up a friend's horse or horses, to hay in winter and grass in summer, when they come to visit her, &c. All to be provided by Solomon, Jr., for her sole use and benefit during her natural life. £15 to be paid her annually by my sons.

Mr. Parkman was acquainted with Mr. Prentice before he came to Grafton, and with two other ministers signs a paper recommending him to the gospel ministry "when it shall please God to engage him in it and heartily pray he may prove a blessing to the churches." This was in 1731.

Mr. Prentice built for himself a house in Grafton, which after his death was occupied by Rev. Aaron Hutchinson, and later by Rev. Daniel Grosvenor; Mr. Parkman doubtless was a frequent visitor to each of its owners. It was moved from its first location and now forms the front of Mr. Henry Prentice's house on Oak Street, having come at last again into the family of the Rev. Solomon.

failed. I repeated Sermon on Heb. 7.25. A very cold day—
very slippery—few at Lecture. Heard by Cousen Winchester y' Sister Ruth Champney at Cambridge was sick.

25. A very cold day again. Ensign Ward of Marlborough here to obtain my Evidence of what the Association which met at Framingham Oct. 16, 1733 judged
concerning Mr. Kent. At eve I gave my Testimony,
confirmed by an Oath before Justice Keyes. Ensign Ward
being there present.

26. At eve came Dr. Thyery but he would go and lodge
at Ensign Maynard's.

27. A. M. on 2 Cor: 13. 14. Sacrament. Dr. Thyery &
Deacon Fay and his wife dind with me. P. M. on Mat: 7.
3. 4. 5. Dr. Thyery at eve, but was called away to visit
Stephen Fay.

28. The weather was very Raw Cold. The Wind was
north and very bleak. I visited Mr. Beeman's[1] Family &
Mr. David Brigham.[1] The Dauter of y⁰ former and y⁰
Wife of y⁰ Latter were ill.

Monsʳ Thyery came to my house P. M. and I had some
Expectations of Mr. Prentice of Grafton, and his wife to
visit me, but yʸ did not come. The Dr. spent y⁰ evening
and good part of y⁰ night with me, but presently after he
got to Bed came Simon Tainter jun. upon a most urgent

---

[1] The Beeman family lived on the Flanders road. David Brigham's house stood about 60 yards east from where the Hospital
now stands. His farm comprised about 500 acres. His house was
burned Oct. 16, of this year (see entry for that day). He rebuilt
the house with the help of his son Jonas, who after his father's
death lived in it.

message from Stephen Fay,[1] to have the Dr. visit him forthwith. Howbeit he would not rise till he had taken several naps. I did not get to bed till past Three o'clock. N. B. Town Meeting to add to ye Seats in ye Meeting House.

MARCH, 1737.

1. It had been very Icy and now by a snow upon ye Ice & it was very Slippery & Troublesome riding. I rode to

---

[1] Stephen Fay, in spite of this severe illness, and lack of attention on the part of Dr. Thyery, lived many years. He was the son of Capt. John Fay and was born May 5, 1715. He lived in Westborough until 1743 when he moved from town, and later became one of the first settlers of Bennington, Vt. He built the first tavern west of the Green Mts., a house which had a stirring history during the Revolution. He had five sons in the Battle of Bennington, and Peter Fay, of Southborough, tells the following touching account of his learning after the battle that his oldest son John had been instantly killed by a ball through the head.

"A messenger was sent to bear the solemn tidings to Capt. Fay as gently as possible. He told him he had something bad to tell him concerning one of his sons. The Captain instantly asked him:

"'Did he disobey orders? Or desert his post?'

"'No.'

"'Did he falter in the charge?'

"'No, worse than that. He is dead,' was the answer.

"'Then it is not worse,' exclaimed the father. 'Bring him in, that I may once more gaze on the face of my darling boy.'

"And when they brought him in, covered with dust and blood, he called for water and a sponge, and with his own hand bathed the disfigured features; declaring at the same time that he had never experienced a more glorious or happy day in his life."

to Mr. Cook's[1] to fix my Horse. Called at Capt. Forbush's.[2]

2. Sister Lydia rode down to Cambridge with me. N. B. We sat out somewhat before 10 A. M., rode double, yet got to Father Champney's at Cambridge promptly at 5 P. M. N. B. Mr. John Jarvis was returning from his journey to Marlborough, whither he had been to wait upon Mrs. Han-

---

[1] Cornelius Cook, the blacksmith, was living at this time in the house still standing on the corner of East-Main and Lyman streets. This house was deeded to Cook, by his father-in-law, Thomas Forbush, in 1732, with four acres of land, for £4. 5s. Cornelius was the father of the famous Tom Cook. (See Aug. 27, 1779.)

OLD COOK HOUSE.

He had eight other children: Jonathan, the oldest, was the father of Molly Cook, almost as well known for her eccentricities as her uncle Thomas.

[2] Capt. Forbush was Samuel Forbush, and he lived in the house now standing on the corner of Lyman Street and the Turnpike. The house has been enlarged since his day, but is probably the oldest

nah Breck, who made a visit yesterday to her sister Mrs. Gott in her illness.

From Father Champney's I rode to Roxbury, called at Mr. Increase Sumner's. Thence I rode to Boston, waited upon my mother, and then went and Supped at Br^r Elias's. N. B. Mr. Bowman y^e wharfinger and his wife at Supper with us. My Horse sent to his Stables. Lodged at Br^r Elias's.

in town. For many years it was used as a tavern. Samuel For-

SAMUEL FORBUSH'S HOUSE.

bush was a brother of Thomas, both of them being among the original settlers of Westborough.

18   DIARY OF REV. EBENEZER PARKMAN.

3. Mr. Mather[1] Lectured on —— against Covetousness. Dined at Br. Samuel's. P. M., visited Mrs. Pierpont, Mrs. Hannah being at Marlborough. Mr. Pierpont also had taken a Journey to New haven. Towards night I rode over to Roxbury. N. B. Mrs. Sumner ill. I proceeded to Capt. Sharp's. By Capt. Sharp's strong Solicitation I tarried all night. N. B. Mrs. Susan not very willing to think of going so far in ye Country as Westborough, &c &c &c.

4. I rode to Father Champney's. Thence I went over to ye Town. N. B. Mr. Jonathan Monnef. Junr. at Father Champney's. I returned P. M. from Town and went again to Capt. Sharp's. N. B. Capt. Sharp & Mm. gone to the Funeral of a Relation at Roxbury. I tarried whilst the Capt. and his Spouse came home. Arguments which be fruitless with Mrs. Susan. I returned to Father Champney's between 8 & 9 in ye Evening.

5. Sister Lydia was willing to go up again to Westborough with me if ye weather would allow. Upon her mentioning her carrying up some other Coloured clothes y^n her black, and our putting off our Mourning it (by Degrees) moved me very much and my Passions flowed almost beyond Controll, till I was obliged to retire away. Every matter was most exceeding Sorrowful to me.—The weather was very

---

[1] Probably Rev. Samuel Mather, the son of Cotton Mather. He was the fourth pastor of the dynasty of the Mathers over the Old North Church. In 1765, he was living in Moon St., and Gov. Hutchinson took refuge in his house when his own elegant mansion was sacked by a mob.

He died June 27, 1785, aged seventy-six, and is buried on Copp's Hill, in the Mather Tomb with Increase and Cotton.

discouraging to Sister Lydia's Design, nor could she in prudence venture tho I tarryed for her till 11 when I sat out. It rained and I had a very wet troublesome Journey. I rode over ye new Bridge in Sudbury & went to Capt. Clark's[1] of Framingham. The Waters flow abundantly, Ice rotts away, ye Snow melts again, ye Rain beats and ye Storm strong. Capt. Clark very urgent to have me stay, but I was resolute to get as far as I could. I called at Mr. Stone's at Southborough, and about nine at night reached home D. O. M. Gratia.

6. Repeated Sermon on Acts, 2. 37. 38. Dr. Thyery at meeting.

7. Dr. Thyery visited me and dind with me. I prayed with ye Town before y^{eir} Elections. Mr. Prentice of Grafton visited me, & note well y^t ye Day I went from home last week both he and his wife came to see me, just after we were gone. A very fine pleasant Day.

8. Cloudy. Some Snow. N. B. Many of ye People gone to Sudbury about Housetonic Rights.

9. The water everywhere exceeding high. Visit Mr. Sam Fay, & Stephen Fay.

10. The Winds more than ordinarily violent. A Barn was blown down at Framingham. A man narrowly escaped drowning at Framingham River. The water being so deep, ye Current so strong and ye Winds so impetuous.

---

[1] Capt. Isaac Clark, of Framingham, was a noted man in his day. He commanded a company of troopers which was out in Father Raile's War in 1725, and on his one hundredth birthday rode horseback to and from Col. Trowbridge's. He lived to be one hundred and two, and died in 1768. His gravestone says: "His offspring that descended from him was two hundred and fifty-one."

11. Divers Neighbours (Mr. Maynard, Mr. Grout & Mr. Chas. Rice), here in ye Evening. Catechizing, but only 4 boys, beside my own. No catechizing P. M. no children came.

12.

13. A. M. on Matt: 7. 6. and P. M. repeated Sermon 46 being ye 4th on Act 2, 37, 38.

14. I visited Stephen Fay, Capt. Fay and old Mr. Rice.[1] David went away.

15. Early in ye morning to Mr. Wipples &c. At noon I was extremely indisposed. Faint &c. Storm, snow. P. M. Dr. Thyery here, I grew better. D. G.

16. Dies. Humill. & Proc. Secret. See my own Memoirs. At eve, Mr. Whipple. N. B. An ewe y^t was gored very ill—fine pleasant Day. Roads extremely hollow. Some of the oldest persons declare y^y scarce ever knew ye Earth to have been so frozen as this winter.

---

[1] Probably Thomas Rice, who was at this time eighty-three years old. He had formerly lived on the same road as the Fays, in the house which had earlier served for many years as a garrison, and near which occurred the sad tragedy of 1704, when two of his sons and two of his nephews were carried into captivity, while his youngest little boy was killed by the attacking Indians.

Thomas was one of the original settlers of the town and one of its most prominent citizens. He served in the Legislature, and did his best to promote the welfare of the Church and town during a long life. He died in 1748.

The house of Mr. Frank V. Bartlett now stands on the site of his old home. This place he had sold, and Abner Newton was living there in 1737, when his dwelling-house was entered in the night-time by Hugh Henderson, who paid the penalty of his crime with his life in November, as recorded in the Journal for that month.

17. A. M. Storm of snow. Rain. Trouble with my sick ewe. Mr. Whipple to Boston.

18. P. M. I rode to Marlborough to Coll. Wood's. Eve at Dr. Gott's.[1] Mrs Gott had been very ill, but is recovering. *Mrs. Hannah Breck with her*, but I spent my time with ye men, scil. ye Dr. Coll. & Mr. Daniel Steward. Late in ye Evening Deacon Woods came to request me to visit a young woman at his House (Dauter of Mr. Samuel Stow) apprehended to be at ye Point of Death. I went, prayed with her &c. I lodged at Coll. Wood's.

19. A. M. To Dr. Gott's, but a short space with Mrs. Hannah. At my Request, she had (she assured me) burnt my Letters, Poems &c. P. M. Funeral of Capt. Eleazar How. Capt. Brigham informed of ye Death of President Wadsworth, ye Night before last, also lately Part of Northampton Meeting-House fell and wounded many, in time of Divine Service, and ye Burning of Young Coll. Chandler's House at Woodstock, and three persons consumed in it, scil, Mrs.

---

[1] Dr. Benj. Gott, a young physician in Marlborough, had married Sarah, daughter of the Rev. Robert Breck. Hannah was a younger sister, at this time being twenty-one years old. Her father had been a good friend of Mr. Parkman, when he first came to Westborough, and was a remarkable man. He was ordained pastor when twenty-two. "As to his learning," says a writer in the News Letter for January 21, 1731, "I suppose it will be no offence to say, there were few of his standing that were even his equals. He was such a master of the learned languages that he could, and did, frequently, to the capacity of his family, read a Chapter of the Hebrew Bible into English, and the Greek was still easier to him. Pride, hypocrisy and affectation were his aversion; and covetousness was what he was a perfect stranger to. His temper was grave

Wright, her son and a man who was asleep with him. I returned home. At eve, Dr. Thiery at my house in great Urgency going to Boston for Drugs, to relieve Stephen Fay, no persuading him to ye Contrary altho ye Roads are extreme bad, the night Dark &c. N. B. A piece of Cotton Linnen of 12 yds. from Mr. Caruths.

20. On Matt., 7: 7, 8. P. M. on Matt., 7: 9, 10, 11.

21. I visited Stephen Fay—was at ye Capt.'s, find Thyery is not a man of Truth or Probity. At Cousin Winchester's, &c.

22. Rain & Cloudy. Visited old Mr. Ward's Family,

and thoughtful, yet cheerful at times, especially with his friends and acquaintances, and his conversation entertaining and agreeable."

Mr. Parkman and Mistress Hannah were married September 11, 1737—all her objections finally overcome. A piece of her wedding dress, and her wedding slippers are still treasured by Mrs. Tuckerman. The dress is a heavy, white gros grain silk—the bodice evidently made with many rows of stitching, between which were run strips of cane.

The slippers are of brocaded silk—a green ground with figures in yellowish white and various shades of red—the heels are high, covered with the silk, and they are lined with a coarse linen.

HANNAH BRECK'S WEDDING SLIPPERS.

reckoned with Mr. Josiah Newton. Rainy—came home in y^e Night & in y^e Rain.

23. Cold northerly wind. P. M. visited old *David Mounanaow*,[1] Indian, he tells me he was 104 last Indian Harvest. Says the name of *Boston* was not *Shawmut* but *Shawwawmuck*. Channcy Pond was called Nawgawwoomcom and Marlboro', ———. N. B. Mr. Seth Rice here about this time to discourse with me on ye life of his sister Thank^f. I visited Mr. D. Brigham's family, and old Capt. Byles.

24. Froze hard again last night. Cold windy day.

25. I rode to Marlb., din'd with Mr. Hovey at Mm. Fish's. Spent ye afternoon at Dr. Gott's—was at ye Coll.'s, but returned to Dr.'s. Mr. Hovey there with a Bass Viol. N. B. Mrs. H.——h B——k at ye Dr.'s still. Our con-

---

[1] After King Philip's War, some of the Marlborough Indians who had been taken prisoners and confined on the islands in Boston harbor, returned to their old homes.

"Among those who returned," says Rev. Dr. Allen, of Northborough, "was David alias David Munnanaow, who joined Philip and, as he afterwards confessed, assisted in the destruction of Medfield. This treacherous Indian had, it is said, a slit thumb, which circumstance led to his conviction. . . .

"His wigwam was on the borders of the pond near the public house long known as Williams' Tavern, where he lived with his family many years and died in extreme old age."

The last members of David's family still made their homes in the field by the pond, within the memory of many persons now living. Until very lately, an extremely old chestnut has been pointed out as the tree under which these Indians had their wigwam. It was called the Wigwam Tree. At last, like old David himself, it has succumbed to extreme old age.

versation of a piece with what it used to be. I mark her admirable Conduct, her Prudence and wisdom, her good manners & her distinguishing Respectfulness to me w^c accompany her Denyals. After it grew late in ye Even'g, I rode home to Westb., through the Dark and the Dirt, but cheerfully and comfortably (comparatively). N. B. My Family all abed.

26. I had appointed to ride to Grafton in order to changing with Mr. Prentice tomorrow, but it proved so very Rainy all day that it was unpracticable.

27. Fair and pleasant Day. Matt. 7: 12 A. M., but P. M. repeated Sermon II, Acts 2: 37, 38. N. B. Mr. Silas Brigham[1] and Mr. Eleazar Pratt of Shrewsbury had desired me to baptize y^{eir} Children. Accordingly, in my usual manner I desired ye Children might be brought forth to

[1] Mr. Silas Brigham, so unfortunately tardy this Sunday morning —had married Mindwell Grout, and the baby Jemima born four days before this, was their first child. She married Constantine Hardy.

Mr. Eleasar Pratt lived near Wild Cat Swamp, and was afterwards set off to Westborough. His baby, Sarah, was nearly six months old, and he hardly deserved so much more credit as Mr. Parkman would seem to give him, for he had his good wife Ruhamah to get the baby attired in its best frock, with the deftness which the care of the three older children had given her.

Poor Silas Brigham, and poor Mindwell! How they must have worried, and how flushed his young face must have been when he marched down the aisle, after all the hurry, to have his pride in his first-born so humbled by the Minister's censure!

The Church Records say under date of April 3, 1737: "Jemima of Silas and Mindwell Brigham baptized by Rev. Mr. Prentice of Grafton."

Baptism. But only one appeared. I looked about till I conceived y^t something had befallen ye other or those concerned with it. I proceeded and baptized Mr. Pratt's (w^c was ye Child y^t was brought) w^n the prayers were over we proceeded to ye last Singing; in ye Time of ye last Singing Mr. Brigham and his Child came in—After ye Blessing and w^{n} I was down in ye Alley going out, Mr. Brigham asked me whether his child could not be baptized. I ans'd, it could not now. My Reasons are these. Besides that, when I am spent with the foregoing Services, it is too much to expect me to repeat over y^m again. Besides that, such a custom indulged would involve us in great irregularity and Difficulty, but this administration for my known Friends would have forced me to make it a custom, and besides the impatience of many of the Congregation to get away home, being they live 4, 5, or 6 miles off. Besides those Reasons, I would urge y^t it was so very sudden upon me y^t I could not judge w^c way I could vindicate it if I should proceed. Again, by ye suddenness I was too much confused to have my Power at command to perform the Devotions; nor was I furnished therefor (Eccl. 5: 1, 2). So y^t it would have been nothing short of horrible Presumption for me to have done it.—Lydia Cutting not well.

28. *Lydia* worse, having a bad Ague in her face & it threw her wholly by; but it was so ordered in Providence, y^t Deborah Ward came to see us and she served us.

Adjournment of Town Meeting. N. B. B^r Hicks had been chosen Constable, but gets off by virtue of a Commission to be Deputy Sheriff. (David Baverick diets here.)

29. Very Rainy. Lydia worse, considerable Fever.

Benj. How with David at his work and din'd with us. Neither of y^m to be persuaded to go for Dr. Gott for Lydia. Jon^n Rogers came to go, but we did not send.

30. *Lydia* somewhat better, very fine weather.

31. *Publick Fast.* I preached on Isa : 1, 9. N. B. Mr. Abr^m Amsden of Marlb. here to desire me to attend the Funeral of his Br^r *Thomas'* only Son, a youth near 21, and very hopeful, who died after a short illness of but a few Days. O y^t I and y^t ye people of Westb., at least some of y^m might be of that small Remnant w^c God has left of truely Godly Ones! and O y^t we might have Grace to Demean and to acquit ourselves as such ; and y^t it might please God to keep off His Judgments y^t this Land may not be made as *Sodom* or like unto *Gomorrah*, but y^t ye Div. Mercy might be afforded to us as we need it & y^t Glory may yet Dwell in our Land !

April., 1737.

1. I rode down to Marlb. to ye Funeral of Joseph Amsden's. Many youth present and seem to be affected. O y^t y^{ere} might be abiding impression on y^{eir} souls! and upon all of us. This is ye second Death in that near Neighbourhood of youth in Flower and Glory within a very little while. N. B. This Joseph Amsden was one of ye Bearers of ye other, scil, ye young woman y^t Dyed at Deacon James Wood's on ye 19th of last month.—After Burial I returned to Capt. Amsden's to afford him w^t consolation I could under his melancholy circumstances. N. B. Coll. Woods with me. N. B. Capt. Nathan Brigham gave further ac-

counts of ye Fury of ye Mob at Boston[1]—assaulting ye Town House &c. At Eve, I was at Dr. Gotts, Mrs. H———h was thought to be gone up to Mr. Week's or Capt. Williams, with design to lodge there, but she returned to ye Doctors. And she gave me her Company till it was very late. Her Conversation was very Friendly, and with divers expressions of Singular and Peculiar Regard. *Memorand^m*. *Oscul:* But she cannot yield to being a step mother.—I lodged there, and with g^{rt} satisfaction & Composure.—

Memorand^m. Ebenezer has begun to learn his 2. Accidence[2] and now makes a Business of it.

SEPTEMBER, 1737.

———w^e were upon y^{eir} journey to Connecticut came to see us, dind with us and prevented us (altho Sister Lydia and Mrs. Bekky were gone already as Earnest of our Going) till so late in ye P. M., then ye Rain coming also y^t we were utterly disappointed.

21. We rode to Cousen Winchester, but they being gone & other neighbors also to Worcester, we struck along up to

---

[1] From Boston News Letter for April 1, 1737:—"On Thursday Night the 24 instant, the middle Market House in this Town, together with several Butchers' Shops near the same, were cut, pulled down and entirely demolished by a number of persons unknown: and several posts of the North Market House were also sawn asunder the same Night."

In consequence of which Gov. Phipps issued a proclamation offering a reward of one hundred pounds for the detection of any of the ringleaders.

[2] The 2. Accidence was a small book containing the rudiments of grammar.

Mr. Prentice's at Grafton. N. B. Their son Nath.l's finger had been wounded, the Top of one of his Fingers being cut off. N. B. Mrs. Sartel of Groton there. Called at Capt. Fay's as we returned home in ev'g.—

22. Visited Capt. Eager's wife[1] who had been some time sick.

23. John Clung so urgent for his money (bec. of his journey to Pensylvania y^t I was obliged to ride about to gather it, till I succeeded at Treasurer Newton's.

24. Message from John Hamilton under condemnation for Burglary requesting y^t I would visit him. N. B. Lydia sick and my wife burthened with ye Business of ye Family. N. B. Fire raging in ye Bushes on ye west side of Powder Hill, drie by ye Drought and ye Frost and ye Wind very high.—Br. Hicks alone there, till I assisted him, & we succeeded. D. G.

25. Mr. Pierpont came to us this morning, having come from Boston but a little before sunset last even'g. N. B. News y^t the vessel in w^c his Goods were had struck upon Martha's Vineyard, but had got off again: he (as he can) pursues his journey to see in what condition y^y are at New Haven. A. M. I Repeated on 1 Chron. 26. 9. P. M. I preached on 1 Pet. 3. 7.

26. Mr. Pierpont and his wife left us. I with my wife accompanied y^m to Shrewsbury. I still continued with y^m

---

[1] Capt. Eager was one of the first settlers in that part of Westborough which afterwards became Northborough. His house was the first built on the New Connecticut Road, between Sam'l Goodenow's Garrison and the Town of Worcester. It was the first tavern opened in the place. He died in 1755.

as far as Worcester and dined with them at Capt. Howard's. P. M. having taken leave of those Excellent Friends, I rode to Mr. Burr's,[1] not finding him at home, I hastened to ye Prison to see ye Criminal. Among other Questions, I asked him his true Name.? he answered Hugh Henderson. he acquainted me with his Birth and Baptism &c. He was much concerned and distressed about his state, and ready to confess himself a great Sinner &c I prayed with him. He requested I would come and see him again. I hastened to Shrewsbury and with my wife, returned in the evening. N. B. John McClung took leave of us.

27. We took up our Flax. We supped at Br.^r Hicks's.
28. I was much indisposed with Headache.

[1] Rev. Isaac Burr was settled over the Old South Church in Worcester in 1725. Mr. Chas. E. Stevens writes: "No portraiture of his person or mind survives; no characteristic anecdote is on record and nothing testifies of his ministry save its continuance for a fifth of a century in a generally peaceful way." Mr. Burr lived on the south corner of Main and Pleasant streets. His house was afterwards removed to Blackstone Street, where it stood until a few years ago. The little sketch of it made for Mr. Caleb Wall's Reminiscences of Worcester, by "an accurate and experienced artist," as he writes, is the only picture of this house in existence.

HOUSE OF REV. ISAAC BURR.

29. Lectured on 1 Sam. 15. 22. At eve Mr. Jarvis came from Boston.
30.

OCTOBER 1737.

1.
2. Sacrament. Ps. 63. 8. Repeated on Is. 53. 1. Patience Forb. came again
3. Catechised at ye Meeting House. Judge Dudley[1] on his return from Springfield made us a visit, and dind with us. Lydia Cutting left us.

[1] Paul Dudley, afterwards Chief Justice of the Province, at this time a judge of the Superior Court, born in 1675, died in 1751. He was the son of Gov. Joseph Dudley, of Massachusetts. He studied law in London. He bequeathed £100 (about $666) to Harvard College for the support of an annual lecture, called, from its founder, the Dudleian lectures. He was a Fellow of the Royal Society, and wrote on natural history and against the Church of Rome.

Seven years after this visit to Mr. Parkman, Judge Dudley had the famous "Dudley parting-stone" erected in Roxbury, where it still stands, with the inscription which has guided so many travellers for more than a hundred and fifty years,

"The Parting Stone. 1744. P. Dudley."

And on one side, "Dedham and Rhode Island," on the other, "Cambridge and Watertown."

He had been Speaker of the House and member of the Executive Council. Judge Sewall writes of him: "Thus, while with pure hands and an upright heart he administered justice in the Circuit thro' the Province, he gained the general esteem and veneration of the people."

The town of Dudley is named "in token of respect to William and Paul Dudley."

4. Mr. Jarvis, Sister Lydia and I rode to Cambridge. Mrs. Susé Champney there. Mr. Jarvis lodged with me at Father Champney's. N. B. I rode down to Mr. Dana's Tavern¹ about my Wife's Trunk.

5. Early this morning we rode to Mr. Dana's again, & saw y ͤ Trunk in good order, in y ͤ Team to be transported up,. and then we proceeded to Boston. Dined at Br ͬ. Elias's.

[1] Dana's Tavern stood near the centre of the town of Brookline and was a famous hostelry for many years. It was a large gambrel-roofed house and stood until 1816, when it was destroyed by fire.

A story of the old tavern is given in Historic Sketches of Brookline, by Harriet F. Woods, in which Tom Cook (see Journal, Aug. 27, 1779) figures as chief actor.

She writes: "There was a notorious thief, well known in Brookline and the adjoining towns by the name of Tom Cook. He had many eccentricities, among which was a habit of stealing from the rich to give to the poor. In horse-stealing he was especially expert. He was frequently arrested, convicted and sentenced to short terms of imprisonment at the 'Castle' (now Fort Independence), that being then the common prison for all offenders in Boston and vicinity.

"On one occasion Tom stole a goose from a countryman's wagon, which was under the shed at Dana's Tavern; not, however, with generous designs for any of his poor protegés, but for the satisfying of his own appetite. But as an uncooked goose would be about as unsatisfactory as no goose at all, Tom resorted to the old schoolhouse,—school not being in session, to cook and devour it."

Squire Sharpe's house was nearest to the schoolhouse, and Squire Sharpe was a grandson of Capt. Robert, and a nephew of Mistress Susanna.

"The Squire, with his *sharp* eye on the interests of the town, discovered a smoke arising from the schoolhouse chimney, and as

My honored Mother in good health. D. G. I returned to Cambridge. found Mrs. Susé Champney there still.

N. B. 6. I sat out from Cambridge before Day—got to Harrington's before sun rising from there first at sunrise, but did not get up to Westb. till nigh one—visited Hannah Bond, who lay sick at Capt. Forb. after that dind at Home. Young men came to gather my Corn. Set y^m to work.

Went to ye private meeting at Mr. Townsend's & preached on 2 Pet: 1. 10. visited Hannah Bond again—about 18 or 20 hands husked out all my Corn. N. B. In my absence Winter Apples gathered in.

7. Mr. John Pratt brought home my cyder which he had made.

8. Mr. Pratt brought home ye remainder of my cyder. Susa Cutting came.

9. I repeated my sermon IV upon Is. 53. 1. from John 10 26. P. M. Sermon 11. on 1. Sam. 15. 22 from Ps. 40. 6. 8.

10. Visited Mrs. Dantforth who is in a languishing state. Was also at Mr. Hayward's & at Mr. Lock's.

'where there is smoke, there must be fire,' he proceeded to reconnoitre and caught Tom in the very act of roasting the goose. Laying the strong hand of the law upon him, he made him confess where he got the fowl and march back with it under his own escort to the Tavern, and, before the assembled inmates of the bar-room, gave him his choice to take then and there a public whipping, or be tried and sent to the Castle. Tom considered briefly and *decided to take the whipping*.

"The countrymen agreed, and flourished their long whips upon him with such vigor, that Tom's appetite for roast goose was abated in a summary manner, and the punishment proved more effectual than his various sojourns at the Castle."

11. Visited Mrs. Rogers who is sick, Hannah Bond and old Mrs. Pratt. N. B. overtook some Travellers on Foot with y^{eir} Muskets: one of em very unmannerly and saucy. —P. M. Mr. Tozer and his wife here. old Mr. Rice visited us. John Clung here.

12. I went to Worcester to see Hugh Henderson, found him in much ye same distressed state y^t I left him in, but I hope more knowing and acquainted with his Condition and with his Duty. N. B. Mr. Burr at ye Goal with me. I prayed with him—a multitude—attending. He earnestly desired me to see him again and wishes over and over y^t I would preach to him.

N. B. When I called at Mr. Cushing's as I went up, Coll. Woods was there, on his return from Rutland. As I returned in the evening, y^{re} rose a storm of Lightening and Rain. Mr. Lock came and carried in Corn.

13. John Clung (who lodged here last night) carried in more of ye Corn from ye Barn. Paid John ye whole and he bid farewell. At evening Br^r Hicks helped in more Corn.

14. Jou^n Rogers got in Pumpkins, & ye remainder of ye Corn.

15. Noah How helped in with Turnips and some of ye Potatoes.

At eve old Mr. Rice, Mr. Jarvis came up.

16. Mat. 3, 1–4. John 16. 8. N. B. I was called away between 8 and 9 in ye morning to see old Capt. Byles, who was very bad with his Throat and at night I visited him again. N. B. The Congregation disturbed P. M. by ye burning of Mr. David Brigham's House but when people gathered in again, and were composed, I went on with y^e

rest of my sermon. A very sorrowful Providence! a great Loss! but I trust y^m and all of us to profit by it, y^t our Hearts may be taken off from temporal transitory Enjoyments.

17. Rainy. Various Company all day and at evening. N. B. Mr. James Fay dind with us. N. B. Mr. Wheeler distressed in Conscience for H. Henderson. Capt. Williams from Marlboro.

18. Visited Capt. Byles who is grown exceeding bad again. Visited ye wife of W^m. Rogers Jr. and proceeded to Mr. Brigham's to see their Desolations. A Sorrowful Sight! I desire heartily to sympathise. Returned to Capt. Byles.[1] He dyed this evening. N. B. Mr. Jarvis went to Boston in ye morning. N. B. Mr. Jon^n. Forbes[2] at my house in ye Evening and after him Messrs Ed and Benj. Goddard.

19. Mr. Brigham's son David fetched away divers things which we lent y^m in y^{eir} necessity. Nathan Maynard P. M. digging Potatoes.

[1] Capt. Joseph Byles had married Rebecca Forbush, the sister of Jonathan, Samuel and Thomas Forbush. He lived on the south side of Chauncy Pond. He was one of the "first inhabitants."

[2] Dea. Jonathan Forbes b. in Marlborough in 1684—married in 1706, when he was a young man of twenty-two, a woman twice married, with a family of four children. At this time he was living near the present town reservoir. He was the first one of the family to write his name Forbes—his other brothers, Samuel and Thomas, and their descendants, being always known by the name of Forbush. The Massachusetts Gazette of March 31, 1768, says:—"His life was exemplary; his departure in the firm hope of a glorious immortality; his progeny numerous."

20. Funeral of Capt. Joseph Byles, my Spouse, Mrs. Richard Burrough and my Dauter Molly all there with me. The deceased was a bright example of Diligence and Industry in his calling, Constancy at ye House of God, diligent attention to ye Worship and Word preached : Truth and Faithfulness to his word and exact Honesty in his Trading. To which add a singularly manly Heroic Spirit. Visited old Mrs. Pratt at Eve. Capt. Eager came home with us.

21. Closely engaged in my preparations. At eve Br^r William Parkman came from ye Council at Concord, which had voted Mr. Whiting unfit to sustain ye holy ministry and advised ye church of Concord to dismiss him, which y^y complied with. N. B. Mr. Francis Pierce here—finished with him about his Boards. N. B. My Br^r left us. Dr. Gott called in.—P. M. I rode to Shrewsbury and met with Mr. Burr at Mr. Cushing's.[1] I proceeded to Worcester and

[1] Rev. Job Cushing, the first minister of Shrewsbury, pastor of the church there from 1723 to his death in 1760. He was the father of Col. Job Cushing—also of Rev. John Cushing, who married in 1769 Mr. Parkman's daughter Sarah. She lived to be eighty-two years of age and died in 1825. Mrs. Tuckerman writes of this daughter Sarah, as follows:—" My grandmother married Dr. John Cushing, of Ashburnham, who taught school in Westborough the year after he graduated from Harvard College. He boarded in the minister's family, and when he was ordained, at the age of twenty-four, he came back and carried off the daughter as his bride. This was in 1768. She was a remarkably bright and capable woman, judging from the family traditions. There were seven children in that large family younger than she, and she had so much to do that her mother could not spare her the time to go to school when it was kept at intervals. But she was ambitious to learn, and her father helped her all he could. She taught herself to write by

stopped at ye Goal at the Grates to speak with the Prisoner and to put him in mind of ye preparations needful for him to make in order to his keeping his *Last Sabbath*. I lodged at Mr. Burr's.

23. Early in ye morning began to write my address to ye Prisoner. A. M on Eccl. 11. 9 a crowded assembly, poor Hugh Henderson present. P. M. on Job: 3. 36. a very great congregation, it being, in y^eir apprehension ye last Sabbath Sermon the poor Criminal is to hear. At evening called at Mr. Eaton's and at ye Sheriff's[1], who went with me to ye Prison. I interrogated ye Prisoner what was ye occasion of his coming to this country—whether he had discovered and acknowledged all that was fit and proper for him to reveal? Whether he had any confederates? A great number flocked in ye Goal when at his Request I prayed with him. I left him between 8 and 9. by that I came to Mr. Cushing's where I intended to lodge. Y^y were all in Bed wherefore, though cold, I proceeded home to my own House.

N. B. Mr. Jarvis came up last night in a chair.

24. Mr. Burr left us early in ye morning. P. M. Mr. Jarvis, my wife, Mrs. Bekky and I rode to ye Great Pond, to Capt. Warren's, and Capt. Forbush's. N. B. Supped at Capt. Forb.

---

copying letters with a piece of chalk on the barn floor, for paper and ink were precious in those days, and not to be unduly wasted."

The house where the Rev. Mr. Cushing lived stood east of the Shrewsbury Town Hall.

[1] The first sheriff of Worcester County was Daniel Gookin, who held the office until 1743.
He was a son of Gen'l Daniel Gookin. Worc. Hist.

25. Mr. Jarvis and Mrs. Bekky Burrough left us. I rode to Hopkinton Association, all y^t came besides were Mr. N. Stone and Mr. S. Prentice. Mr. Barrett concio on 1 Pet. 4. 11. If any man speaketh.

26. Public lecture by Mr. Sol. Prentice on Job. 12. 35. first part. N. B. I had a very Sudden Turn of Sharp Pain in my Side after Dinner, but thro Mercy, I recovered.

Mr. Prentice went home with me and lodged at our House.

27. Rode with Mr. Prentice to Grafton and preached his Lecture on Jude 10. 21. Returned to Westboro at night. N. B. The Governor has reprieved Hugh Henderson for a month at the request of Mr. Burr and Mr. Prentice.

28. Ah! what sad grounds of Severe Reflection upon myself for my wretched negligence and unfaithfulness! How great need of renewing and fixing my Resolutions of Reformation. But especially of crying unto God for pardon of what is past and Grace to assist and quicken me henceforward!

29.

30. All day on Job,: 3. 36 Rain A. M. High winds at even. N. B. Mr. Chamberlain din'd with us.

NOVEMBER 1737.

1. Visited Mr. Dantforth.
2.
3. Stormy.
4. Very cold.

5. I rode to Southboro'. Met Mr. Stone by Capt. Warren's. Very cold. Mr. Peabody and Mr. Moquet of Framingham here.

6. Preached at Southborough, on Job,: 3. 36 A. & P. M. At eve, Coll. Ward and his wife came in to Mr. Stone's. N. B. Y^e Coll. exceptions against that passage in my forenoon sermon, p. 2–*too Small for the Divine Oracle to have been exprest about either*.

7. At Mr. Tim Brigham's. Mr. Stone brought Mrs. Parkman to his House, we dind there, after which I rode to visit old Mrs. Morse at Marlboro', confined by her Broken Bone, and in great distress of mind, whilst Mr. Stone went with my wife up to Dr. Gott's. There we tarried all night.

8. Called at Capt. Williams, and at Mr. Eb. Beeman's on our way home. P. M. Funeral of one of Mrs. Seth Rice's Dawters who dyed by a Quinsy. Rain. N. B. The Floor of ye Room at Mr. Rice's broke under us.

9. Stormy.

10. I rode to Mr. Wheeler's, called at Mr. Dantforth as I went, but dined at Mr. Wheeler's. N. B. Mr. Thos. Ward at Mr. Nathan Balls's. I was at Mr. Lawrence's, and at Mr. Gershom Fay's and at Mr. Collister's. N. B Disappointment about Swine notwithstanding my long Dependence.

11. We first tyed up our Cattle in ye Barn. My oxen were at work for Mr. David Brigham's to cart stones for y^{er} chimneys. I was at Mr. Grout's about Beef.

12. Fine warm day.

13. John 3. 36 & P. M. on Joh. 16. 8. Capt. Eager sick.

14. Bʳ Hicks went to Cambridge upon my Horse.

15. Trooping and Training—prayed with yᵉ foot before Dinner and dind with yᵉ officers of both Horse and Foot— prayed with ye whole Body at eve. N. B. Capt. Eager detained by his sickness and Lieut. Baker[1] also absent. N. B. I wrote to Worcester by Capt. Moses Rice, being I could not visit yᵉ Prisoner.

16. Bʳ Hicks came up with Sister Willard.

17. Mr. Tainter came to me before Sunrise and informed me of a most Sudden and awful accident in yᵉⁱʳ neibourhood. That the wife of Mr. Joshua Harrington (who came up with his Family to Dwell among us, but this Day three weeks) was Shot in the head last evening, a little before Sundown, by a servant named Ebenezer Chubb in his 15ᵗʰ year, and she dyed upon the Spot. Mr. Tainter was going for yᵉ Coroner. *Public Thanksgiving*. Preached on Lev. 3. 1. After yᵉ publick exercises, yᵉ Coroner's Inquest sat on yᵉ body of Mrs. Harrington and yᵉⁱʳ verdict was *Accidental Death*.

[1] Lieut. Edward Baker was one of Mr. Parkman's first friends in Westborough, for he and James Eager had been the committee who brought him the news that he had been called to be the town minister. He was always prominent in town and church affairs, and chairman of the committee which built the old Arcade.

He lived on Main Street, on the Pollard place, where his son, Squire Baker, afterwards had his home. He had ten children, of whom one, Joseph, born in 1736, was "the Squire."

His house was moved and is now part of Mrs. Gleason's house.

He died in 1763, and his stone still marks his last resting place in the old burying ground, although that of Persis his wife has long since disappeared.

18. My wife and Sister were with me at ye funeral of Mrs. Harrington.

19.

20. Sacrament. Joh: 16. 8, repeated. Mat. 10. 29. 30 P. M. N. B. Mrs. Trewsdale of Newton, mother of Mrs. Harrington, above mentioned, dind with us.

21. I rode up to Worcester to see Hugh Henderson again. Was sorry to find he had tried to make his escape by filing the Goal[1] door. We talked more of other matters, and kept longer off from ye main point of his case yⁿ heretofore. I'm more put to it to judge of his Frame. Mr. Burr came to me, requested me to preach to him on Wednesday. Hugh desires it of me, and several of the people repeatedly and urgently insist and plead for it. I prayed with the prisoner and took leave at about seven o'clock. N. B. his Discourses of ye Jury, not going by the laws of God & ye Country in Condemning him, having but Circumstantial Evidence. As to Newton, he offered him all reasonable Satysfaction &c: But he added, that he was guilty, and his many sins had provoked God to anger &c: —

[1] The goal or jail where Hugh Henderson was confined stood on the west side of Lincoln Street, a short distance from Lincoln Square. It was a building forty-one feet by eighteen. "The prison part," writes Caleb Wall, "was eighteen feet square, made of white oak timber set with studs, four inches thick and five inches broad, and floored, roofed and ceiled with two-inch planks spiked together. A stone dungeon was underneath. The north end of the structure, finished as a dwelling, afterwards became part of the old 'Hancock Arms.'" Probably at this time it was the dwelling-house of the jailer, Luke Brown.

I called at Mr. Cushing's and supped there. Thence I rode home.

22. Deacon Miles of Concord here to bring the Request of ye Church y^t I would assist in ye Fast y^y have appointed in order to ye Calling another Minister.

23. The wife and younger son of Mr. Increase Ward very bad. I visited y^m and old Mrs. Pratt A. M. P. M. I rode up to Worcester at the Request of ye Criminal and others to preach to him. There were so many at ye Goal y^t we were obliged to go to ye Meeting-House. I preached on 1 Tim. 1. 15. Supped (with Mr. Campbell) at Deacon Haywards.[1] We visited ye Prisoner. He spoke of having a solemn warning taken from his mouth, but chose to have it deferred to ye morning, but prayed I would be early. We lodged at Mr. Burr's.

24. I went to the Prisoner as early as I could, and Mr. Burr was with me to assist in penning down what ye Prisoner[2] had to deliver by way of Confession and Warning to

---

[1] Daniel Haywood, one of the first deacons of the Old South Church in Worcester. He kept the first tavern in that town—he, his son, and grandson keeping for nearly a hundred years a hotel on the site of the Bay State. This old hotel is still standing in Worcester, having been moved years ago to the southeast corner of Salem and Madison streets.

[2] The sad story of Hugh Henderson we learn from these dying confessions, which, together with a poem on his untimely death, were published as a broadside and sold as a warning to all youth.

He was of Scotch-Irish descent and came to Massachusetts about 1735, and for two years indulged his wicked practices, when he was arrested and convicted of breaking and entering the house of Abner Newton, of Westborough, who lived at this time in the old Thomas Rice garrison. (See note for March 14, 1737.)

46   DIARY OF REV. EBENEZER PARKMAN.

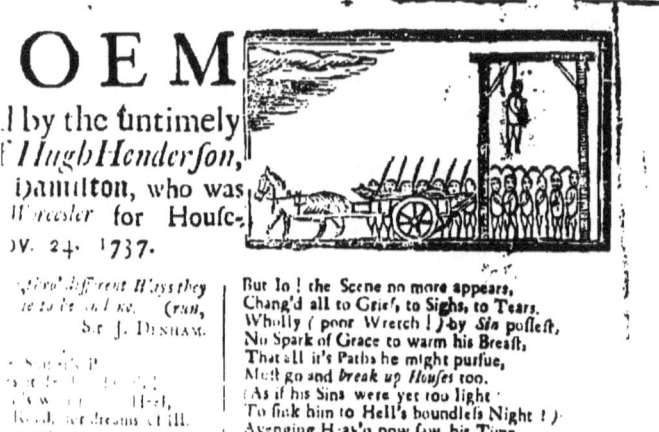

y^e World before his Execution. In it I was as punctual

Four indictments were found against him, two for burglary and two for larceny, and he was tried, convicted and sentenced to be hanged on one for burglary. The Court was the Superior Court of Judicature sitting at Worcester in September, with the following named judges on the bench: Benj. Lynde, Paul Dudley, Edmund Quincy, Jonathan Remington and Richard Saltonstall.

In the following extracts from the Confession, we can detect Mr. Parkman's pen:

"The Confession and Dying Warning of Hugh Henderson Who was executed at Worcester in the County of Worcester, Nov. 26 1737. Signed by him in the Presence of four of the Ministers, the Morning of the Day of his Execution.

" I, Hugh Henderson, otherwise through my wickedness called

and strict as I could be in inserting his own words as near
as I could, and when any others were used, It—

John Hamilton of about 28 or 29 Years of Age, was born in Armagh
in the Kingdom of Ireland, received Baptism in the Manner of the
Presbyterians and was brought up by my uncle, who was obliged
to give me suitable Learning, but did not; which Neglect, together
with my own Neglect of learning the word of God afterwards, was
a great reason of my taking to such wicked Courses as have brought
me to my unhappy, untimely End.

"I began with smaller Sins, while I was Young: with but stealing Pins: against which I received warning oftentimes, but persisted in it, and was very disobedient, till I increased further in Sin."

Then follows warning to various classes of people and confession of various sins, and the confession ends:

"Having given this Warning, I desire to commend myself to the Charity and Prayers of all God's People for me, and that You would lift up your Hearts to God for me, for the Pardon of my Sins, an interest in Christ, and that I may be sanctified by the Spirit of God: But above all I commend myself to the infinite Mercy of God, in my dear Redeemer, begging and beseeching that through the Merits of His Blood, I may this Day be with Him in Paradise.

"HUGH HENDERSON
"Signed with his Mark.

"A True Copy Examined
"Per EBR. PARKMAN."

The Poem is entitled:

"A Poem occasioned by the Untimely Death of Hugh Henderson alias John Hamilton who was hanged at Worcester for House Breaking, Nov. 24, 1737"—and an extract therefrom reads:—

"The Scene we did but lately view
Too well evinces this is true—
A Man with healthful Vigour bless'd
The Morn of life but hardly past.

Introduction to the Latter Part of the Journal.
1778.

Many changes had come to Mr. Parkman, his family, and to the town, since he wrote the accounts of his courtship of Susanna Sharpe and of Hannah Breck. Forty-one years had slipped away. The little church on the hill had given place to a larger but still unpretentious meeting-house on the Common. He was living now, he had been for many years, in his own handsome house on Main Street.

> Compelled to leave the pleasing Light,
> And *stretch away* to endless Night;
> Because regardless of his Peace,
> He chose the flowery Path of Vice."

The uncle receives his deserts in the poem as follows:

> " But when he met with no Restraint,
> And found his Uncle was no Saint,
> In Vice's pleasing Steps he ran."

The N. E. Weekly Journal, Dec. 6, 1737, says:

"On the day of his Execution the Rev. Mr. Campbell of Oxford preached to the Prisoner and a great assembly, a very suitable sermon on 1 Peter 4-5. The Prisoner was exceedingly moved and in such Anguish of soul that the Expressions of it in the face of the congregation, in crying and moans, in prayers and tears and passionate gesture there were even to disturbance.

"At the place of execution, after the Rev. Mr. Hall of Sutton had prayed, the prisoner with great earnestness desired all that were present to hearken well to what was going to be read to them, and to mind to take the warning contained in it, after which he put up a most importunate and pathetical prayer himself which manifested more of knowledge of religion, sense of his own state and humble faith and hope in God, than anything that has been received from him before."

So was ended this sad chapter in the history of Worcester County—her first execution!

THE PARSONAGE.

By deed of date April 5, 1750, he had purchased the following-described tract of land from Nathan Brigham, of Southborough:

"A certain tract of land measuring five acres and a hundred and twenty-six rods, situate on the Plain Northerly of the Burying Place in the first Parish in Westborough, Westerly of the road leading to Sutton and is bounded easterly and southerly by land left for a way & by Forty rods of land left for the Meeting House and four Rods for Stables, and likewise by the Burying Place. Westerly by land of Capt. John Maynard, Northerly by sd Parkman's land & Northwesterly by Common land."

His house, which he built where Dr. Curtis' old residence now stands, can still be seen on High Street just beyond the schoolhouse.

The house was well built, and considered by some even extravagant, and Mr. Parkman himself records that he was criticized rather sharply by Lieut. Tainter because his window frames were so large. "And although," writes Mr. Parkman, "I rebuked him for thus speaking, especially as there were many persons present, yet I was disturbed thereat; and the frames *were* larger than I intended, and I would rather they had been smaller."

About 1753 the new meeting-house was finished, and here Mr. Parkman preached until his death. Here were held the town meetings and nearly all the important gatherings of the people. Originally there was no steeple, and as it began its career so it ended it, for the steeple and porches were removed about 1835, when it was converted to business purposes. As the old Arcade, it stood until a few years ago. Now nothing remains of it but the round window in the possession of the Historical Society, and much of its rich old oak converted into picture frames and bookcases and spoons and rulers, treasured in many a house in town as a memento of the days of Mr. Parkman and the people he loved and tended.

The forty-one years had made many changes in the people, too. We miss the old names of 1737, and greet new ones in these later years. The young minister had become an old man, and feebleness and infirmity hampered his work. But, aside from the physical debility, we recognize the same man,—still doubting his own worthiness, still striving to rightly discharge his duty, still imploring Divine grace, and finding in the most straitened circumstances abundant evidence of the loving and merciful hand of Providence. His happiness now is largely in his friendships, and especially in the children and grandchildren which so fill his heart. We read the entry of these latter years with less amusement, but with more tenderness and reverence, as he lays before us the motives and thoughts of his daily life. And the people of his day go in and out before us—our own familiar friends.

NOVEMBER 1778.

I bless God for ye Light & Privileges of another of the blessed Days of ye Son of Man. May I be in the Spirit on ye Lord's Day! I preached A. M. with some Fervency once more on Ps. 92. 7 and beseech God to grant Success!

Mrs. Ruth Godfry with her little Son,—dind here. P. M. I went on in Repeating Sermon on Gal. 3. 14, which it is with God alone to render effectual! May He graciously vouchsafe it!

N. B. The Singers more generally sat today in ye Front, & some no. stood up. Mr. Lemuel Badcock was among y^m. We were not so happy as to have any singing in my Family today—not in ye Evening. Mr. Jonas Bradish did not come to me in any part of ye Day, notwithstanding all that he said yesterday. I am sorry he gives no more reason of y^t conduct.

2. No Mr. Bradish here today neither. Altho he assured me he would come today, on y^e Account of showing me some Bounds. Perhaps the weather might hinder that Business,

THE ARCADE

but I think to have come and conferred with me on y^e Several affairs depending. Dr. Hawes[1] acquaints me with his Mother's Death and y^t he is going to her Funeral Improving this opportunity I write to Mr. Moore and send it to Man's at Wrentham for Conveyance.

3. Mr. Bradish came, but gives me no reason to think he is at all sensible of any Guilt or Blame on account of ye Neglect of his Duty. And as to Bounds of ye Land which he laid out for me, he says he has been there and ye Land being now cleared, the monuments are all gone, and it is impossible to find them. Mr. Ezra Houghton of Chauxit came with a message from Mr. Mellen to request me to go up there, inasmuch as the Arbitrators on their Affairs were to meet, and he has sent to Mr Stone likewise. But I was obliged to deny. I must be otherwise employed, it is too cold, I have no horse, and know I can't get one &c. &c. Mr. Houghton dined here,—left me to go to Southboro'. Elias tries to get a horse to go to Cambridge, but in vain. P. M. I preached at Mr. Tainters' on Rev. 2. 10. Borrow

[1] James Hawes came to Westborough from Wrentham in 1764, and immediately took an influential position in town and church, which he held until his death, in 1821. He bought the house which in 1737 belonged to Cornelius Cook, and paid £80 for it with ten acres of land. He added the rooms beyond the small hallway to the original house. In his day it was painted red. In more recent years it has been plastered. James Hawes was lawyer and justice as well as physician. The Court was usually held in his dwellinghouse, and he entertained many travellers, charging for " loging " —supper—or brandy—as the case might be. A night's lodging was 6d, while two glasses of brandy were 9d.

He was always a good friend and neighbor of Mr. Parkman.

Mr. Tainter's Horse for Elias. Deacon Wood rides home with me. Mr. Potter has made Elias a coat.

4. Elias,[1] on Mr. Tainter's Horse returned to Cam-

HARVARD COLLEGE.

bridge. I gave him 14 dollars, my newest Shooes, a variety of cloatheing, half a large cheese &c &c. May God incline his Heart to Religion & Learning!

5. Mr Winslow Packard of Pelham brings Mr. Rob. Abercrombie's Salutation and ye gift of Mr. Eben^r Erskines Sermon on Ps. 118. 22 & on Isa. 9. 6. with ye true state of ye Process against him: To which is added a number of Sermons of the same eminent man, from various Texts.

---

[1] Elias, Mr. Parkman's youngest son, figures very prominently in the Journal. He was born January 6, 1761, consequently was now seventeen years old. He was educated as a physician and

The book is very acceptable to me and I am very thankful for it.

6. Mr. Amariah Frost jun^r was here and dined with us. I perceive that he has lately married Miss Esther Messinger of Wrentham, his first cousin. Mr. Caldwell of Sutton brought ye Horse which Elias rode and gratis. Toward night (being earnestly sent for) I went to see Mrs. Sarah (wife of Mr. Eb^r Maynard) who was very ill of Dysentery &c. prayed with her and ye Family. N. B. A letter from Elias by Caldwell.

7. A letter from my friend Quincy[1] at Medfield, dated

practiced medicine in Preston, Conn., and in Holliston, Mass. About 1792 he went to Milford, Mass., where his rich brother Samuel purchased a place for him. Breck and Samuel stocked a store for him; an apothecary and grocery combined. In 1793 he was licensed to sell spirituous liquors and in 1810 as an innholder. The Milford History calls him "A very social, kind-hearted and courteous man, but too easy in general temperament and habits to achieve financial success."

He married, in 1785, Alethina Belcher, of Preston, Conn. His oldest son was named Samuel Breck, after the two brothers who helped him so generously. This son afterwards went South, but he and all his family were drowned when the ill-starred Pulaski was lost. Dr. Elias' first wife died in 1792, and he married, in 1794, Susannah (Learned) Johnson. He named the eldest daughter of this marriage Alethina for his first wife, and the eldest son Johnson for her first husband. After he had eight children he adopted a little girl—Marie Antoinette.

Dr. Elias died Sept. 30, 1828, aged sixty-seven.

[1] This was Edmund Quincy, Judge of the Court of Common Pleas, and for many years a merchant of Boston. We can identify him from the son Henry (see Journal, June 5, 1780), who was born in 1726 and died May 27, 1780.

Sept 17. & Oct 1. ult. We hear that Nanny Beeton is in such Insanity as to go from her B^r John's in ye Night, and wandered up to Sutton. Word is left here from those at whose House she is to her Father, who is accordingly going after her to bring her home.

Edmund Quincy was born in 1703 and graduated at Harvard College in 1722, being therefore exactly the same age as Mr. Parkman, although the latter graduated a year earlier.

He had a large family of sons and daughters, among them Dorothy, who married John Hancock, noted for her beauty, wit and dignity.

She was born May 10, 1747.

During the summer of 1775, she visited at the house of her father's friend, Thaddeus Burr, in Fairfield, and there she met Aaron Burr. She was then engaged to Hancock, and she complains that her aunt would not allow Aaron Burr and herself to pass a moment in each other's company.

In the fall of this year she was married in the old Burr mansion, having a brilliant wedding, which proved to be the last merry-making ever held there, as it was burned in 1779 by order of Gov. Tryon.

Another daughter of Judge Quincy married Samuel Sewell, the old Judge's grandson.

Dr. Jacob Quincy was one of his sons.

The famous " Dorothy Q " of Holmes' poem was a sister of the Judge. She died in 1762.

A number of Judge Quincy's Letters are published in the Salisbury Memorial.

His house and store were on Summer Street and his brother Josiah's on Marlboro Street. He had a large garden, which joined his brother's. This house is called the Summer Street mansion.

He died in 1788, aged eighty-five, outliving Mr. Parkman by six years and being at the time of his death an acting magistrate of Suffolk County.

8. So kind and gracious is God y^t we are permitted to see ye light & enjoy the privileges of this day, which begins the 55th year since ye founding this church and my Ordination. While I bless God for His long Suffering, I would humble myself for my unfaithfulness and unprofitableness, imploring pardoning Mercy through the great Redeemer, and Grace to help me, and y^t may be sufficient for me for the Future. Preached on II. Pet: 1. 12. 13. P. M. on v. 14 with proper alterations of ye last, which had been delivered before. N. B. Several gentlemen were at meeting, P. M. which I suppose came from ye Arbitration at Chauxit.

9. Mr. Timothy Whitney was here to trade with me about my Oxen. Mr. Isaac Parker, where they have been kept, having refused to give what one after another judged they were worth viz. Eighty Pounds L. M. P. M. Visit Mr. Eb^r Maynard's wife & prayed with her. Visit old Mrs. Kelly and prayed there. N. B. Nanny Beeton seems composed. Mr. Robert Wilson and his wife (who was Patty Dunlap, grown hugely fat) were there. I rode to Mr. Han^h Parker's to enquire after wood, for we are reduced. At eve Mr. Andrews here to desire me to marry him tomorrow.

10. Mr. Timo. Whitney has got my oxen and pays me 40 £ L. M., and gives me his Horse for 40 £ more in three months with interest. N. B. Old Mr. Thos. Whitney is present and promises his son shall fulfill ye Engagement, and Breck[1]

[1] Breck, Mr. Parkman's eleventh child, was born in 1748. His wife, Susannah, whom he married in 1777, was the daughter of Col. Levi Brigham, of Northborough. Soon after his marriage, he opened a store in one end of the little house still standing on South

60 DIARY OF REV. EBENEZER PARKMAN.

was witness. Sophy[1] to Concord. Mr. Thos. Kendal hav-

B. Parkman,

Street, using the other end for a dwelling-place. At this time it stood between the parsonage and the church.

Breck left seven children, and was the ancestor of all the Parkmans who remained in Westborough.

[1] Sophy was the fourteenth child of Mr. Parkman, born in 1755. A little Journal kept by her for parts of the years 1777 and 1778 is still in existence, but unfortunately ends in July, 1778. She knits her

ing left Grafton, comes and takes what things he left here, dines with us, and goes for Framingham.

BRECK PARKMAN'S SHOP.

own stockings and gloves, spins thread, makes a skirt for Mrs. Baker, helps in quiltings, weaves shirts for Elias, bucks yarn, combs flax, scours pewter, &c., for her daily work. Her recreation consists in going to singing school, visiting her friends in the "hospital" sick with small pox, and making little trips to Northborough and even to Boston.

She married Elijah Brigham.   See note for Nov. 12.

P. M. Went to Widow Baker's, according to Mr. Andrews' Request. I married y^m, supped and we sing Watts' Ps. 128. 6 Dol.

11. This day as I suppose is ye Time appointed for ye Ordination of Mr. Ripley of Concord, but it's Rainy and by Noon a very Severe Storm of Wind and Rain. Thro Divine Favour we had wood brot yesterday by two of Capt. Maynard's[1] sons. He had sent none (y^t I know of) till now. But now we feel the Good of it; and are thankful.

[1] Capt. Stephen Maynard has the reputation of being the wealthiest man of his day in Westborough, and his house, burned a few years ago, was solid and handsome, and well fitted for the residence of a wealthy farmer. The work on his farm for many years was performed by slaves, and he was very loth to give them up, so loth, that the heavy stone walls by the side of the avenue leading to his house, are said to be among the very last labor performed by slaves in Massachusetts. In the house was one small room, reached by a sliding panel. This had brick walls with an arched ceiling and no window, and tradition affirms was used in the discipline of refractory slaves. The fire laid this chamber bare to the sunlight, for it was built in the chimney.

Capt. Maynard's wife—"Cousin Maynard," as Mr. Parkman calls her, was formerly Anna Gott, daughter of Dr. Benj. Gott, where Mr. Parkman visited so frequently in 1737, and of Sarah Breck, Madam Hannah Parkman's sister. She had previously married Dr. Samuel Brigham, and she was Capt. Maynard's second wife. Her daughter, Anne Brigham, married Isaac Davis, a neighbor of Capt. Maynard, and became the mother of many Davises, including Governor John.

Capt. Maynard, after a life of much activity and usefulness, died in 1806. His personal property was sold at auction, and included fifty old books and "a right in the Westborough Library"—besides all kinds of wearing apparel and household utensils—"puter" platters and "puter plats"—basens old and poor, &c., &c.

DIARY OF REV. EBENEZER PARKMAN.   65

12. Was at Deacon's Woods and with Squire Baker,[1] providing a team to plough my Orchard. I dind at Breck's, and P. M. at Mr. Nathan Maynard's, Bond's and Warren's. Master Elijah Brigham[2] returns with Sophy from Concord.

THE STEPHEN MAYNARD CHIMNEY.

[1] Perhaps no name appears more frequently in Mr. Parkman's Journal than that of Squire Baker, son of Lieut. Edward Baker. Like his father, he held many town offices. He was born May 10, 1736, and was married by Mr. Parkman, in 1758, to Martha Death. They had a son John.
[2] Elijah Brigham was the son of Col. Levi Brigham, whose father, David, is mentioned several times in the Journal for 1737. His

& informs that yesterday, Mr. Ripley was ordained. Rev. Josiah Bridge of Sudbury began with prayer. Mr. Haven father deeded him the north part of his farm where the Heath house now stands. It was a little further from the road than the Heath house, a low two-story house with rooms either side of the front door. After the death of Col. Levi, his son Winslow lived in the house. Elijah was the fourth child, born in 1751. Winslow, who is often mentioned in the Journal, was five years younger, and between the two brothers in age, was Susanna, Breck Parkman's wife. Josiah, born in 1758, was a doctor, and died unmarried when he was thirty years old, while Mindwell and Anna, at this time girls of eighteen and fifteen, both died unmarried; Mindwell when twenty-four and Anna when twenty-seven.

Elijah graduated from Dartmouth College and studied law. On September 21, 1780, he married Anna Sophia,—as related in the Journal. She lived three years after her marriage and left two children. Nov. 26, 1783, her brother Ebenezer writes: "Dear sister Brigham departed this life in full hopes of a glorious Resurrection to eternal Life! Alas!"

Elijah Brigham, after Mr. Parkman's death, continued to live in the parsonage, which is generally called the "Judge Brigham house." He served Westborough for many years as representative, senator and councillor, and Worcester County for sixteen years as Judge of the Court of Common Pleas, was elected to Congress in 1810, and was a member of that body until his death, in 1816.

He figures so prominently in the Journal that it may not be amiss to quote from Mr. Abner Morse who in writing of him says: "Of this man, I cannot speak in justice to convictions and escape the suspicion of extravagance among strangers; while among his acquaintance who survive, nothing would fail of a hearty response which I might say commendatory of his social and domestic virtues, his commercial integrity and honor, his great common sense and refinement, his patriotism and political integrity, his wisdom and benevolence, his fidelity to every official and important trust, and his services in the advancement of the moral, civil, and educational

of Dedham preached on ——. Mr. Eb' Bridge of Chelmsford prayed before ye charge and delivered it. Mr. Dana of Barre prayed after ye charge, Mr. Clark of Lexington gave ye Right Hand of Fellowship. May God graciously accept their Work and their Offerings, and may ye Ordained be Strong in ye Grace of our Lord Jesus Christ!

Mr. Jon^n Child kindly brings me a Barrell of Cyder. The Cyder is gratis. I gave him a Dollar for bringing it.

Mr. Ben How mends the Oven.

13. Old Mr. Nathan Maynard came with a yoke of oxen. Ben Wood with a yoke and my Tim. fetches a yoke of Squire's and his plough, and they plough ye Orchard, and a while at ye Island. Several loads of Wood were brought me: which is a great Comfort to me. I desire to thank God therefor. At eve, Mr. Jonas Bond of Sutton and his dauter here. They are returning home. They ask Sister Lydia to go up and stay awhile among them.

14. Mr. Joseph Farrar here going again to preach at Grafton.

The weather is now grown so cold and ye feed gone, we give the cattle dry meat and house the Cows and Calves.

15. On consideration of the New Year with this Church (which commenced last Sabbath) I went on A. M. with 2 Pet. 1. 14 & P. M. I put them in mind of what had been, and what still is, the subject of our preaching: viz: The Gospel of Christ from 1 Cor. xv. 1.

interests of the community in which he lived. 'Stranger, tread lightly at the grave of one such as thou ought to be, true to his conscience and country.'"

Sr. Brigham (Elijah) dind here. He delivers me a letter from Dr. Crosby who is in the Army, at Woodbury.

16. On this day was the Town Meeting, to Consider my Support, and by reason of ye extraordinariness of ye Depression of ye Medium of Commerce, & being persuaded y^t many persons were unknowing to my Circumstances and Some were desirous I would say something to inform y^m, probably Also if I did not send my mind to y^m, nor go to the Meeting, would make an Handle of that, and resest, say they did not know y^t I desired anything, what should they impose it for? therefore I sent y^m a paper (which see) drawn with as much wisdom and Care as I could. But it had not the Success that might reasonably be expected, except with regard to ye Wood, which they provided for handsomely. But as to sallery, they voted only £300 where every one asks in Lawful Money what they used to in old Tenor. Batherick was here at evening, & seemed very sorry the Town had done no more. Parkman Bradshaw came from Brookfield, and informs that his brother Benjamin grows worse. He lodged here.

17. Bradshaw leaves us to go to Cambridge, Boston &c. Wrote by him to my Dauter-in-law Sally. I attended the Association at Southboro. Messrs. Smith, Goss, Bridge and Whitney there. A committee from Mr. Goss's Church to ask advice about ye gathering of a Church in ye south part of Bolton. I returned home at eve. Henry Marble has been here in my Absence.

18. It was so fowl weather was disappointed as to killing a fat cow as designed.

19. I preached at Mr. Gale's[1] to his aged Parents on 2 Cor 4. 16. May God be pleased to grant Success! In returning called to see Mrs. Mallet &c.

20. Messrs. Newton and Thad Warrin came and killed a fat cow for me. Mr. Levi Frisby of Ipswich called and dind here. Bradshaw returned & lodged here.

21. He left us for Brookfield. Mr. Joseph Harrington

GALE TAVERN.

[1] Abijah Gale, innholder, lived on the road to Southborough, in the house recently occupied by Dennis Fitzpatrick. The large L has been burned, but the front of the house is substantially the same. He was selectman for the years 1778-80, and held other town offices during his life.

came to see me & talked about y̆ᵉ late Grant of y̆ᵉ Town and about y̆ᵉ Singing. He brot an extraordinary Present of Butter! P. M. Mr. Caleb Harrington came kindly and cut out and Salted my Beef. I desire to praise God for all His Favour!

22. Preached A. M. on 1 Cor. 15. 2 P M. repeated sermon on James 1. 22 which may God graciously accept & Bless!

Not a large Assembly by reason of y̆ᵉ rough, cold weather.

23. I visited Mr. Ebenezer Maynard's wife who is still sick and prayed P. M. Mr. Henry Marble makes me a Visit.

24. I am closely engaged in my Studys, tho it is not without difficulty by reason of y̆ᵉ Cold and ruggedness of y̆ᵉ Season.

25. Mr. Joshua Johnson came for y̆ᵉ Paper of advice of y̆ᵉ Association, which I have transcribed for y̆ᵉ Bolton committee. He dined here. Elias came up on foot from Cambridge, arrived seasonably and well. Susé came up with her child and lodged here.

26. *Thanksgiving.* I had prepared in part, but could not finish it. I improved part of sermon on Ps. 147. 1. 7; to page 7 and wrote additions on loose papers. Breck and all his were here at y̆ᵉ Entertainment, also Sr. Brigham (Elijah). May y̆ᵉ Lord accept our gratulations, and bless the Holy Word dispensed! - had excellent singing. I wrote by Bradshaw to my son Ebʳ at New Braintry.

27. Mrs. P.— poorly. Town meeting by adjournment. I hear yᵗ y̆ᵉ Town Committee is getting my Wood to Mr. Newton.

I wrote in part, the Conference between Q—— and W—— concerning ye Support of Ministers.

28. Elias was to have returned to Cambridge, but his Linnen &c was not ready. P. M. I rode to Southborough, and Mr. Stone came here. His Son, Mr. Thomas Stone and his wife, were both confined by Illness.

29. I preached at Southborough on Rev. 22. 17. A. & P. M. May a Divine Power accompany and render ye Word effectual, and especially to my own Soul! At eve. I returned home, as did Mr. Stone; who preached for me A. & P. M. on Phil: 2. 4. 5 which I pray God to bless and prosper!—I brot from Mr. Stone's Pike and Hayward's Cases of Conscience. Sr. Fay, Mrs. Maynard and her Niece, Miss — Witt dind here. I had a letter from Rev. Ezra Ripley of Concord, concerning his Ordination &c.

30. It is too great a storm for Elias to leave home.

I read part of Pike & Hayward's Cases. The Town meet by Adjournment & having dispatched their Business dissolved ye meeting. Sister Champney remains under much trouble by an almost constant Diarrhœa. Mr. Levi Warren here on account of ye private Meeting tomorrow.

Numerara dies nostras sic doce nos, Domine &c.

DECEMBER, 1778.

Breck sets up an Iron Stove in his shop.

I preached at Lieut. Levi Warren's, a third Exercise on Rev. 2. 10. May God be graciously pleased to add His own efficacious Blessing! N. B. Mr. Daniel Hardy was at Mr. Warren's before ye Exercise began and manifested his Disgust at my sermon on ye late Thanksgiving. He found fault with my saying so much about Singing ye praises of God. I replied y^t it was the very Business of the Day.—the present Truth—y^t if he was dissatisfied with it, he had need ask himself whether it was not because he *himself was out of Tune.*—After ye Exercises, Mr. Badcock and his Scholers sang a number of good Tunes, in Parts. We had also a plentiful Table Spread and agreeable Entertainment.

2. Elias sat out early to return to Cambridge & Timothy with him to bring back ye mare which he was to ride upon as far as Framingham. Timothy returns about 2 o'clock, and brings Patty Forbush, one of Mr. Eb^r Forbush's [1] Dauters to spin here. Mr. Dan'l Forbes [2] came

[1] Mr. Ebenezer Forbush and his father (Lieut. Forbush) are often mentioned in the Journal. The father, whom Mr. Parkman usually calls the old Lieut., was Thomas, son of Thomas, the original settler, and brother-in-law of Cornelius Cook. His house stood, until destroyed by fire two or three years ago, on the corner of East Main and Lyman streets, opposite the Tom Cook house. His son Ebenezer lived with him, and took the place after his father's death. His oldest daughter had married Thomas Andrews in 1776.

This house was probably built among the first in Westborough, but it would seem from the cellar that it originally was smaller, as the rooms on the west of the front door were built with no cellar under them.

Ebenezer at this time was forty-eight, the old Lieutenant eighty-four, while Ebenezer's daughter Hannah, married to Thos. Andrews and perhaps living in this house, was twenty-three.

Patty Forbush, whom Mr. Parkman mentions as coming to spin for Mrs. Parkman, was the second daughter of Mr. Ebenezer Forbush, who two years later married Fortunatus Miller.

[2] Daniel Forbes was a son of Dea. Jonathan, an original settler of

LIEUT. FORBUSH HOUSE.

kindly to inform Mrs. P—— of a Medicine, which he would send her some of, to cure her Indispositions.

3. Sophy carrys yarn to Miss Molly Harrington, to be wove for a great coat for Elias. P. M. Mrs. Green and her Sister, ye Widow Whipple made us a kind Visit. The latter being about to leave us and live at Prince-town.

4. At eve came Mr. Elisha Forbes and his Wife to Visit us, and brought an extraordinary present. 31 pounds of Meat, Beef and Pork and a Cheese of 12 lbs., and supped with us. Mr. Forbes also offered y^t if I would take one of ye Boston newspaper, he would pay for a year. May God reward his Benevolence and Generosity!

5. Mr. Nathaniel Sherman in his journey home to Mt. Carmel in New Haven called and broke fast here. I wrote by him to the Widow Pierpoint for my Notes on Job. 19, 25 &c. Rev. Buckminster of Rutland[1] hindered by

---

Westborough. He was born in 1710. He lived on that part of his father's farm known as Jackstraw, and his cellar can still be traced in the pasture near the road over the hill. He was selectman, representative in the Legislature, and one of the Committee of Correspondence. For an account of his death and strange funeral see the Journal for January 14, 1780.

Mr. Elisha Forbes, of whom Mr. Parkman often speaks, was a son of Daniel's born in 1745. He lived in the house formerly occupied (1737) by Dea. Simon Tainter.

[1] Rev. Joseph Buckminster, of Rutland, "had a dignified and ministerial appearance, wore a gray or white wig, cocked hat, and white bands; was a man of talent and learning, and set his face like a flint against immorality of every kind." He was what was called a "Sublapsarian Calvinist." "It is a comfort to think," writes Mrs. Lee, " that the thing itself is not so harsh as its name; for it seems an effort to soften the stern features of Calvinism

weather from proceeding on his journee home. Stopt and tarrys here with us. Send his horse to Deacon Wood's. Mr. Charles Newton begins to bring wood from Ministerial Lot, viz. 5. feet.

6. I administer ye Lord's Supper: but Mr. Buckminster preached A. M. on Job: 5. 4. P. M. on Mat. 16. 26. Mrs. Mainard and Miss Patty Fisk dind here.

May it please God to accept our Offerings and bless His Word and Ordinances to us! Deac. Wood came after meeting.

7. Mr. Buckminster went up to ye Deacon's to Breakfast, before he left us. I rejoice in God's great Gifts to him. May it be continued!

8. I wrote Sundry Letters, particularly to my Grandson Isaac Baldwin at Dummer School in Byfield, & to Rev. Mr. Levi Frisbie minister at Ipswich.

9. Tho exceeding cold and windy, Breck sat out for Boston. Mr. Chas. Newton brot wood, 5 feet and dind here. P. M. he brot 6 feet. Master Fisk and his sister Patty, Mrs. Fisher, Miss Nabby Martyn visit here. Fisk is going to keep school in ye South part of ye Town. I finished *Drexelius*.

10. Newton brings a load A. M. 6 feet (he says) P. M. his man another load 6 ft. | yet it proves very stormy.

I would bless God for my many Comforts. Concerned for Breck who is I suppose at Boston, and has sent a load of corn.

and to mingle a little human clay in the iron and granite of its image."

He was pastor in Rutland for fifty years—from 1742 to 1792.

11. The earth covered with snow. Windy and cold. But we have supplys. D. G. Sad news from Otter Creek & Cherry Valley.

12. Breck returns from Boston, to our Joy safe, tho thro' much Hardship. Says a Murder was committed the night before last at Charlestown Neck, of a countryman found next morning, two clubbs lying by him. N. B. No Murder but a man perished in the storm. (This evidently written in later.)

13. Breck is out of Wood. Susé herself and the child, her sister Mindwell & Billy Spring came up here to be with us over ye Sabbath. I preached A. M. what I had prepared further on 1 Cor. 15. now on ye 2. middle clause, "if ye keep in memory what I preached unto you." It was a storm of Rain and difficult getting to Meeting.

Breck, his Family & Br. Josiah dind here. P. M. delivered with variations and large additions my Sermon on Ps: 147. 19-20. May a merciful God forgive my Defects and bless what was agreeable to his Will! N. B. Squire Baker was very kind in coming with his Sleigh, and carrying me and Sophy to meeting, bring us back, both A. & P. M.

14. Breck had wood brot him. Susé &c. returned home. I finished Mr. Locke on Toleration. At eve Mr. Elisha Forbes here.

15. Timothy goes to Mrs. Temple at Upton for Cloth, but in vain.

I am entertained with Dr. Fuller's England's Worthys.

16. It being moderate air, I rode in ye Sleigh—to see old Mrs. Baker, who has been sick. I dind there and

thence I proceeded to visit Mr. Joseph Grout[1] and family, being out of health; but Mrs. Grout herself is sick of a Fever. Their son Joseph this day returned home from Warfare, but Mr. Grout is greatly concerned about his son W^m. at Fishskill, and Benj. is gone a great while after him, and hear nothing. I prayed with y^m. Called at Lieut. Jonⁿ. Grout's, who is come home, from the Service. Newton's man, Thos. Harrington, 2 Load. 6 feet each.

17. Sent 9 yards of cloth to Deacon Brown's to be dressed for a great coat for Elias. At eve there were two marriages, viz: Mr. David Goodell[2] to Miss Eliz. Brigham (Cousin

---

[1] Joseph Grout and Sarah his wife had twelve children, the oldest, Joseph, Jr., a young man of twenty-three, the youngest, baby Lucy, two years old. William was just twenty, and Benjamin twenty-one. The family lived about a mile from the village on Main Street, on the place now owned by James McTaggart.

He and his wife are buried under one stone in the old burying-ground—on the bottom of which can faintly be deciphered the words:—

"Death like an overflowing flood—
Hath swept us both away—"

Lieutenant Jonathan Grout and his wife Hannah had two sons among their seven children, Moses and Jonathan, Jr.

He died in 1801, and is buried also in the old burying-ground, with the inscription:—

"Consider this as you pass by
That you likewise are born to die
And there 's a work assigned to the
Prepare for death & follow me."

[2] Cousin Maynard's daughter, Elizabeth Brigham, was at this time twenty-six years old, while David Goodale, of Marlborough, was born in 1716, which would make him a man of sixty-two. As Mr. Parkman the following Sunday speaks of his "new spouse," he probably was a widower. The "new spouse" died in 1798.

Maynard's Dauter) 8 Dollars, and Mr. William Acock to Mrs. Mary Lewis. 3 Dollars.

18.

19. Breck has a fine fat Turkey roasted here.

20. Preach A. M. on 1 Cor: 15. 2 last clause which may God succeed!

Mr. David Goodell the Bridegroom and his Bride together with her mother Maynard dind here, as did Master Elijah Brigham. P. M. The Bridegroom preached on 1 Cor: 6. 19-20, and I hope to ye Glory of God. He went from ye Meeting House, with his new Spouse, to Capt. Maynard's.

21. Messrs. Nathan Maynard Junr and Caleb Harrington killed a large sow for me. I lent Maynard sixty-six dollars. Mrs. P. kills 5 Geese, & 6 dunghill Fowls for market with ye Pork. For it appears necessary to make some money of what we raise that we may be able to purchase what is wanting in other respects

22. Exceeding tedious time for Cold Snow blowing &c.

Patty Forbush came here to Spin. My days are a Shadow.

23. Mr. Joseph Harrington goes with his Team for Marblehead, and takes my Pork, Geese and Fowls, to the care of Mr. Elisha Forbes for Marketing. Am engaged in Sermonizing somewhat, but oh! my leanness. Breck trades with two swine drovers, and buys two shoats for me, at between 17 & 18 pence ye pound.

Hear the sorrowful news of aged, pious Master Minot's death. The Righteous are taken away from the Evil to come, but we that remain lose much in losing their Prayers.

The Lord sanctifie this Death to ye surviving widow & Son; and to me under ye Loss of such a worthy Friend!

24. Breck and his dine here on a roast Turkey of his providing. Elias came home on foot from Cambridge. He came from there yesterday, & with him Young Nathan Fisk, a Freshman. They dind here. It is so very cold, Fisk lodges with Elias at Breck's.

25. It remains exceeding cold. They breakfast here. I write by Fisk to Mr. Benj. Bradshaw, who I hear is worse. Fisk sets out for Brookfield. Mr. Nathan Maynard brings a piece of Camblet,[1] 14 yds from Mr. Benj. Howell of Worcester, for which Mr. Maynard delivered to him from me 20 dollars. Mr. Han{h} Parker, late Constable, is here and pays me what Money was behind in ye Wood rate, which was about £6. 12. For which I gave him a receipt in full; only it is to be remembered yt Messrs. Joseph Grout, Jos. Green and Benaj Brigham have not brot theirs. At night Patty Forbush goes home.

26. An extraordinary tedious Time Cold, blowing, snowing. How invaluable ye Mercies I enjoy. I am thro great goodness, in health, Habitation, Cloths, Food, Fewel: my son and Timothy &c tend the Fires, the Cattle, get Wood and Water &c. but how many are at this time exposed to terrible *Hardships*, both by land and Sea! May

---

[1] Camlet, according to the Century Dictionary, "A very durable plain cloth, used for cloaks and the like; a water-proof material in common use before the introduction of India rubber. All the kinds of camlet are, in a certain sense, imitations of Oriental camel's-hair cloth; they are made of hair, especially that of goats, with wool or silk, and present a veined or wavy appearance."

God extend pity to y⁴ miserable poor,— to Sailors, to Soldiers, to Teamers abroad & their destitute Families at home!

27. Cloudy and cold, but sun broke out, but still very cold. Very few came to Meeting. On consideration of severe storms and intense cold, I repeated with some additions Sermon on Ps. 148, 7-8. P. M. preached what I had prepared on Mark 9. 24. Read the proclamation for Continental Thanksgiving, which I received but this day at noon.

28. Mr. Elisha Forbes pays me for my Pork & 6 Geese £38. 18.

29.

30. CONTINENTAL THANKSGIVING. preach on Isa: 1. 11. Breck &c dind.

31. Elias rides to Cambridge. Mr. John Fay dines here and kills two Hogs for me. Mr. Harr. helping. Cousen Maynard made us a Visit. Master Fisk also. Drank tea & y⁴ last tarrys in the evening. My dear dauter Cushing came in a Sleigh with Mr. Neh⁵ Maynard.

JANUARY, 1779

I bless God for y⁴ Light of another morning, which begins A NEW YEAR of y⁴ divine patience and Long suffering towards me, which (I confess) am most unworthy. With Thanksgiving for y⁴ Mercies received and penitently acknowledgement of my ingratitude & innumerable offences, I implore Remission, thro the Merits and Mediation of my only and most dear Saviour, and humbly beseech the divine Favour to be extended to me and mine still; I desire devoutly to renew my Solemn engagements by Covenant to be y⁰ Lord's, and commit to Him, y⁰ Sovereign of my Life, all my Cares and Concernments, all y⁰ Changes and Events of this peculiarly difficult year, or what part of it, it shall please y⁰ great Supreme to vouchsafe me to continue in this frail uncertain State!

—— But my dauter Cushing being here, & soon to return, and Col. Job Cushing dining with us, Breck also and his, I was much interrupted and prevented: very unavoidably. May y⁰ Lord extend compassion!

2. My dauter leaves us to return with Mr. Neh. Maynard. I lent her Pool's Annot.ⁿˢ. Vol. 1. Fuller's Pisgah Light, and the Life of Dr. Inc. Mather. Elias returns from Cambridge. He says y⁰ Dr. Appleton is ill.

3. I have prepared one sermon on Ps. 90. 2, & delivered it. A. M. Master Elisha Fisk, which keeps y⁰ South School, dined here. I thought it best to deliver P. M. part of my discourse on Matt. 22. 37-38 to page 6. with additions according to y⁰ occasion.

4. Walked A. M. to Dr. Hawes Wrote Letter to Mr. Forbes.¹ Col. Cushing dind here. At eve came from Brookfield my kinsman Mr. Alexander Oliver, and lodged here.

---

¹ Probably his son-in-law, Rev. Eli Forbes—a son of the first Jonathan, and brother of Daniel Forbes. He had married in 1752, Mr. Parkman's daughter Mary who had died in 1776. He married again eight months later Mrs. Lucy Sanders, whose children, Charlotte and Jo, visit at Mr. Parkman, as recorded in the Journal. Mrs. Lucy Forbes died in 1780, and after one more marriage of eleven years, he married for his fourth wife Mr. Parkman's daughter Lucy, the widow of Col. Jeduthan Baldwin, of Brookfield.

After graduating at Harvard College, Eli Forbes was settled as

5. Oliver goes on his journey to Boston. I preached at Deac. Wood's on 2 Tim. 1. 13. omitting in many parts, & adding such passages as were necessary to accommodate it to ye Present times. N. B. Breck agrees with a Post to bring Newspapers &c.

6. Capt. Jonas Brigham[1] and his wife were so benevolent as to present me a Cheese. I take ye more notice of this because he has been so long aloof, but I rejoice in his friendly Disposition. Elias is Cyphering.

7. I rode in ye Sleigh to see ye Widow Rice (widow of ye late Mr. Edmund Rice.) As I went I called to see old Mr. James Maynard and his Wife. I visited and dined at Mr. J. Crooks. N. B. He lately lost his pocket book with 300 dollars & other papers. In returning home I called at Mr. Amasa Maynard's. At evening, Mr. Nathan Maynard, jun^r here, and returns me 50 Dollars (in one Bill) of ye money he lately borrowed. Sixteen Dollars are yet behind.

minister in North Brookfield. In 1759, he went as chaplain in the army, with the regiment of which Stephen Maynard was captain, and, as Constantine Hardy records in his small journal, he preached many a faithful sermon at Ticonderoga and Crown Point, on texts singularly appropriate to the occasions. He is called the Rev. Mr. Forbush, but after his return from the campaign, he adopted the more correct spelling of Forbes.

In 1776, he was installed over the Church in Gloucester where he died in 1804, leaving a fine portrait of himself and a goodly estate.

[1] Capt. Jonas Brigham was an uncle of Elijah, and lived in his father David's old home. He was elected to many town offices,—serving for seven years as selectman—was a member of the Vigilance Committee, and a delegate to the County Congress at the beginning of the Revolution. His wife was Persis Baker.

8. I reckoned with Breck, & paid y⁰ full of his Account. The Ballance from Sept. 1777 to Dec. 31. 1778 (likewise Mr. Stockwell's account of 5 ⅛ & some change borrowed 7/6) was £57. 19. 2. lawful money.

9. Mr. Badcock (the singer) brought me from Mr. R. Cranch's of (Old) Braintree, Vol. I of y⁰ Universal and historical Biographical Dictionary in large 8vo. This volume goes no further than A. there are 11 vol. more. A small piece of Cloth for Elias, a great Coat received from Deac. Brown's.

10. I preached what I had composed on Mark 9. 24. P. M. I went on & finished Repeating on Matt 22. 37-38. May God graciously concur!

11. I diligently read Biography. Dr. Hawes in the Evening. He offers to pay me money for Timothy's work for him last year (15 days in y⁰ whole, Stephen Maynard worked 2½ for me, Timmy's at 2 Dolls. and Stephen's at 3,) but I told y⁰ Doctor it was in y⁰ way of exchanging work, & therefore I expected to have work again for it. N. B. I wrote by y⁰ Doctor to Dav. Sanger.

12. *Biography.* have y⁰ Surprising News of y⁰ awful Death of Benj. Andrews of Boston Esq. who last —— shot himself through y⁰ Head by a Pistol, which he was handling, & not aware y' it was loaded. Lord, what is Man!

13. Susé rode to Capt. Maynard's in y⁰ Sleigh and safely, but in returning y⁰ Mare took a start, and tore away with Speed from Susé, who had got out of the Sleigh, and came home o' foot: but y⁰ mare first, broke y⁰ Sleigh and threw out a Case of Gin—however broke but one Bottle (which

might at this time stand at — Dollars, but no Mischief done to Life or Limb. The praise to God!

14. Yesterday and today much engaged in Biography. Sent to Mr. Cushing, President Edwards on Free Will, and wrote to him, by ye Widow of ye late Major Brigham. Young Mr. Frost here and lodges.

15. Mr. Frost leaves me, but goes to Breck, and I perceive he is about to set up a Store at Mill River.

16. Closely applied as I have been for some days before on my preparations. Yet all I can by my slow writing is one sermon.

17. Preached A. M. on Mark 14. 24, and finish my present Design upon this Text. May God graciously succeed it! Mrs. Maynard dines with us, as well as Master Fisk. P. M. Repeated on Joh. 15. 5.

18. Dr. Hall of Sutton[1] in his Journey to Concord calls here.

[1] Rev. David Hall was settled as pastor of the Sutton Church in 1729, with an "Honorable Selery" of £100 a year of Province Bills or its equivalent in supplies. After a pastorate of sixty years, he died in 1789. The Worcester Spy for May 12 of that year says:—

"His character as an able orthodox divine, pungent, zealous preacher, and his steady regard to the distinguishing doctrines of Christianity, with the sobriety and exemplary gravity of his life, and his tender affection for his family and flock, are too well known to require illustration; it may suffice to notice, that the general esteem and respect for him was manifested by the large concourse of people (estimated at more than a thousand) who attended his funeral, with a solemnity becoming the occasion."

He had a family of thirteen children, and many of his descendants have distinguished themselves as doctors, lawyers and minis-

At eve came Mr. Daniel Forbes jun^r from Brookfield. Says Mr. Bradshaw grows very weak, presently came his Brother Nathan from Walpole, going to see him. The latter lodges here. N. B. Mr. Badcock keeps a singing-school at Mr. Barn. Newton's. Elias and Timothy go to it to hear.

19. A. M. Mr. Badcock here. An uncommonly rigorous Season. By reason of Breck's agreeing with a post to ride this Road, I have ye Benefit to read two of ye Boston Newspapers ; Saturdays and Mondays, which arrive here on Tuesday evening.

20. Mr. John Forbes of Rutland on Otter Creek which (thro mistake) we heard was taken by ye enemy, came to see us, being well and safe. In reading ye Biographical Dictionary—Life of Dr. Atterbury.——

21. Tho very Cold yet Breck goes in ye sleigh to Boston.

22. At eve came my Kinsman, Nathaniel Bradshaw from Brookfield—tells me his Bro^r Benj. is so low y^t he himself gives up & thinks he shall soon depart. Nathl lodges here.

23. Cousin Bradshaw leaves us to return to Stoughton-ham. At eve Breck returns from Boston. Inform. y^t his sister Sally is become more sociable and chearful.

24. Delivered A. M. to a small congregation, an exercise y^t is part of Expos. of Mat. 17. 17 to 21. but it being a continuation of ye Discourse on Mark 9. 24. I read on in

ters. His youngest daughter, Deborah, married Rev. Daniel Grosvenor, who is occasionally mentioned in the Journal as the pastor of the Grafton Church.

Rev. David Hall, as well as Mr. Parkman, kept a Diary for many years, which is preserved in the rooms of the Massachusetts Historical Society.

Mark 9 to 29. P. M. preached on Mat. 22. 39-40. which I designed as a second part to y⁰ Discourse on Mat. 22. 37-38. Master Moses Brigham[1] who keeps school at y⁰ East Quarter of y⁰ Town dind here.

25. Being at y⁰ Shop, Capt. Fisher and Mr. Badcock were there and acquainted me with the Desire of y⁰ Singing

FORBES HOMESTEAD.

[1] Moses Brigham was the oldest son of Moses Brigham, Sen., and Mehitable Grout, who were living at this time in the house known as the old Forbes homestead and now occupied by Geo. A. Ferguson. It is situated on East Main Street, about a mile from the village. His sister Sarah had married, seven years before this, Jonathan Forbes—the third of the name, and through this marriage the Moses Brigham house passed into the Forbes family.

School to have a Lecture preached to ym, and though (as they say) they would be glad if Mr. P. would himself preach, yet because of the disquietment among ye People, about singing, and for ye sake of drawing in people, it was mentioned to ask one of the neighboring Ministers, particularly Mr. Sumner[1] to preach it. I replyed with Consent.

JOSEPH SUMNER.

Moses Brigham, Jun., the school teacher, left Westborough and settled in Hanover, N. H., and afterwards in London, C. W.
As we learn from the entry for March 26, he was lodging at that time at Mr. Andrews', who lived on East Main Street. Probably he "boarded 'round" during the week.

[1] Joseph Sumner, for many years an intimate friend of Mr. Parkman, was pastor of the Shrewsbury Church.

provided they would acquaint ye appointed Choristers with it, and endeavor to have them lead in ye Affair.

26. Mr. Elisha Parker here A. M. on ye Same Business, of ye Singing Lecture—to write to Mr. Sumner &c. but I answered him as I did Capt. Fisher yesterday.

P. M. Deac. Wood. here—brot. a large Spare Rib, advised with him ab't Singing Lecture and he approved of ye Steps proposed.

Mr. Peter Whitney,[1] his Wife & Child, also Mr. Ham-

> He was born in 1740—January 19—so at this time had just passed his thirty-ninth birthday. He was settled in Shrewsbury in 1762, Mr. Parkman making the ordaining prayer.
>
> He lived until 1824, when he was eighty-five years of age, having been settled in Shrewsbury for sixty-two years.
>
> He was a very large man, being six feet and four inches in height and of commanding presence. He wore a white wig and three-cornered hat.
>
> Mrs. Sumner is not only mentioned in the Journal, but Mr. Parkman owed her many a pleasant evening and comfortable night. "She was," says Rev. Peter Whitney, "descended from a family respectable from the infancy of the country to this time. Such was her deportment in her station as not to diminish the lustre of the name nor detract from its deserved distinction." She was Lucy Williams, of Pomfret.
>
> [1] Rev. Peter Whitney, of Northborough, is best known to fame as the author of the History of Worcester County, a fact which perhaps he did not foresee when he wrote in the preface: "Had the writer of these sheets known before he began what a labor it would have been, he would not have attempted it, but having begun he was unwilling to desist."
>
> The historian of Northborough says "that he was distinguished for the urbanity of his manners, easy and familiar in his intercourse with his people, hospitable to strangers and always ready to

mock, came over in a Sleigh to visit us. and N. B. Mr. Daniel Forbes was here, tarrying after y^e Company & gave me great Disquietment about y^e Support of my Family,

give a hearty welcome to his numerous friends; punctual to his engagements; observing an exact method in the distribution of his time; having a time for everything and doing everything in its time, without hurry or confusion; conscientious in the discharge

what number in it they were willing to maintain, and what not—that 300 and my wood was an honorable sufficiency &c. But it was too apparent y^t he was put out of Humour by my consulting him about my advising ye Singers to invite ye Choristers to lead in ye proposed plan of ye Singing Lecture. For he said those men had been too much courted already, and had conducted but indecently towards ye Singers; so that they did not deserve such respect to be shown y^m. On ye other Hand, I conceived it would be most prudent in me, in time of so much Difficulty, to advise to a Method y^t must needs be most conciliating, and prevent further Complaint. May God graciously impart the Wisdom y^t may be profitable to direct, under such trying Circumstances.

of his duties as a Christian minister; catholic in his principles and in his conduct; always taking an interest in whatever concerned the prosperity of the town and the interests of religion,— he was for many years the happy minister of a kind and affectionate people."

He was the son of Rev. Aaron Whitney, of Petersham, and was born there Sept. 6, 1744, being at this time thirty-five years old. He had been ordained in Northborough in 1767. He was a staunch patriot, and in 1776 preached a sermon in which he enumerated twenty-six crimes of which King George was guilty. This discourse was dedicated to John Hancock, and every sentence in it was calculated to arouse a love of freedom and a resolve to use the sword boldly in doing the work of the Lord.

He married Julia Lambert, of Reading.

"He passed," says a notice of his death, "his long ministry in perfect peace and harmony both with the church and society."

In 1888 a memorial tablet was erected to his memory in the First Congregational Church of Northborough.

27. Mr. Newton, at eve, after his sledding wood today, thinks he has brot ye Quantity agreed for: but it was not so in my Memorandum Book.

28. Mr. Newton brings more wood, and brings his own Account which I copy and cast up, but we find that now he has brot enough to make up 35 cord. Mr. N. Maynard jun^r. came with a load of six feet: half of which was for Mr. Joseph Green, & ye other half for Mr. Newton. There is still more wood brot out from ye Lot to Beeton's: the charge for cutting and sledding out so far, he throws in, and we part in peace.

One Mr. W^m. Parkhurst of Coi's Hill, calls to inform y^t on Monday deceased and yesterday was buryed Mr. Benjamin Bradshaw at Brookfield!!!

May God graciously support all of us under this His holy Stroke! Especially may my Grand Dauter have grace to improve suitably this Sorrowful Bereavement!

At eve Mr. Eli Whitney and Mr. Elisha Parker here, and desire me to appoint a Singing Lecture, and to write to Mr. Sumner to come and preach it: on Thursday next (the 4th of February) at 2 P. M. Breck, Susè with her Baby, Molly Pratt, go in a Double Sleigh, and Mr. Elijah Brigham and Sophy are with y^m to Mr. Daniel Grout's at Grafton. Elias and Timothy to ye Singing School (as hearers) at Mr. Barn. Newton's.

We have ye sad news y^t Mr. Peter Adams, heretofore of this Town (son of ye late Mr. Elephalet Adams) was suddenly killed by ye Falling of a Tree, at New Guildford N. H. May God sanctifie so awful a Dispensation to all Survivors, and in particular to ye mournful Widow (who was Susanna Pratt of this place) and her Orphan Children!

29. This Day is memorable for ye Sorrows I was plunged into in ye year 36 (43 years since) when ye first Partner of my Joys and Divider and Sharer of my Griefs was taken away: I remember still ye Wormwood and ye Gall—my Soul is yet humbled within me. May God grant me true and thorow Humiliation!

I was interrupted by two setts of Company: first Mrs. Parker & Mrs. Davis, which rode over here to making a Visit, but especially by Rev. Grosvenor[1] and his Wife & child, accompanied by Rev. Mr. Farrar and Mr. Grosvenor's young Brother Nathan—in a Sleigh—all of y^m dind here.

I wrote to Mr. Sumner & sent it by Mr. Elisha Parker to come and preach to ye Singers next Thursday.

30. Mr. Jonⁿ Maynard brot a load of Wood to me for Breck, in Return for a load which he borrowed of me, and Mr. Maynard brot gratis a load of that wood which Mr. Ch. Newton left at Beeton's.

[1] "Rev. Daniel Grosvenor," says the Grafton History, "was a man of very pleasing manners, both in the pulpit and out of it, dignified in his bearing, courteous and engaging in his address. Rare conversational powers, united with these qualities, made him everywhere a pleasant companion. His fondness of anecdote, ready wit and pleutiful resources also served to make his presence always welcome to those who loved society. . . . . The years of his ministry embraced the period of our revolutionary struggle, in which crisis he evinced his attachment to the cause of his country 'by leaving his pulpit, taking his musket and joining the company of minute men that went to Cambridge on the 19th of April.'" At this time he was thirty years old.

N. B. Mr. Badcock has been with me to speak about ye Singing. (viz. how many times, and what times they desire to sing) on proposed Lecture Day. At eve. Mr. Elisha Parker here, to let me know y^t Mr. Sumner will come (extras accepted) to preach ye proposed Lecture, & asks me to his on Wednesday.

31. I preached on Mat: 22. 39. P. M. repeated Sermon 1. on 2 Cor. 3. 15., but read from X. 12. bec. of ye long Explic^n of ye Context, proceeded to ye forepart of ye Amplification in p. 5 & added cotempore.

I appointed a Singing Lecture to be next Thursday at 2 P. M. Dr. Hawes delivered me a Packet from Col. White, Rept. for Rochester. I found it contained principally Rev. Mr. West's (of Dartmouth) anniversary Sermon at Plymouth, Dec. 22. 1777 with a folio letter of his to me, in six numbers, opening further the prophecy's in Isaiah, Ezekiel, Daniel, Micah, & ye Revelation, which as he conjectures, point at ye present Times in America, accompanyed by a letter from my son Moore, & his Transcript of Mr. West's Letter (of 16 pages octavo) lest I should not be able to read Mr. West's autography. Which were very acceptable.

In ye evening, read Mr. West's sermon above mentioned, as well as Mr. Moore's letter. Thus I finish this month, and may a gracious God forgive the Miscarriages & Deficientys I have been chargeable with! and ye Day past in Special!

FEBRUARY 1779

At eve came my Kinsman, Mr. W^m. Bradshaw, who has been to Brookfield, but did not arrive there till after his brother Benjamin's Funeral.—He lodges here as does Master Fisk.

2. I preached at Mr. Barnabas Newton's on Ps. 44. 15 to p. 73d.

N. B. We Sung twice, because y[e] Singing School was there, and I tarried to hear y[m] Sing after my Exercise.

3. Rode to Shrewsbury (at Mr. Sumner's Request) dind there.[1]

[1] Mr. Sumner was living at this time in the old parsonage, formerly the residence of Gen'l Artemas Ward of Revolutionary fame. The "Meeting-house land" adjoined. In 1797, Mr. Sumner built the new house which still remains as it was in his day—his bed, desk and bookcase, his clock and portraits, each piece of furniture in its own place as it was when he last saw it. The old house in which Mr. Parkman so often "dind" and lodged, also still stands:

SUMNER HOUSES.

Mr. Fairbank preached y^e Lecture on 1 Joh. 4. 16. latter part. After sermon we had some Conversation about several passages delivered concerning God permitting Evil—and on ye Fallen Spirits & Pharaoh, y^t they ought to bless God for their Existence. I answered (among other things) our Lord's saying of ye Traytor, "it were good for that man if he had never been born." I returned home at Evening.

4. A SINGING LECTURE at ye Request of ye Singing School.

Mr. Sumner preached. His text was Ps. 149. 1. It was conducted thus. After Dinner (at which besides Mr. Sumner & Col. Job Cushing y^t came with him, was Mr. Stone of Southboro) when we first went into ye Meeting House, An Anthem was sung. Then Mr. Stone made a short Prayer. After which I appointed and read Ps. 149. which was Sung without Reading the Lines by the Deacon. then Mr. Sumner prayed. after which we sung Ps. 113, Deacon reading as usual, & ye Sermon next followed. Mr. Sumner prayed again and we sung ye 5th Hymn without reading, except my first reading over ye whole. In Conclusion of the Exercise, I pronounced the Blessing. But then Mr. Badcock, the Master began an exercise of Singing—of Anthems and Tunes—which was very grateful, and may God graciously Condescend to accept ye Sacrifice!

At eve a number of other Gentlemen here, viz: Dr. Crosby,

but enlarged into a tenement house, and moved from its original site, neither of the two ministers would know it now. In 1830, it was substantially the same as on this February morning, when Mr. Parkman "dind there."

Master Benj. Stone of Shrewsbury, Masters Brigham (Elijah and Moses) & Fisk.

5. Sermonizing.

6. Do.

7. On Mat. 22. 39. A. M. Master Fisk dined here. P. M. on 2 Cor. 3. 14 former part. But all depends on Divine Blessing! In ye eve read Pike and Hayward,—also Benj. Foster against Mr. Fisk on Baptism. "God dwelling in ye Tents of Them."

3. Bills of two Emissions viz. of May 20, 1777 & of Apr. 11. 1778. are refused in common Trade. I acquainted Squire Baker with this Difficulty with respect to some part of my Money, and some Considerable which I received of him. He told me he would change such bills as I had of Those Emissions. This day I went up to him, & his clerk changed 142 Dollars for me.

P. M. I wrote to Mrs. Moore.

9. Wrote again to Mr. Forbes about his Sheep.

10. Transcribed from biographical Dictionary P. M. went up to ye Singing School (by desire) to hear ye Singing. This is Mr. Badcock's last Day. In ye Evening. I was seized with shivering and went to Bed not well.

11. Mr. Badcock leaves us. I sent by him Mr. Cranch his Vol. I. of Biographical Dictionary, and a Letter to Mr. Forbes to ye care of Col. Coffin, Rep for Gloucester. At Eve. Master Fisk, Sophy, Elias carries Susè to see her Father who is confined with Indispositions—and Breck goes at evening & they tarry there.

12. Mr. Thos. Warrin & Stephen Maynard cutt up part

of y⁶ woodpile today to pay Mrs. Parkman for knitting for y⁶ latter of yᵐ. They dind. They work till evening. Nathan Maynard junʳ gives me a note for 16 Dollars (lent him with much more) Dec. 21. last.

At Even I rec'd a Letter dated January 25, from my son Forbes, acquainting with y⁶ Death of one of Mr. Forbes' Dauters, by a Fever, and y⁶ Distress Cape Ann is in by y⁶ Small Pox, yᵗ he, being desired by y⁶ Selectmen and y⁶ Doctors Plummer & Coffin to assist, has innoculated and administered physic to near 100: Col. Stevens and his Wife have got safely through. But alas for y⁶ poor people, who want Bread, and Cloths & Fuel! May God pity yᵐ and grant Supplys, especially of his Almighty Grace and Spirit: that they may duly improve providences, and the Seasons and means of Salvation!

A sad disappointment in ye over rotted flax, which appeared by y⁶ breaking & swingling a part of it. The young man (Phin Brigham) desists as working in vain, throws in his pains and leaves it. A. M. Breck goes to Brookfield to look after his Bradshaw affairs. Dr. Stimson[1] was here from Marlborough & tells me old Mr. Thos. Biglo an old Friend (perhaps about 86) is dead, And old Mr. Jonas Morse (about 84) is dead also, & to be buryed this day. May God grant Me to be ready, in all respects so for y⁶ Time is hastening upon me.

14. Rain A. M. A thin congregation. Preached again on Mat. 22. 39. Master Fisk dind here. P. M. go on with repeating (with incidental variations) on 2. Cor. 3. 14 for-

---

[1] Dr. Jeremy Stimpson, of Hopkinton, author of a short history of Hopkinton.

mer part. used from Artic. 6th in continuation of page 8 to middle of page 11.

After our evening Exercise Mrs. read good part of ye Touchstone of Saving Faith O y^t God would add His Blessing to these fervant and powerful means of Grace!—

15. Elias is so much taken with a pair of Steers at Mr. Harrington's, that he prevails with me to go and trade with him for them. I went to his House and drank Coffee with his Mother and Wife.

16. Elias with Mr. Harrington about ye Steers, & I compleated a Bargain with him: His steers are coming 3. he asks 80£ for y^m. I give him my large Steer and 35£, and paid him ye Bills in Hand. The steers are duly exchanged. Elias P. M. makes a Business of trimming ye great Apple trees in ye Garden &c. Mrs. Harrington, both, here. Breck returns from Brookfield and New Braintree. Gives me but a Sorrowful account of ye Insolvency of ye late Mr. Bradshaw of ye Afflicted state of my Dauter Baldwin, by reason of her Husband's absence so long from his Farm & Business &c. Also Ebenezer's Affairs difficult.

17. I was chiefly recluse. Recollect. Mr. Nasmith's (a Scotchman's) Directory and Exemplar for Self-Examination & Willard's Blessed Man from page 188 on X 5 treating of Confession &c.

18. Cousin Maynard with her son-in law Goodell and his wife came to see us. They came on foot. P. M. drank Tea and returned as y^y came. Mr. Goodell has lately been at Henneker, & says Mr. Rice is so well as to preach steddily again. To God be Glory!

17. Capt. Morse[1] came here and brot me an handsome Cheese which he says his Wife made on purpose for me. N. B. This was unexpected as I had apprehended he had been under Disgust from Thanksgiving Time. But I hope it is gone over. Breck here and asks for Liberty to build a Smith's shop at ye Corner of my Land next the Burying Place.[2] At eve came Master Fisk to see us with Elias at Even to a Singing Meeting. at Mr. Newton's but lodges here.

20. A Letter from my Son Samuel[3] to his Br. Breck,

[1] Capt. Morse was Capt. Seth Morse, who lived on South Street where Mrs. J. D. Potter lives now. He led the troops from Westborough in the Revolution. He laid out the present garden.

[2] The only burying-place in Westborough until many years after Mr. Parkman's death, was the small plot of land on Main Street that we now call Memorial Cemetery.

The first burial is said by tradition to have been that of Thomas Rice's little son Nahor, who was so cruelly slain by the Indians in 1704.

Mr. Parkman's land adjoined the burying-ground, and he seems also to have had a right to use that, as we see him pasturing his guests' horses there on a later occasion.

In 1747 this land was granted to the Town of Westborough by the Proprietors of Marlborough, as recorded in their Great Book. It is referred to in that record as one and a half acres of land " where the Inhabitants have always buried their dead."

[3] Samuel Parkman, at this time only twenty-eight years old, was already a prosperous merchant in Boston. He had married, half a dozen years before, Sarah Shaw—the daughter Sallie to whom Mr. Parkman so often refers. At this time he had four children— Samuel born in 1774, Sarah in 1775, Hannah in 1777 and the baby Abigail six days old. Little Abigail lived until 1807, and we trust realized all her grandfather's wish for her. In 1780 the " fine fat

SAMUEL PARKMAN.

informs y⁺ Sally had a Dauter born on ye 14th at 4 A. M. was baptized P. M. and called Abigail. The praise and

dauter " Sukey was born on June 4, who lived until 1824 and was the grandmother of Col. Robert G. Shaw, and one other child, John, was born in 1782. Two months later "dauter" Sally died, and in 1784 Samuel married again, Sarah Rogers, and had five children, among them Francis, who was the father of Francis Parkman, the historian, a corresponding member and generous donor, as also has been his sister, Miss Eliza S. Parkman, to our Historical Society.

Samuel Parkman's store was on Merchants' Row. His house stood on the corner of Green and Chardon streets. The Electric Railway Station now occupies his old site. He built two houses for his two daughters on a part of his large garden, which still stand facing Bowdoin Square between Green and Cambridge streets.

Samuel Parkman, with Elias Hasket Derby, of Salem, Samuel and William Shaw, of Boston, and a few other merchants of the day, amassed a large fortune in exporting indigo, tar, turpentine, masts, etc., and bringing back from India and China vessels laden with the rich manufactures of those countries.

In 1801 he presented to the Westborough Church the first bell which had ever rung to call the people to worship, and the day that they voted their thanks to him they decided to add a steeple to their plain meeting-house. This was afterwards taken down, and the "old Arcade," as we know it, may have resembled the church as it was in the minister's day more nearly than the building reconstructed from the recollections of our "oldest inhabitants." The bell, cast by Paul Revere, is now in the belfry of the Baptist Church.

Among the portraits hanging in Faneuil Hall are two presented by Samuel Parkman; one of Peter Faneuil, by Col. Henry Sargent, the other a full-length of Washington, standing by his white horse, by Stuart.

Mr. Parkman also subscribed $4,000 in 1798 towards the building

Glory to God & may y`e` Child be a rich Blessing ! Mr. Eb`r` Maynard jun`r` from Conway to see me.

21. I preached once more on Mat : 22. 39. 40. P M Repeated Sermon on 2 Cor. 3. 14. last clause. N. B. Mrs.

of the war-frigate Boston, given as a free-will offering to the Government by the merchants of Boston. Only one subscription was larger than his.

Samuel Parkman died June 18, 1824, aged seventy-three.

A niece of his second wife writes : " My remembrances of him are limited to the Sunday calls, which he often made at our house, after the morning service.

" He was a very genial man, and so fond of children that he never forgot to bring us some sugar-plums, which were a much greater rarity then than in our modern days.

"After making his call, he would step to the sideboard, put his package into a covered dish and go, without saying anything about his gift. You may judge of the excitement, after he had gone, in opening and sharing its contents."

An old man still living in Westborough, at the age of ninety-five, describes him as a very straight, stoutly-built man, fine looking, who made very little talk with any one. He tells the following story of him, after he became one of the wealthiest men in New England :

He owned many houses, which he rented. One day one of his tenants dropped into his store, made some small purchases and asked :

" Who can I get to carry these things up ? "

" I'll carry them up," said Mr. Parkman, from another part of the store. So, when the time came for closing the door that night, Mr. Parkman took the packages and knocked at his tenant's house. The man came to the door, saw Mr. Parkman, and was overwhelmed with confusion.

He delivered the bundles with the remark : " When I began the world, I did my own lugging."

Maynard as well as Mr. Fisk dind. At evening Exercise, Breck brot his brother Josiah Brigham here.

22. I could not visit ye Sick by reason of a Storm. I review & Set in order great numbers of Letters. I give way to Timothy's cyphering, tho (besides his taking Care of ye Cattle) there are many things to be done.

23. I go on reviewing and disposing Letters, Papers & Collections.

Mr. Goodall, who preached at Southboro' last Sabbath, came to me to ask Advice abt his going to preach at Otter Creek. N. B. I sent by him to Mr. Joh^n Loring his Book of ye Life of ye renowned Piereskins.

Breck and Elias P. M. go over to Upton to singing meeting there.

24. I rode to Mr. Elijah Hardy's to see their little Elijah, who had been very ill, but was much better—to Mr. Joseph Grout's to see his William who languished, but is recovering—proceeded to Mr. Grosvenor's, but he was gone to Pomfret. I dind there, with Mr. Farrar. He went with me to see Mr. Joseph Brown, who was gone to Providence. Viewed his Library, but not his Electrical Machine. To this Mrs. Brown invited me and to bring Mrs. P—— when Mr. Brown may be at Home. In returning from Grafton, had Capt'n Woods and his Wife's Company from Dr. Jos. Woods, where we drank Tea.

In ye evening came Moses Warren to let himself to me for six months. & asks an hundred pounds lawful money for that term. I defer giving him an answer till next Monday. My son Ebenezer came from Brookfield, in his way to Watertown, tells me Col. Baldwin is come home, and Alexander

Oliver is dismissed, but is suffered to stay, his Wife's Circumstances considered till April. Ebr lodges here.

25. I walked to Mr. Thad. Warrin's to hire him to get out Fencing stuff, posts and Rails; thence to Mr. Isaac Parker's to see and talk with his brother Ephraim about living with me, and he seems disposed. At eve, my son relates somewhat of his sorrowful case, and how his son in law had beguiled him to give a Warrantee Deed of his Place, without a proper Security, an unhappy step!

26. Ebr. leaves us to go to Watertown and Boston. I send by him to Mr. David Sawyer at Framingham; Breck sends quantity of money by him to his brother Samuel. Joseph Grout Junr is examined in order to his joining in full Communion with ye Church, & I consent.

27. Mrs. P. has made up my Camlet gown, lined with Green Baise.[1]

28. A. M. Repeat on 1 Cor. 3. 17, for P. M. on Isa. 28. 1-2, A long sermon, which could not be divided. Application was occasioned, by Town Meeting on ye Morrow. Mrs. Maynard Messrs. Elijah and Moses Brigham & Mr. Fisk dind here.

MARCH 1779.

The Town met. They sent two to ask me to go and pray with ym. I complied, and at their Request, I read ye King of Britain's Speech to his Parliament. November last. Mr.

---

[1] Baize was a coarse woolen cloth made in Norwich and Colchester, England. It was sometimes white, sometimes blue and white, red or green, as in Mr. Parkman's cloak lining. It was used largely for the dresses for servants and in earlier days for slaves. It had a nap on one side.

Daniel Forbes was here to ask me to preach at his House tomorrow. My son Ebenezer returned from Watertown, Boston &c. He brings a letter from Mr. Forbes of Gloucester, concerning y[e] Sickness of his son-in-law, Charles Saunders of about 8 &c. &c. The choristers Chamberlain and Whitney, say they want to be dismissed and desire there may be a new choir. Eb[r] lodges here. N. B. Moses Warren was released from serving me this season.

2. I preached to y[e] private Meeting at Mr. D. Forbes's on Ps. 44. 18, recommending Stedfastness in Religion and rebuking Inconstancy Declining and Apostacy — and Isaac Millar, a Delinquent, was there. N. B. Mr. Forbes repeatedly desires I would revive y[e] Public Reading of y[e] Scriptures. N. B. My son Eben[r] went with me to y[e] Meeting, tarrys and lodges here.

3. Eph[m] Parker (brother of Elisha and Isaac) came to work by y[e] Day for me. He goes to y[e] Ministerial Lot to get Posts and Rails. I went to Squire Baker's, and acknowledged a power of Attorney, to be sent to Mr. David Hitchcock of Brookfield to recover a Debt from James Smith of Western; to be carried with a letter to Mr. Hitchcock by my son Ebenezer. N. B. Hon[ble] Sam[l] Baker was there. The Town meets by adjournment. Messrs. Belknap and Forbes here, and acquaint me y[t] the Chief of y[e] Town have expressed their desire y[t] I would revive y[e] public Reading of y[e] Scriptures, and say there were but two (Mr. Andrews and Mr. Han[h] Parker, y[t] said any Thing against it: also Messrs. Chamberlain and Whitney, the choristers, were here y[t] they might see what I had drawn up, to lay before y[e]

Congregation, praying there may be a New Choice in their Stead. Eb^r lodges here. So does Ephraim Parker.

4. I don't send ye power of Attorney to Mr. Hitchcock nor Breck's Letter to him, but have writ myself, and have agreed with my son Ebenezer (who now leaves us) to go to Mr. James Smith of Western, and apprize him of what I am about to do, y^t he may prevent ye Evil by discharging ye Bond. Mrs. P—— disposes of Baize Lining to Ebenezer, and with ye money, and some additions (that of 34s.) purchases — yds. of Bear Skin to make him (Elias) a Straight-bodyd coat. (Designed Lining of a New Red homespun Camblet gown for Elias.)

5.

6. Eph.^{m} left me by agreement and to return again:

7. A Stormy, snowy Day—but a small Assembly.

I read A. M. ye former part of ye first Ch. of Zechariah and delivered expository observations for ye forenoon exercise.

Sr. Brigham (Elijah) and Master Fisk dined here.

P. M. Read Rev. 14. first 7 or 8 x & repeated what I had delivered upon it three years ago to page 7. May God graciously own and bless what has been done agreeable to His Will! Both before and after our evening Family exercise Mrs. P. read to me Pike and H. , and I read part of *Charnock* on Gen. 6. 5. The Sinfulness and Care of Thought, both which were very quickening to me. To God be ye Glory!

8. Went to see Sam Dalrymple, whose Leggs were lately scalled with hot wort. Mr. Harrington sleds away with my four Steers, 4 logs of Maple to his door.

9. At Squire Baker's who takes my acknowledgment of another power of Attorney to Mr. David Hitchcock instead of that of ye 3^d which upon reviewing was not agreeable, and therefore was not sent.

The Squire was exceeding Friendly and generous. He gave me 20 lbs. of tryed Tallow and to Mr. Stone 12 lb. being all he spoke for. Moreover he would have me, whenever I am in any Straight, to let him know of it. I called to see Mrs. Wheelock. She has a bad Breast: and Mrs. Keens.

10. Eph. Parker came again. Breck goes to Boston. I wrote to Mr. Ripley of Concord for my Books and for Sister Champney's Chest. Also to my Son W^m. to hasten my Cart Wheels. P. M. came my son and Dauter Baldwin from Brookfield and with y^m Oliver How to wait on y^m, and by Tea Time came Dr. Stimson & young Mr. Sam. Woodward of Weston. The two latter returned to Marlboro'. The others lodged here: the Horses were taken in to keeping by Capt. Morse. Eph^m. Parker lodges here.

11. Mr. Baldwin and my Dauter leave us to go towards Byfield, but she is in doubt of her reaching there. Their man returns back to Brookfield. At eve came my son Moore,[1] who has been at Oxford and Charleton, & goes this

---

[1] Rev. Jonathan Moore, of Rochester, had married, in 1768, Susanna Parkman. She had died in 1777 and soon after her death, as Anna Sophia writes in her Journal, "brother Moore" came to Westborough and brought her a "black satten cloke that was my sisters, also an under Petticoat, and some of Sukey's knit Lace for a tucker."

Tuckers were worn for nearly a hundred years as an essential

way in his return home. He brings me another Letter from Mr. West, containing No VII & VIII of Prophetic Computations and Remarks. He lodges here.

12. At noon came my son Alexander of Marlb. in New Hampshire. I am so short out for good Hay that I send one horse to Mr. Eben^r. Maynard, the other to Mr. Jon^n. Forbes^2 to be kept. For Mr. Moore will Tarry over ye Sabbath.

13. Alexander leaves us to go to some part of Connecticut to pay ye woman he bought his place of.

part of a woman's dress. They were made of linen or lace and covered the neck and shoulders above the bodice, which was usually cut low. The latest form of a tucker was merely a handkerchief crossed in front and tucked under the edge of the dress. Sometimes called neckpiece or modesty-piece.

^{2}Jonathan Forbes is a very prominent name for many years in the history of Westborough. There were four of the name. The first Jonathan was one of the original settlers of the town, an original member of the church and one of its early deacons. He lived near the site of the town reservoir. He died in 1768.

His son Jonathan, born in 1715, married a daughter of Dea. Simon Tainter, and was also a deacon of the church. He died in 1756, leaving three children.

His son Jonathan, the only one of the name living at this time, except his only little boy of four years, had married the daughter of Moses Brigham, and afterwards lived in his house on West Main Street. He lived at this time on the old homestead near the reservoir.

He is buried in Memorial Cemetery, with only the inscription on the monument to give us any hint of the latter years of his life:

> "Afflictions sore long time I bore,
> Physicians were in vain,
> Till God did please with death to seize
> And ease me from my pains."

14. I read and briefly expound Zech. 1. 7. Mr. Moore preached A. M. on Luke (?) 6. 46. Mrs. Maynard dined here. I did not read P. M. Mr. Moore preached on 1 Joh. 5. 3. Jos. Grout J^r. was admitted into ye Church. I appointed ye Communion & Lecture and by Desire notified the Congregation to make a new choice of Choristers, after ye next Lecture. At eve Mr. Moore repeated ye Heads of ye afternoon Sermon, viz. on 1. Joh. 5. 3. I earnestly pray for Success may attend both ye Exercises, and y^t we may all be inspired with that love of God which produces new Obedience.

15. Mr. Moore leaves us to return to Rochester. I wrote by him to Mr. West. I rode in ye Sleigh to visit poor Mr. Daniel How, who has a mortification in one of his Feet. But I first dind at Mr. Davis's. At Mr. Fessenden's, (where Mr. How lives) I talked with him (Mr. Fessenden) about his not coming to meeting—but he gave me no Answer—

Mr. Davis[1] furnished me with his Horse to ride back— for Elias proceeded in ye Sleigh to Northboro'. I made a visit to old Mrs. Kelley (who is about 85) was born March 6 old Style 1694) and prayed there.

16. Visit Deacon Wood. N. B. Yesterday a Thief stole out of his Bar about 100 Dollars. They pursued and found ye Villian, one Waters at Marlb. recovered in part and a Note for ye rest. The Deacon made up, but Col.

---

[1] Isaac Davis, a young tanner, who came to town to teach his trade to Capt. Stephen Maynard's son, had married Anne Brigham, step-daughter of Capt. Maynard, in 1772. They had four sons, Phineas, Isaac, Joseph, and John,—Governor of Massachusetts and

Johⁿ Ward sent him to Prison. I went in to see Capt. J. Wood's wife and prayed there.

17. Mr. Stone came, dind with me. He tells me his people have voted to sing Tate & Brady's Version, & began last Lord's Day. The High Sheriff of this County, W^m. Greenleaf Esq. dind with us. He is going to Medfield to see his father Quiney, and called to take my Commands, but I had no letter writ. Mr. Stone preached my Lecture

Senator of the United States. They were living at this time in the house recently occupied by Hiram Broaders. In 1781 they bought the Dea. Tomlin place, which has been known since as the Davis homestead. Isaac and his sons became wealthy men, and they and their descendants, who take pride in the name of Davis, have held many positions of honor and trust.

FIRST DAVIS HOUSE.

on Ps. 103. 3. first clause. After Sermon and Blessing, the Church were by y^e Desire of y^e Deacons, stayed concerning Contributions. The Congregation staid also at y^e request of ye Choristers, y^t they might resign and ye People might make a new Choice.

They chose Mr. Eli Whitney by 41 votes: Mr. Eb^r Chamberlain jr. by 31, Mr. Johnathan Batherick by 29, Mr. Elisha Parker by 23. My son Alexander came from Connecticut and lodged here. I wrote to President Langdon to excuse Elias' tardiness. And delivered Elias 100 Dollars.

18. Elias sat out on Breck's mare for Cambridge, Alexander, after dinner, undertook his Journey home. Rec'd a Letter from Mr. Ebenezer Sparhawk of Templeton, which related to some uneasiness's there, I wrote an Answer.

At eve came two of Timothy's brothers. Elias and John Bryant from Stoneham on Foot. They lodged here.

19. Mr. Timothy Parker of Templeton came in, to whom I committed my Letter to Mr. Sparhawk. The rigorous weather excites Pity to Elias at Coll.

20. The Bryants left us A. M. to go to Littleton and thence home, when I had prepared nigh as much as I intended to deliver came a young gentleman with Mr. Elijah Brigham, viz. Mr. Caleb Alexander, who was from Northfield, and lodged here. He was graduated at Yale College, approbated by the Association at New London.

21. Mr. Aaron Hutchinson jun^r came from Marlboro', to preach for me, today, but Mr. Alexander preached A. M. on Isa: 5. 4. I read Isa: 53. both ye young Gentlemen attended with us at ye Sacrament, which was administered. Mrs. Maynard dind here. P. M. Mr. Hutchinson on Mat:

25. 46. I detained ye Church and read a Letter from ye South-west Parish in Bolton, requesting assistance in a Fast and gathering a Church.   The Church voted compliance and Dr. Hawes and Dea. Wood Delegates.   Mr. Hutchinson goes to Grafton. Mr. Alexander lodges here. His horse at Mr. Elijah Hardy's.

22. Mr. Alexander here for it is a great storm. He lodges here.

23. Mr. Hardy came to wait on Mr. Alexander to his house.

I am in great Doubt about my going to ye Fast &c. at Bolton. P. M. Dea. Wood here to see what I shall be like to do. I have endeavored to prepare my S. if I should. Both ye Roads and ye Weather very unpromising.

24. Instead of going to Mr. Whitney's in ye way of Bolton (as I had planned) it proved so tempestuous, so violent a snow-storm, y^t I could scarcely go out of Doors at all. Ephraim's brother Elisha was here and dind with us. He speaks of ye Straits and Difficulties to which many of ye People of Bolton are reduced, for want of Bread and how scarce Meat is there. May ye great Provider Pity y^m, especially at this Season, and all others y^t are exposed in this terrible Storm! in Special y^t are at Sea.

25. *The Storm continues: and ye Snow is very deep.* Going to Bolton Fast and Council, I suppose is utterly impracticable.   I am employed by my s. in my Study.

But about 10 or 11 the Fierceness of ye Storm abated and the Sun appeared. Yet P. M. ye Heavens are clouded again.

26. Go on with my preparations for ye Sabbath.

P. M. came Mr. Alexander accompanied by his uncle Miller. Stays not long. Mr. Caleb Harrington invites and waits upon him to his House, and thence he intends to go to Master Moses Brigham's, who is to be found at his School, or at his Lodging, Mr. Andrews.

27. Tho ye Snow was troublesome, yet Ephraim is employed in fetching two load of Posts and Rails (partly finished) from Beeton's.

28. A. M. on Zech. 11. thro' out. P. M. on Rev: 14. 7 to P 14. with addition of four uses in a loose Paper. No stranger to dine. At eve. Mr. Elijah Brigham came with Breck, and such of his Family as could come, to join in ye Repet^n Singing &c.

29. John Baker undertakes his Journey to Andover, where he is going to School to learn Latin. He calls here to borrow an Accidence, which I let him have. May God be his Guardian and grant Success!

30. Engaged in Various Readings &c A. M.—P. M. came Parkman Bradshaw from Brookfield. I understand y^t ye Circumstances of my Son Ebenezer are difficult. He has hired of Mr. Hitchcock ye House which his son Bradshaw took a Lease of. Sent Mr. Joseph Bond Mr. Bradshaw's Horse to keep. He himself lodges here. Rec'd Letters from Mr. Whitney about a Contribution for Rhode Island people and concerning ye Fast &c. at Bolton.

31. Mr. Bradshaw sett out for Cambridge. I rode to visit Mr. Stone, of Southboro' Dind there. He tells me his son-in-law Bangs of Hardwick is dead. P. M. I went with Mr. Stone to ye Meeting House where Mr. Luke Wilder held a Singing. In returning, I borrowed and brot home Clark's Lives of eminent Persons Fol. Called at Mr. Gale's, his

Father being poorly. At Mr. Andrews—have not been there since their Marriage till now.

The roads are exceeding Dirty, ye snow melting apace. This Ride was followed by Bad Cramp in ye Night.

May ye Lord pardon ye Sins of this Month, & spare me &c.

APRIL. 1779.

Mr. Baldwin and his wife came from Boston. This morning from Gale's, where they lodged last night, but here to Breakfast. He says ye Vessel which Breck and Samuel had interest in, was presently upon Sailing out, was captured in Cape Cod Harbour, by a privateer of only 6, 2 pounders whereas they had 8 4 pounders. But ye Capt. had carried ye Cash which was ½ ye Worth ashore, quilted in his Jacket, and therefore saved it. Mr. Baldwin lodges here.

2. My son and Dauter Baldwin left us to go to Brookfield, a Marvellous Day for Warmth. Col. Baldwin says if I send my Cattle to his pasture they shall fare as well as his will. Mr. John Forbes[1] here and dines with us. He brings me and I read y^e *Constitution of ye State of Vermont*. Mr. Fish wrote a Letter to me to desire me to forward a Subscription for his Reply to Mr Foster of Leicester, concerning

---

[1] Mr. John Forbes was a son of the second Jonathan Forbes and Joanna Tainter. Otter Creek, where he settled with his family, is a stream in Rutland County, Vermont, emptying into Lake Champlain. A year before this, as we learn from the Church Records, the Westborough Church had contributed £22. 18/. od, for his relief on account of being driven away from his home by the enemy, and also on account of the sickness and death of his wife. Although he had eight children, the genealogical record ends with them.

Infant Baptism. I headed a paper, subscribed and set it agoing. Several Young Gentlemen being present, viz. Sr. Crosby, Elijah Brigham and Abraham Holland. The weather wonderful warm &c.

3. Alter and enlarge ye Garden. Eph Parker setts out stumps, roots &c. I read ye Constitution of Gov'n^{mt} in ye State of Vermont.

4. Read Zech III. and my exercise was upon ye first 5 Verses. Mrs. Maynard dind with us. P. M. on Rev: 14. 7 middle clauses, which may God be graciously pleased to bless to all of us!

5. Capt. Fisher here A. M. borrows ye London minister's Sermons on Prayer. I write to Mrs. Brown, widow at my son Samuel's at Boston, concerning Letters sent by a Female Society at Boston to Father Loring.

P. M. I had Dr. Hawes' mare to go to Bolton. I first rode over to see Mr. Daniel How, whose case, with his mortifying Toe is deplorable! He was somewhat free to speak. I prayed with him. Proceeded to Mr. Whitney's and lodged there.

6. Mr. Whitney and I rode to Mr. Benj. Baily's in Bolton, where ye Pastors and Churches of Westb. ye first in Shrewsbury, Northboro and Stow met. The East Church in Sudbury did not come.

It was appointed a day of Prayer, Humiliation and Fasting. We assembled at Mr. Samuel Jones' House, Mr. Newel prayed. Mr. Sumner preached a seasonable sermon on Ps. 122. 8. I prayed after ye Sermon. We sung twice, but had only one Exercise. After refreshing, formed into a Council. I was Moderator and Mr. Whitney Scribe. The

Candidates for Communion met us at Mr. Bailey's and expressed their desires to be formed into a church state. The members of divers Churches presented their Dismissions. We made the needful Enquirys into their agreement and mutual Satisfaction with one another. And tho they had in times past been in unhappy Disquietments, yet condescended and were united, thro' ye great Goodness of God and preparations were made for accomplishing ye Solemn Work. I lodged there.

7. The Council met, and ye Brethren assembled. After prayer, conferred. Something was prepared for ye Brethren, by way of mutual Concession and acknowledgement of past offences, especially ye Wally Brethren in setting up that church & some of the members disturbing other churches and Mutual forgiveness. From such Material, drawn up, one of ye Council compiled Result: At Mr. Benj. Baily's, to whose son I find Sally Crosby is married and lives there.

P. M. The Result was finished and read, was voted by ye Council, then Read to and it was voted by ye Brethren to accept of and conform to it, except Col. Silas Bailey, who was unavoidably obliged to withdraw: and Mr. Eph. Fairbank, who wanted some Liberty about communicating with Mr. Walley's Church, if he was there *accidentally*, but nothing could be granted to him of that kind, upon which he chose to wave joining with y^m. for ye present. A *Covenant* was read to y^m in which they term themselves Congregational (not Independents) to which they consented and signed it. And if ye other Brethren should within a few days incline to come and consent, and sign as they had done, it should be accepted as if it had been done today. This very solemn Transaction performed, they were by ye Moderator openly announced and declared to be a Church of ye Lord Jesus Christ, by ye Name of ye South Church of Christ in Bolton, who were then presented to God in an address of Gratulation and Supplication by ye Moderator. In ye Council ye Votes were unanimous, in the Church, next to; For which may all Glory be given to ye most High!

The Church chose Mr. Whitney to be their Moderator *pro temp.* I returned with Mr. Whitney so far as to his House & lodged there again.

8. Returned home (calling a little while at Capt. Maynard's) and found thro God's Goodness all in safety. P. M. Miss Patty Fish here. N. B., Polly Howard works here for Sophy, making Lace.

9. Capt. Maynard here, and wants to be about ye Work of Straitning ye Road,[1] through my land back of ye Meeting

[1] Unfortunately no map exists of the Westborough of Mr. Parkman's day, and we have to reconstruct the roads from the lay-outs. This road toward Nurse's was probably towards Ebenezer Nurse whose land adjoined John Maynard's, and in the direction of the present Summer Street.

In 1756, according to the Town Records, a road was laid out as follows: "Beginning at the Road running through Mr. Samuel William's land, then running partly on land that was left for a highway and partly on Capt. John Maynard's land, then turning and running through John Maynard's land to the Rev. Mr. Parkman's land, then running through Mr. Parkman's land to the land the Meeting-house now stands on, and to the Great Road South of the Meeting-house."

This is evidently the road that was straightened—John Maynard's land was bounded westerly and northerly by the Buryingplace, easterly by Samuel William's land, and southerly by land of Ebenezer Nurse.

House toward Nurse's. My son Cushing and his son John came—lodged here: but Mr. C's horse is sent to Mr. Bond's. N. B. My Dauter C. has been exceedingly ill for some time: and is reduced to a very weak State.

10. Mr. Cushing and Dr. Stinsson dind here.

11. Mr. Cushing preached. A. M on Psal. 16. 11. P. M. on Eccl. 8. 11. N. B. He read ye Ch. & Psalm.

May God grant His Blessing on ye Exercises of ye Day!

12. Dr. Hall of Sutton going to Boston calls and dines here. (with Mr. Cushing). P. M. tho it rained, they both took leave. Mr. C. goes to Shrewsbury, but leaves his son John here to live with us a while.

13. My sheep grow very troublesome, to Mr. Newton. I rode over to Mr. John Kelley's to see his wife—prayed with her. Reproved him for his absenting from public Worship. Visited at Mr. Stephen Cook's.[1]

Elias came home, rode upon Dr. Hawes' horse. N. B. He went from College this morning to Boston, and yet came home before night, ye Sun considerable Heighth.

14. Fine weather—Gardening, plant Trees—move ye Bees. W^m. Deadman a soldier from Stoneham going to ye Camp near —— Manor, breaks fast here—he brings a Letter from Tim's Mother—she writes of ye death of her Son-in-law, Lt. Daniel Bryant.

---

[1] Stephen Cook was a brother of Thomas, and son of Cornelius. He had been imprisoned twenty-five years before this, with his brother Robert, for killing an Indian at Stockbridge, but it seems to have been a less heinous offence than robbing Abner Newton's house.

He seemed to have been the best of Cornelius Cook's family, and served on the school committee in 1780.

15. Old Mr. Wm Nurse[1] dies this morning, aged 8-years. I walked over to see old Mr. Jonah Warrin & prayed there. Cousin Maynard sent over an Horse for her aunt, and Stephen to wait upon her, not immediately to return.

Dr. Hall returning from Boston called here.

N. B. I hear that Mr. Grosvenor has asked a dismission from his Pastoral-Relation. I read Mr. Wigglesworth's and Mr. Tucker's Dudleian Lectures.

16. Attended and prayed at ye Funeral of Old Mr. W^m. Nurse. He was 83 sometime in last month. I had considerable discourse with Ensign Fay. Elias went P. M. to Concord with Cart, Boxes and Horse. Mr. Amos Parker, Eph^{m}'s Father here. He is obliged with a No. of *Lelock Trees*. At eve Mrs. P. returns home. Hear that a girl has set Fire to Mr. Kendal's House at New Salem, the same that fired Mr. Fessenden's at Walpole. She is committed to Jayl.

[1] William Nurse, son of Benj. Nurse, of Framingham, and grandson of that Rebecca Nurse, of Salem, who was hanged as a witch. He had married Rebecca Fay, of Westborough, and settled in 1729, on Shrewsbury house lot No. 3, which was set off to Westborough in 1741, and was the same farm still owned and occupied by his descendants, the family of the late Dea. B. A. Nourse.

He left six children, some of whom Mr. Parkman occasionally mentions in the Journal.

Mary, married Eleazar Williams, of Westborough.
Lydia, born in 1727.
Daniel, in 1729.
Benjamin, in 1731.
Rebecca, in 1734, and
Priscilla, in 1736.

17. Elias returns from Concord: and relates a tragical story of one Whitney of Townsend, who is suspected to have poisoned his Wife.

18. A. M. on Zech. 3. 6–7. P. M. on 1 Thes. 4. 13. Occasioned by ye Death of Mr. W^m. Nurse. May Divine Blessing accompany!

19. Breck went to Boston. I sent by him 28 Letters, of ye private female Society to ye late venerable Father Loring, to ye care of Mrs. Elizabeth Brown, widow, heretofore Leazenby: and a number more to and from Mrs. Mehitabel Hystop of Brookline, to ye care of ye Rev. Mr. Jackson.

20. A. M. Was at Dea. Wood's, at his Son's, and at Mr. Dix's (who lives at Capt. Wood's) but he was not at home. P. M. Visit Mrs. Mallet, who is sick of a Fever. rode to Col. Brigham's, to Capt. Jonas Brigham's. Neither of ye Men at home.

Rec'd a letter from Elijah Brigham A. B. respecting Sophy.

21. Capt. Maynard Solicits me about moving my Walls on ye north west, and straightening ye Road from ye Meeting House to ye Northward. He promises it shall not be to my Damage. He will be at ye Charge and will measure ye Land, that I may have Equivalent. N. B. In some perplexity about getting up a pair of Cart Wheels from Monroe's, which Billy has made for me. Capt. undertakes to get y^m up, Breck returns from Boston, and brot me a letter from Mrs. Eliz. Brown of ye Female Society of Boston.

22. Mr. Grosvenor, on his Journey to Dr. Kittredge, at Tewkesbury, for help in his utterance, calls here. May God grant success! Mr. Solomon Maynard for Capt. May-

nard brings my Cart Wheels in a Waggon, and goes with y^m to Mr. Joseph Smith's to have ye Tire put onto y^m. Isaac Baldwin from Dummer School, going to Brookfield, calls and refreshes here.

23. Capt. Maynard and his people, with two Wallers from Sutton, begin to move my Wall beyond ye Orchard to make ye Road from ye Meeting House towards Nurse's straight. Hannah Whitney, (sister of Mr. John Harrington's Wife) came to me, confessing ye sin of Fornication and desires to make her Peace with God and his people.

24. Mr. Grosvenor returns from Tewkesbury and dines here. P. M. my son Samuel and his Wife came from Boston two days ago, and today here. Sally is still but indisposed.

By reason of variety of company, was necessarily obliged to desist from what I was preparing for ye Public tomorrow.

25. Very much on consideration of my Dauter-in-law I chose ye Subject of ye Day. Read Cantic. 8 and delivered ye Sermons formerly preached on V. 5.[1] A. M. to p. 8. P. M. to p. 15. Which may God graciously accept!

26. I was much taken up in trying (tho fruitlessly) to get an Horse for Elias to go with ye Cattle to Brookfield.

[1] The text is: "Who is this that cometh up from the wilderness leaning upon her beloved? I raised thee up under the appletree, there thy mother brought thee forth; there she brought thee forth that bare thee."

We wonder if "dauter Sally" did not feel that she and "her beloved" had come up to the wilderness, instead of from it, and if she realized that the two long sermons, fifteen pages in Mr. Parkman's minute hand, were preached especially for her.

The next Sunday he gives her another sermon on the same subject.

27. My son Samuel returned to Boston, leaving his Wife, with his Chaise here; who before dinner grew so uneasy, that with Tears, she prayed me to get some Neighbors to carry her in her chaise to Boston. Indeed her husband was but just out of sight, when she repented her staying behind, and would have had him called back.

N. B. I sent by my Son to Mrs. Eliz. Brown, at her request for some of his papers, two manuscript sermons of Mr. Loring, one on I. Joh. 4. 9. the other on Gal. 2, 20

We are every day perplexed by ye unruliness of ye Sheep.

28. The Sheep were so disorderly I was forced to go to my Friend, Squire Baker, to request him, again to take ye Sheep to pasture, and to assist me in getting my young Cattle to Brookfield, both which he consents to.

29. The Sheep are sent to Squire Baker's pasture to be kept there till after Shearing. P. M. came Mr. Wm May and with him, Mr. Solomon Walcott, a young preacher, from Mansfield, Mr. May went to ye Squire's, Mr. Walcott lodged at ye Shop.

30. Elias left us to go to Cambridge, and to Charleston, on Mr Jon^n Fay's Horse. Mr. May went with Elias to Cambridge. Eli Forbes, from Cape Ann, by ye way of Boston, came and lodged here. He brings me a Letter from his Father, which relates many sorrowful things, which have befallen them, particularly ye death of Col. John Stevens, Mr. Solomon Parsons and his wife. Mr. Rogers has left his people for want of Support. Mr. Cleaveland at Sandy Bay is on ye wing, Mr. Parsons of Squam at present under disgrace &c. &c.

MAY 1779.

My Dauter in Law, Salley, rides in her Chaise with Eli Forbes to Brookfield.

2. Did not read publickly because I had not done with ye former passages already read. viz. Zeph. 3. 8, which I preached on A. M. and on Cant 8. 1. P. M. Mr. Adonijah's Rice's wife dind here. May God bless ye Word delivered.

Mr. W^m. May came at eve lodged here.

3. Mrs. Mallet remains ill. I visited her, and there was also old Mrs. Stone (one of ye poor from Charlestown) I prayed with y^m.

N. B. I was met by Mr. Stockwell Shoemaker, and could not avoid discoursing with him concerning ye amazing alteration of ye Price of Things, for I this day paid *Six Dollars* for only ye making of a pair of Shooes for me, viz. by Mr. James Smith who works at Capt. Fisher's, which is 12 times as much as I gave for ye last Pair but one, for which I gave half a Dollar, at Mr. Barn. Newton's. N. B. Mr. May has bought of Joseph Lee of Cambridge Esq. 1420 acres of Land in Montague, and has paid for it. It stood him between 4 and 5 Thousand pounds. L. M.

N. B. As I received a Letter yesterday noon from Ensign Aaron Warrin, desiring me to preach next Fast Day on 1 Chron. 4. 10. today began to write upon it.

4. Mr. David Clark of Ashburnham came to see us. N. B. No word of Complaint about his son Ben: who is in ye Continental service. Mr. Amos Parker of Shrewsbury here, his business with his son.

5. My Dauter-in-law returns with Eli Forbes from

Brookfield. Benj. Bancroft of Sutton Stores his Load in my Barn.

6. General Fast throout y⁵ United States. The forenoon exercises were (not designedly) exceeding long. A. M. on the text requested by Ensign Warren, viz. 1 Chron. 4. 10, but I read and made some remarks upon v. 9. P. M. Used part of sermon on Jer. 8. 5, but with many enlargements. O y' God would please to accept our sacrifices, and quicken us to conform to his holy Word!

Col. Job. Cushing, Maj' Ezra Beeman were at meeting P. M, and refreshed themselves with us at eve. They were here upon y⁵ Business of Raising a number of Men to go to Rhode Island.

7. Eli Forbes Returns to Cambridge and Boston. Sally tarries with us. I send by Eli to Elias, Ferguson's Astronomy, with a Letter against his Selling Books, which he has had of me, and have writ to Eli's Father, particularly to send for his Sheep after Shearing.

N. B. Breck has bought another horse, which his brother Samuel procured for him, of Major Stillman at Boston. P. M. I rode to Mr. Thomas Bellows to see him in his weak and low condition, and prayed with him and his son's Family—thence I proceed to divers Other of y⁵ Families in y' corner, viz. Mr. Chamberlain.[1] N. B. his son Daniel gives me half a bushel of Indian Corn, and lends

---

[1] Mr. Parkman, this lovely May day, rode down the Flanders Road, a street which took its name, according to tradition, from the quarrelsome habits of the farmers living thereon, a tradition which seems well authenticated from the fact that in some old deeds it is called "Contention Road."

me a bushel and half more. I called at Mr. Nat. Chamberlain's went into widow Bellow's, and stayed some time at Ensign Snow's—drank Tea there &c. At home found Capt. John Wood & his Lady, who make a visit here.

8. Wrote to Mr. Whitney of Northboro' for ye Result of Bolton Council. Breck goes to Holden P. M. Mr. George Stimson was here and carried away from my barn four bushels (as he says) of Indian Corn, which is part of ye load stored there by Benj. Bancroft on last Wednesday. for which he gave me his Receipt. He says the load is his, & that he Shall soon take away ye Rest of it. Mr. Isaac Miller was here and signed an acknowledgement.

9. With some amendments I went on A. M. and finished on Jer. 8. 5 last clause. Administered ye Lord's Supper. N. B. Br. Isaac Miller was restored. Mrs. Maynard dind here, as did one Daniel Holbrook, whom Mrs. Parkman saw to be a stranger and invited in. P. M. on Jer. 5. 20–25 to page 9.

10. I visited Mrs. Mallet, and old Lieut. Thomas Forbush and his wife. Breck and his Family brot and eat their dinner with us, which was so much ye more agreeable and sociable.

P. M. Mr. Waters who has been preaching at Newtown here and informs me of ye Death of Dr. Wheelock, president of ye College at Dartmouth, and of Dr. Winthrop, professor of Matham. & Philosophy at Cambridge. The last was buryed at Cambridge May 1. O y^t God would show compassion on ye bereaved Semenerrys!

Mr. Noah Hardy's wife here. Mr. Elijah Brigham brings his classmate Mr. —— Foot. They all drink coffee.

At eve. Mr. George Stimson here about y⁶ Load Stored in my Barn, but took none of it away. N. B. John Forbes came to spin.

11. Visit Mr. Daniel How, & prayed with him—went to Mr. Benj. Howe's—called to see Mrs. Kelly. Sophy goes to Mr. Amos Parkers at Shrewsbury. Col. Baldwin & his son Isaac came. Sarah Miller came to spin. Isaac Forbush takes away by order of Benj. Bancroft the remainder of y⁶ Load above said. Col. Baldwin and his son lodge at Breck's. Their horses are put into y⁶ burying-place, our Hay being gone.

12. Col. Baldwin puts one of his horses into Salley's Chaise, and waits upon her to Boston. Isaac to Boston in his way to Byfield. I read Logan's Cicero of Old Age.

13. Breck undertakes to new modell y⁶ Frame for the Grape Vine in y⁶ Garden to run upon; and Parker and Timothy help him. I am still engaged in Logan's Cicero of old age, with very useful notes.

14. Breck, Parker and Tim. are still upon y⁶ Vine and garden.

15. Mr. Parker (Eph^m's Father) here. Eph.^{m}. goes home, & carries John Cushing to Shrewsbury.

16. Preached again on 1 Chron. 4. 10. Mr. Elijah Brigham dind with us.

P. M. repeated on Jer. 5. 25 with many omissions and alterations.

17. Visit old Mr. Bellows, who is become weaker. Prayed and discoursed with him. Visit at Mr. Eb^r Chamberlain jun^r. He presents me half a bushel of Indian meal

—tells me his Br' Daniel went to Marblehead with a load of Indian and Rye, and had 25 Dollars p. Bushel.

18. I rode Breck's mare to Bolton, it being Association, Messrs. Smith,[1] Harrington, Bigelow, Newell present—Messrs. Stone, Bridge and Whitney absent. Mr. Goss[2] prayed and gave a Concio on Joh. 4. 36. especially latter part, with a particular application to what was lately done at ye Council in Bolton, accompanyed with Sad Complaints —which after ye exercise was over, I made reply to. But we parted in peace. In returning I called at Capt. Edward Johnson's and drank Tea there. Stopped at Mr. Whitney's and lodged there.

[1] Rev. Aaron Smith was ordained pastor of the Marlborough Church in 1740. He was dismissed a year before this, ostensibly on "account of his infirmity and weakness, which greatly affected his lungs and his voice in particular." The Mr. Bridge of whom Mr. Parkman often speaks was settled in East Sudbury, and had married Mr. Smith's daughter. Mr. Smith lived with them until his death, two years after this, at the age of sixty-seven.

He was rather unpopular as a minister, and supposed to have an inclination to the tory cause. Some one had even gone so far, two years before, as to discharge two loaded guns into his room through the window. His house still stands in Marlborough, and some years ago the present owner extracted the bullets from a beam.

[2] Mr. Goss, of Bolton, "A tall spare man of stern aspect and not of gentle or winning manners. He appears to be a man of indomitable will and somewhat forbidding presence. With many of his brethren, he entertained high notions of clerical authority, a *high church Puritan*, as he might be styled. In the war of our Independence, he took sides with the royalists, and was a thoroughgoing Tory, as was his son Thomas, who fled to Annapolis, N. S., where he ended his days."

19. In my way home I went to see Mrs. Dolly Rice. N. B. her Dauter Adams resides there. I called at Mr. ――― Andrews, newly come to live in y⁶ house y⁴ was Mr. Tinney's. Visited Mr. Dan¹ How who still grows worse— at Capt. Maynard's to see Stephen who has been languishing. Dind at home. P. M. Mr. Waters on his way to Newtown to preach for Mr. Merriam. Capt. Goddard of Sutton here. Informs me of his raising Madder and Malage Grapes.

20. A. M. Mr. Belknap came in to see me and discoursed abt my circumstances and y⁶ necessary supplies. The affairs coming on in y⁶ Town Meeting P. M. Mr. Daniel Nurse here to renew the Request of his two Sisters, y⁴ there may be a Fast kept at theirs. I am obliged to take some time to consider of it.

N. B. The Town debated upon making me some further allowance, considering the vast increase of y⁶ Necessaries of Life. But it passed negatively.

21. The proceedings of y⁶ Town yesterday were to my Surprise.

22. Mrs. Scott is improved to work here. Sophy droops.

23. A. M. on Zech. III. 9. 10. Cousen Samuel Brigham,[1] besides our Spinners, John Forbes and Sarah Miller,

---

[1] Dr. Samuel Brigham, a son of Mrs. Stephen Maynard, consequently Mrs. Parkman's nephew. He was a graduate of Dartmouth College, although in 1777 he served as paymaster in Washington's army. He studied medicine with Dr. Ball, of Northborough, and married the doctor's sister, Mary. He practiced for a while in Shrewsbury, until "a casualty befel him which forced him for life almost entirely from practice."

dind here. N. B. Mr. Batherick stops me in my going to meeting P. M. and acquaints me that Mr. Jonas Bradish was here, and desired ye Church might be desired to stay after ye Exercises. It was sudden, and at that juncture, an interruption. But I spoke to Mr. Bradish and several of ye Brethren, who he had been talking with, viz. Capt. Jonas Brigham, & Mr. Saml Forbush who joined in y^e (verbal) Request y^t the Church might be spoke to, and a meeting appointed.

P. M. I read Eph. 5 and preached on v. 6.

I detained ye Church, and appointed a Meeting on Tuesday next at 2 P. M. Sophy not well and took physick this morning, but knew it not till it worked.

24. I went to Squire Baker's. Mr. Jonas Bradish there, who gives me reason to expect today some such Paper from him as he designs to lay before ye Church, but (as usual) disappoints me. Squire Baker again relieves me as to pasturing my sheep, if I will obtain of Mr. Elisha Forbes to keep his uncle Eli's nine.

Miss Eliza Beals came in to see me and consult me upon her Spiritual State—mentions several Scriptures She would have me preach upon, but which I have already. As to her bodily State, she is grown exceeding dropsical.

At eve came Mr. John Belknap Junr of New Braintree, and is full of exceptions against Mr. Foster—has got also Mr. Isaac Foster's (the father's) ordination sermon preached at New Braintree. He leaves it for me to read.

25. I sent for Mr. Elisha Forbes, who came and told me he would take care of his uncle's nine sheep, that they may not trouble me any more. No Mr. Bradish though I staid

at home to wait on him. At half after 10 I received his Letter to be laid before ye Church. P. M. Church Meeting, but not till after three by reason of ye member's Delinquency. Mr. Bradish came—his paper read. I answered it. Many debates ensued. At length he confesses in such a manner as that the Church voted Acceptance, and for ye Sake of peace, I conceived it best to forgive him, and thus we emerged from this Difficulty, for which I am heartily thankful! We began and ended with prayer.

26. Wrote (and copied) a Certificate concerning Jonas Bradish directed to Rev. Mr. Jos. Brown of Winchendon.

This day of great Solemnity when ye Heads of ye Tribes assemble together for ye grand purposes of Seeking ye God of our Fathers, and hearing what God ye Lord has to say to us as likewise to exercise that invaluable privilege of choosing ye Counsellors for this State—and this happy Season for ye Convention of Ministers. I am obliged in prudence all things considered to stay at Home, where, however may my Heart join with all those who gratefully celebrate ye praises of God giving thanks to His Name, and would earnestly implore pardoning Mercy for ye whole Land! and the continuance of all public and personal Blessing, that the judgments of God may be removed, that we may be extricated out of our Difficulties, and be lead in ye Paths of Rest and Peace!

27. Visited poor John Bond, under grievous lameness, and prayed with him—dined at Col. Brigham's, in my way to old Mrs. Beaman, who I visited and prayed with. Mr. John Belknap jun. here again, about Mr. Daniel Foster's

Doctrines. I have read his F's sermon, with the notes. Mr. Ithamar Bellows dies about 5 P. M.

28. Mr. John Belknap calls once more, as he is returning home takes ye Book he lent me—is very free, against Mr. Foster and deeply concerned what will be ye Event.

P. M. Mr. W^m. Brigham's wife, near neighbor to Col. Brigham here, drinks Coffee with us &c. My kinsman, Mr. Thos. Needham, returning from camp at Fish-kill to his family at Salem, comes in to see me—he is more out of Health than when he was here last year, and thinks not to go to ye Army again.

29. Attended Mr. Ithamar Bellows Funeral and prayed. May God please to sanctifie ye Death of ye aged Brother to us!

30. A. M. Read Zech. IV. and gave expository notes on ye former part, but preached on Eph. 5. 6. Preached P. M. on Rom. 8. 11. by reason of Mr. Bellows death. Mr. Sam. Barrett of Hopkinton and Mrs. Maynard dind here.

31. Mr. Broaders comes and informs me of ye Death of Mr. Danl How, which occurred yesterday towards night. Aged 54 last October. N. B. I appointed a Catechizing on next Thursday A. & P. M., and am. (by divine assistance) to preach at ye private Meeting tomorrow: so that the Funeral must be tomorrow morning, and he must be buryed in Northboro in that south part[1] where his Father and Mother were interred.

[1] This burying-ground was used when Westborough and Northborough were one town. It is now overgrown with large trees, but very many graves can still be traced. A few are marked with names and dates on the headstones, more, simply by a common field stone

Mr. Willard of Mendon and Mr. Edmund Foster, preacher at Marlboro' having changed yesterday, met and baited here. Breck receives of me £.300 which I commit to him as either lending it to him or partly to pay for a yoke of oxen bot of Mr. Crooks for £200, and ye remaining 100 to trade with as may be most prudent to save ye sinking. Old Mr. Wait of Ashburham here. Lt. Grout here to enquire into ye meeting at his House.

June 1779

I attended ye Funeral of Mr. Daniel How, who dyed at Mr. Fessenden's. Mr. Woodward of Weston and his Ladie, on a journey to Hartford, Springfield &c. called and dind here.

P. M. I preached at Lt. Grout's on Lam. 1. 9. into page 8th.

2. Breck returns from Boston. Eph^m. Parker is preparing to go with the Oxen and Horse to Waltham for earthen Ware. I wrote a letter for Sister Champney to Mr. Ripley of Concord, about her Chest. I covered it with a Letter to my Son W^m in reply to his of May 24, received by Breck.

3. Eph^m. went to Waltham, sat out about 3 A. M. N. B. Timothy Bryant's Time being out, he went with Parker, in order to return to his Mother at Stoneham. I gave him eight dollars, which was as much as I could spare. I wrote by him to his Mother May God be the guardian of his Youth! Mr. Elisha Forbes directs that his uncle Eli's sheep be sent to his pasture, and his brother

at the head and foot. The burying-ground is now in Northborough, on Brigham Street, a short distance from the Westborough line.

Simon, with Billy Spring, drives y^m there. I catechize at ye Meeting House. 34 Boys. 44 Girls. After catechizing I married Phineas Hardy to Sarah Wiman. He gave me Eight Dollars.

N. B. Mr. Joseph Harrington was here and manifested Disgust at ye Proceedings of ye late Council at Bolton. At eve, but before Sunsetting, I by Request of Mr. Sam'l Forbush, went to his House. He has been raising a new Barn,[1] and moving part of an Old One. I was at their Supper, after which we Sang part of Ps. 112.

4. Eph^m Parker returned from Waltham with a load of earthen ware for Breck. Mrs. Ruth Godfrey came to see us, and tarrys over night with us.

5. Mrs. Godfrey returns home. She is very much out of Health, and (I understand) reduced in worldly Circumstances.

6. Preached on Zech. IV. 6-10. Mrs. Maynard dind here.

P. M. preached on Rom. 8. 11. I did not read today.

7. Col. Cushing brot my Grandson John Cushing from Shrewsbury, to reside a while with us. Breck acquaints me with his great Losses by ye Remarkable Depreciation of ye medium. P. M. Messrs. Daniel Forbes and Joseph Harrington here to talk with me about Mr. Daniel Adams and his wife's indecent living apart: and what method must be taken with them: But most probably their design was (and Mr. Gale came in to join them) to find fault with y^e

---

[1] Mr. Samuel Forbush's barn still stands facing Lyman Street. In 1812, the soldiers enlisted for the war, used it for their barracks.

Result of ye late Council at Bolton. And they request they may have it read to ym again on the next Lecture Day.

8. I rode to Mr. Nat. Whitney's in Grafton to talk with Hannah Whitney about her Humiliation and joining with ye Church. Then proceeded to Mr. Grosvenor's, but neither he nor she was at home. I went into Mr. Joseph Brown's, with hope to see his *Electrical Machine*, but he was again gone to Providence. His lady was generous in entertaining me. I dind there and she sent her son Obadiah to call Mr. Henstick, the baptist Minister, to show me ye said Machine. Mr. Grosvenor had by this time returned from Sutton, and came to me, and kindly assisted Mr. Henstick in ye Electrical Operations, which were wonderful. I was electrized a number of times, the rather as it was said to be a Remedy against ye Cramp, which I am much subject to. The Experiments led me to utter, "how Manifold are thy Works, O Lord, in Wysdom hast thou Made ym all." In returning home, I came by Mr. Isaiah Fairbanks and Mr. Nurse's Miss Lydia and Miss Rebecca request a Fast may be kept at their House, and that Mr. Sumner and Mr. Fisk may be sought to perform on that occasion. The time, to be, God Willing, this day Fortnight. I came home safely through the Divine Goodness to me.

9. Sophy with Mr. Brigham, in Mr. Newton's Chaise, goes to Marlboro. Mr. Goodall here and shows me ye Certificate of his Ordination at large, or as a Missionary, to go to the State of Vermont. Mr. Elijah Hardy's wife makes us a visit.

10. Sister Champney is putting up her things in order to leave us. Mr. Mellen and his wife call and drink Coffee.

A Training Day with ye South Company. Much imprudent Firing. Read Roman's Annals of ye Netherlands, Vol. I.

11. Sister Champney left us to go to Mr. Jonas Bond's in Sutton. My son Breck went with her in Mr. Barn. Newton's Chaise, & left her at Mr Bond's. We have bad news of a Fleet supposed to be British, on our Coast, and some other Evil Tidings.

12.

13. Delivered another exercise on Zech. IV. viz. from v. 11 to ye End.

The widow of ye late Capt. Benj. Fay dined with us.

P. M. Considering y^t this is ye Time when Invasions and a new campaign are feared, I delivered again a sermon on Isa. 1.19 to ye beginning of page 7. with divers alterations and additions.

14. Send by Dr. Hawes, a Letter to Mr. Moore, also to Mr. Thos. Adams.

15. Rain ye Forenoon. I could not go to Northboro' Association, dined at home, but P. M. I went to Mr. Whitneys. Mr. Stone, Smith and Goss there. I returned at Eve. Breck and his Wife & Dauter, Mr. Brigham & Sophy are gone, in two Chaises, to Boston. Mr. Forbes and Miss Charlotte Saunders came at eve, & lodged here Capt. Maynard's work men are moving ye Walls.

16. Mr. Forbes and his Dauter left us to go to Brookfield. N. B Before he went, his cousin Elisha came, and they agree about ye nine Sheep of Mr. F. which I have heretofore kept. Mr. Aaron Smith came—dind with us—Lt. Bond, and with him a yoke of Oxen and Horse—my Eph.

Parker with my oxen and Breck's mare go on in plowing fallow ground at ye Island.

17. I looked for Mr. Whitney to preach my Lecture, but he did not come. I preached myself on Ps. 139. 23. to ye latter part of page 6 & concluded with a few warm Expositions extemp.

Mr. Daniel Forbes, Mr. Gale & Mr. Joseph Harrington tother Day requested ye Church might be stopped and ye late Result at Bolton might be read again to y^m. I therefore gratified them, but it was at ye sad Cost of our Peace: for there were presently bitter Exceptions against ye Result and against ye Council y^t formed it. I endeavored to open and to explain every Difficulty, and ease every Complaint — but it was in vain. They were not quiet when we parted. I desire to be humble before God on acct. of this sorrowful Token of his holy Displeasure, and pray for Divine Pity.

At my House were Messrs. Johnⁿ Fay and Eli Brigham, who also eat with me: and we were chearful notwithstanding what I had met with.

N. B. One Mr. Haden of Grafton tells me that they are in great Confusion, having had a meeting there to see whether they should build a new Meeting House: or whether they should repair ye old one: and whether they would grant Mr. Grosvenor some Relief; but they contended and would do neither. For which I am sorely grieved.

18. I am in some Fear y^t the disquieted Brethren will desire to have the Communion deferred, but none came to me.

19. We are in anxiety about Mr. Forbes and Dauter,

which should have come last night, Commencement at Cambridge.

20. Administered ye Lord's Supper—preached A. M on Ps. 139. 24. (having read the Ps. publicly) P. M. on Ps. 36. 1-7. Squire Whipple and his wife and Mrs. Maynard dind here.

N. B. Congress's Address to ye States about ye Currency, tho long, it was read partly by me and partly by Deacon Bond and Mr. Elijah Brigham, in ye Congregation. Mr. Daniel Nurse tells me that the designed Fast at his Sister's, is put off till after ye busy Season.

21. Mr. Forbes and Dauter Charlotte came from Spencer, he having preached there yesterday: and sent Mr. Maccarty to Concord, they lodge here. Town Meeting and Training to raise nine men forthwith; but they do not succeed.

22. Mr. Forbes and dauter leave us to go to Concord, Camb. and Boston. Wrote to Elias by him.

P. M. came Mr. Joh.^n Hobby from Concord, and brot Mrs. Minot to see us. They lodge here.

23. Eph^m. Parker begins to Mowe.

Mr. Hobby, Mrs. Minot and Sophy walk up to Squire Baker's. but return to dine with us. P. M. our Company leave us to go to Northboro, and Mr. Brigham and Sophy accompany y^m. Mr. Fitch visits, to tell me he is engaged to Change with Mr. Sanford next Sabbath, but will change ye 11 of July. Mr. Cushing and Mr. Wm May came and lodged here.

24. I was a while at ye Hay. Mr. Cushing after Dinner

goes to Lancaster, and carrys his son John with him, to go home.

25. Mr. Henry Quincy[1] came to Break fast with Breck —refreshed himself with me at 10. By him I wrote to his Father now at Newtown and to Mr. Thos. Adams of Medfield, who I hear is much out of Health.

26. Received from Mr. Moore two Letters dated

He informs me that his Negro Man, Cato, is taken by ye british force, and y^t he has lost 1500 wt. of Rice. I hear of Rejoicings lately at Boston and Cambridge, on account of Gen'l Lincoln's Victory over ye English Army in South Carolina.

For several days I have drooped, and have but low Appetite, especially at dining. I am become thinner, but P's. 73. 26.

27. Was but faint and my Exercises too long.

Read Zech. V. from 1 to 4 v was ye Exercise A. M. On Isa. 1. 19. to page 11 P. M. Admitted Hannah Whitney to

---

[1] Mr. Henry Quincy, called "the handsomest man in Boston," the 2d son of Mr. Parkman's dear friend, Judge Edmund Quincy, b. Jan'y 26, 1726–27. He was twice married and had a family of twelve children. Soon after his death in Cambridge, in 1780 (see Journal June 5, 1780), his family moved to Boston, with Judge Quincy, and were obliged to take boarders. Among these was the young French Consul to the United States, Mons. Joseph Dupas de Valnais, his secretary and friends. In 1781, he married the daughter, Eunice Quincy, and two years afterwards she went to Paris, where she died about a dozen years later. Her husband and daughter returned later to this country, in 1816, where they were welcomed by the Quincy family.

MADAM HANNAH PARKMAN

Charity, and into Church Fellowship, and baptized a Child of Mr. Benj. Warrin's.

28. Read Bell's Travels—thro' Siberia and Tartary to Pekin. I was somewhat lively, yet not as heretofore. I thank God for my Preservation and earnestly wish for Grace to improve my Time and Talents.

29. I opened and spread Hay a while A. M. Mrs. P. has rid unto ye South of ye Town to procure Worsted Combings. She went to ye Outermost House and returned in Safety. P. M. the News Papers which contain Gen'l Lincoln's Victory over the british Forces in South Carolina. To God be glory! I wrote to Mr. Jonas Bond of ye North of Sutton concerning Sister Champney.

30. Some part of ye Day I was feeble and faint, heartless and do but little—"Cur mundus, militat sub vana Gloria" &c. &c.

Afterwards I had somewhat more of Vivacity D. G. The Lord is Long-Suffering to astonishment!

July 1779

Read part of Dr. Cotton Mather's Agathangelus & Celestinus. Thus far it appears to be a very useful quickening Book. I have reason to bless God and would heartily do so, for the eminent Writings of that pious and learned man.

Dr. Hawes, who has returned from Court, was here and communicated to me some of the Transactions of ye Assembly, and what ye Town of Boston have, by their Committee of Correspondence, sent to ye Committee of Westboro' relative to some fresh Efforts for ye Appreciation of y^e

public Currency. N. B. Thomas's Spy[1] comes again to the Shop for a Numbers of yᵉ Neighbors.

2.

3.

4. Preached A. M. on Zech. 3. 4 P. M. went on with Repetition of Sermon on Isa. 1. v. 19-20 to p. 15.

5. Visited Mr. Belknap[2] and dind there. He has a Widow Sister that lives there. Her name is Flagg. I called at Mrs. Seth Wood's, & obtained of her to weave for us. I also made a Business of visiting and prayed with old Mrs. Chamberlain. She was very ill and under hysteric Affections. I called at Mr. Wᵐ. Johnson's. Young Mrs. Belknap went with me to her Father's, Ensign Snow's.

---

[1] The Massachusetts Spy was established in Boston, nine years before this time. In 1775, for greater safety, it was removed to Worcester, where it has since been published, and is now the oldest newspaper in Massachusetts, and in the United States. It was printed by Isaiah Thomas, until 1802, a modest little sheet of four small pages.

[2] The Belknap farm was Mr. Parkman's farthest point this day, being near Rocklawn. John Belknap had come, a young man, to Westborough soon after the incorporation of the town, and built a log hut on his farm, where he was besieged by wolves and Indians, but escaped from both, and lived to a good old age. At the age of eighty, he married the widow of the 2d Jonathan Forbes, Joanna Tainter. He was now eighty-two.

On the way home, Mr. Parkman would go by the Chamberlain houses, Mr. Beeman's, and probably that of Mr. Thomas Andrews, who may have lived at this time with Thomas Forbush, his father-in-law, in the house he afterwards owned. In this century the house has always been known as the Andrews house. The Andrews family came from Salem.

who put a Cheese into my Saddle Baggs. I called at Mr. Beeman's and at Mr. Thos. Andrew's. On my way home I went into ye Workhouse[1] to see a Stranger who was taken sick on ye Road from Fishkill and going to his Family at Casco Bay.

6. I went to ye Private Meeting at Mr. Joseph Grout's I preached on Lam. 1. 9 from page 8 to 13. I was handsomely entertained, but principally request ye divine Blessing.

7. Read Smalley's discourse on Joh. 6. 44. Visit ye poor Sick Stranger at ye Workhouse,—and prayed with him. His name is James Webber of Purpoodock and has a Wife and two Children; he is ill of bilious Fever and Camp-Distemper.

8. I sent my Watch by Mr. Moses Nurse to Mr. Simon Willard[2] of Grafton: the chain being loose, unhooked.

[1] This was a house built according to a vote passed in the March meeting of 1767—"To see if the Town will agree to build a workhouse and where to set it." They decided "it should be set and stand on a corner of Mr. Timothy Warrin's land." Mr. Timothy Warren lived on the road to Southboro', on the Warren farm just beyond where the turnpike crosses.

[2] Mr. Simon Willard, a famous clock-maker of Grafton and Boston. He was a great-grandson of Capt. Benj. Willard, the 15th child of Major Simon Willard. Capt. Benjamin was one of the first settlers of Grafton. Simon's father, also a Benj. Willard, had twelve children, nine of whom were sons, and the second son, Benjamin, was probably the first clock-maker in New England. He advertises his clocks as made by his workmen in Grafton as well as in Roxbury. Aaron and Simon were his brothers, and both were distinguished as clock-makers; Simon, especially, who lived until

N. B.   Mr. Nurse has brought from Mrs. Lydia Garfield 31 & ½ yds of tow cloth which she has wove, and for which I paid 21 Dollars and 5 Shillings.

9.   I was in some perplexity about my Haying, because nothing is done about it all this Week (except One Load on Monday) and yet Parker is going to work at Harrington's.

10.   I prepare for Hopkinton and P. M. I rode there. I called to see old Mr. Jonas Warrin. I carryed to Mr. Barrett his first Volume of Henry's Exposition. I lodged at Mr. Fitch's.   Mr. Fitch to Westboro.

11.   I preached at Hopkinton on Joel 3. 13 A. & P. M. It rained at eve. It was so wet and uncomfortable that I tarried there: but yet Mr. Fitch himself got home.

12.   Went to Mr. Barretts, where I was very affectionately received. He lent me the third volume of Mr. Henry, viz. on Job, Psalms &c: he lent me also the third volume of the History of England in Folio and Howel's Familiar Letters. 4 vols bound in one Oct. Book. but in his Generosity he gave me the Folio which contains Dr. Stillingfleet's Sermons, twelve, and his Discourse on the True Reason of the Sufferings of Jesus Christ. This Cargo of Books I brot Home.

Having understood that Mr. James Webber was still sick

1848, and died then in Roxbury at the age of 96—leaving a son of the same name.

At this time, when Mr. Parkman entrusted his watch to him, he was twenty-seven years old.

The houses of the Willards were in the "Farms Deestrict," near Wild Cat Swamp. Only a cellar hole shows where Simon's once stood, but Benjamin's still defies the winds and storms of our New England winters.

at ye Work house, I went there P. M. to see him and prayed with him. Mr. Thomas Adams of Medfield came at Evening with a number of Books and lodged here.

We have a Sad Report y^t New Haven is taken by ye Enemy.

13. Mr. Adams has brought home to me at length Sir Wm Temple. He has led me also into an Exchange of a number of Books viz. For Voetius 3 vols. I have Dr. Stanhope's Thomas a Kempis Dr. Calamy, of Vows; Horneck's crucified Jesus, & Dr Goodman's Old Religion. For Monsr. Boileau's 2^d vol and Mat Prior's Works 2 vols. I have Dr. Hammond's Annotations in large Folio. For the Lay Monastery, I have Herman Prudence, & Three Select Pieces of Mr. Thos. Shepherd. For Comin's Real Christian, unbound, I gave him at his proposal a Pound of Sugar. He presented me a Pamphlet, Dr. Gibson on ye Sinfulness of Neglecting and profaning the Lord's Day. N. B. I returned him his Drexilius on Eternity. He showed me a Manuscript of his Dauter's forming in 4to Alphabetical, and contains an account of all manner of Errors, Sects, &c in every age of Chty. He sold Breck a number of unbound Books, Firmin, Shaw, Shepherd, Doelittle &c. After dinner he left us to go to Sherburn.

14. Mr. Joh^n Hall of Hopkinton here. I visited and prayed with ye sick Stranger, Mr. James Webber. He is grown worse. May God prepare him and us for His Sovereign Will!

Mr. John Pigeon of Brookfield here and dind with us.

15. Am variously employed among the Books which I lately had from Mr. Adams and Mr. Barrett. P. M. attended Mr. Webber's Funeral, & prayed. We have ye Sad News

of ye British Forces invading New Haven, Fairfield, Stratford &c.

16. The news from New Haven is confirmed. Susè not well.

17. Isaac Baldwin came up from Cambridge where he has been examined and approved, tho not admitted into College. lodges here. A Letter by Baldwin from Mr. I. Quincy. Eph^m on Breck's Horse, at ye Close of ye Day, to Shrewsbury.

18. Read Ps. 103 and preached on v. 14. Sam. Brigham dines. P. M. on Isa. 1. 20, & finish that Discourse. At eve I read in Stanhope's à Kempis on Death. May God grant His almighty Blessing to accompany my Weak Efforts!

19. Parker returned from Shrewsbury to his Work. Mr. Eleazar Fairbank of North Shrewsbury, trades with Breck, and visits, dines, and spends good part of ye P. M. with me.

20. Read preface to Shaw's Immanuel. Newspaper from Boston, but am chiefly impressed and taken up with ye weighty, important Things, which relate to my Dissolution and an eternal World. It is wonderful that I am no more affected with them.

21. Breck goes to Boston. Mr. Elisha Forbes with his Team goes down to load up for him. Miss Polly Howard here making Lace for my Dauter Cushing. Mr. John Pidgeon came in his way to Brookfield, and lodges here. He brings fresh news of our Success against ye Enemy in recovering ye Fort on Hudson's River, which they had lately taken from ye States, & fortified more Strongly, which is called Stoney Point, near King's Ferry: May

God grant to His people a suitable Frame of Mind upon Such Occasions!

Elias came from Cambridge.

22. Sr. Fisk (as now I suppose he is honored) made us a Visit and dind here. Mrs. Lamson ill, her aunt Knowlton, who tends on her, lodges here.

23. Mr. Eben.^{r} Allen, a Stranger, born at ye Vineyard, his parents live at Rochester, himself a Preacher, came here to see me, stayed and dind, is going to Needham to preach there.

Breck returns from Boston, tells me Salley is very comfortable.

24. I have very much left my Husbandry Business with Parker., and betake myself to my Studys.

25. Preached A. M. on Zech. v. 3.4. Mrs. Maynard dind here. P. M. for ye sake of some Disconsolate persons, and a View to ye Communion next Sabbath, I repeated with some Additions sermon on Ps. 69.32, which may God graciously succeed! At eve read a Kempis Book IV. Chap. 1. the Communion being appointed.

26. Applyed myself to Studys and began my Preparations. Mr. Waters from Newtown, where he has been preaching calls here. The Rain upon our Hay, it much perplexes and disappoints in various Respects.

27. Mrs. P. is with my N^r. Harrington's wife in her Travail.

28. They have a Dauter born. I read Bell's Travels to Pekin, & went to see Mrs. Harrington. Mrs. Dolly Rice here.

29. Mrs. Lamson being still in a very unfit Situation to

be alone, has Mrs. Drury, Daughter of her aunt Knowlton with her from Day to Day, but she lodges here—ever since last Saturday night.

30. Drury Fairbank, who sometime ago was Sick and languishing, under a dangerous consumptive Cough, is strangely raised to Health, and is going into ye Service. P. M. came from Worcester, my Dauter Baldwin, with her son Isaac waiting upon her. She has been of late much borne down with her Disorders, but is (just now) somewhat brighter. They lodge here, as does Mrs. Ellwell, who in coming to help Mrs. Lamson, had a Fall from her Horse, and is rendered incapable to help her.

31. Isaac Baldwin returns to Brookfield, but leaves his Mother and her Chaise here. Mr. Waters returning to Newtown. How swiftly this month has fled! So teach us to number our Days that we may apply our Hearts to Wisdom!

AUGUST 1779.

A. M. on Ps: 36. 7. Administered the Lord's Supper, which may God graciously accept. Mrs. Maynard dind here.

P. M. preached on Ps: 4. 7. to p. 9. O y^t this might be ye Frame of my own Soul! N. B. Did not read publickly.

At eve, read Mr. Dolittle's XIII Chapter on duty after receiving ye Sacrament.

2. Breck has found sundry books for me, viz: Dr. Scott's Serm. Vol. II. Which is on ye Love of God: Firmin's Real Christian and Shepherd's Three Select Pieces, and mended several others. Mr. Joseph Harrington has brot a

Loin of Veal, which I would take a grateful notice of.—Rumours of a British Fleet.

The Town meet on a number of important Articles relative to the affairs of ye State; particularly to choose several Delegates for ye Conventions. We are to meet for Preparing a plan of Government in this State, and another respecting the Depreciation of money, &c. Mr. Nathan Maynard jun^r goes to Boston for Breck and carries in his Team Mr. Eli Forbes' Trunk.—old Mr. David Maynard here and carrys to Mr. Peter Whitney's, Henry on Psalms &c.

3. I preach at ye private Meeting at Dea. Bond's on Lam. 1. 9. & finished ye Subject. Mr. P. Whitney communicates some Letters. Elias went to Mr. Simon Willard of Grafton, and brot from him my Watch mended and cleaned, and Transactions of Mr. Goss and ye Brethren of ye South Church in Bolton. He has lately preached at ye Dedication of ye new Meeting House there, on that Text 2 Chron: 6. 41.

4. Moses Warren of Upton came from Mr. Fitch's of Hopkinton, and bought a Greek Grammar of my son Elias.

I read the Art of Speaking, y^t is ye first part which is the Essay on Rules &c. At eve, Mr. Isaac Parker, who is very friendly and generous.

5. Elias goes to Worcester for Mr. Isaac Parker to bring ye Newspapers. Capt. Fisher here. He listens to Geographical Description. Read ye admirable Character of Dr. Sol. Way by Mr. Cogswell. Mrs. Eliz Pratt of Worcester came in to see me.

Elias returning home, brings me word from Mrs. Parker

of Shrewsbury (where he dind), y^t my Sister Cushing[1] is sick.

6. I left my Study to visit Sister Cushing. Mr. Moses Nurse has bought my son Breck's fine mare so y^t (tho' it was more tedious to me) I rode his grey Horse, to Shrewsbury, dined at Mr. Sumner's. Visit old Madam Cushing, who is sick of a Fever, &c, but is somewhat better today. At her Request, I prayed with her. I rode to Mr. Amos Parker's. In returning I stopt at Mr. Isaac Davis about soal leather.

7. By reason of Various Hindrances & Interruptions, I made but a little Preparation for ye Sabbath It is a more than ordinary rainy Season. Mrs. P——n's lameness is much increased and fills her with Smart.

8. It is still wet Weather. I preached A. & P. M. ye rest of ye Discourse on Ps: 4. 7. which may we all be duely effected with !

Mr. Samuel Barrett of Hopkinton and his Wife came over to our Meeting (Mr Fitch and his lady being gone to Connecticut) dined &c. here. At eve, I read in ye Family some Chap. of Thomas á Kempis. N. B. The Widow Sarah Smith is in Glooms again.

9. I visit old Mrs. Smith, but she is exceedingly changed: and is not willing to talk with me. Mr. Child also is very much exercised with Pains I prayed with y^m and greatly pityed y^m. Went to Mr. Daniel Nurse's and his Sisters—

---

[1] His sister Cushing was the mother of his son-in-law, the wife of the Rev. Job Cushing. She lived nearly twenty years after this, and died at the age of ninety.

to Mr. Thos. Whitney's[1] and dind there. He tells me he will have another talk with Mr. Benj. Fay in order to

[1] Thomas Whitney lived in that part of Shrewsbury called "the Shoe," in the house on the North Grafton road, next easterly to that of Dea. Nourse.

THOS. WHITNEY HOUSE.

He and his wife both lived to a green old age, and their gravestones still stand in the Memorial Cemetery.

In 1762, when most of the farms in the Shoe were annexed to Westborough, he was left behind in Shrewsbury entirely surrounded by Westborough. "We do not know," says the Westborough Historian, "whether he loved Shrewsbury more or Westborough less; but the General Court, with more regards for individual wishes than in town divisions of the present day, allowed his farm to remain a part of Shrewsbury." In 1793 this farm was

154   DIARY OF REV. EBENEZER PARKMAN.

make up their Difference—was informed by him also y^t Mr. Samuel Fay would have me go to his House. I went in to Timothy Whitney's, visited at Mr. Joseph Hardy's, went to see Mr. Eli Whitney and his new Wife—called at Mr. Phin. Hardy's—went to Mr. Elisha Forbes, Mr. Tainter and his

annexed to Westborough, in response to a petition of Elijah Whitney, his son. Eli Whitney was of another family, and was the father of Eli Whitney, the inventor of the cotton-gin. He lived on the well-known farm on Eli Whitney Street, in the house whose picture has been preserved for us by Barbour's Historical Collections. The son Eli, at this time, was a boy of fourteen. The large monument in the Memorial Cemetery, near the Whitney house, marks the spot where Eli Whitney and his first wife, Elizabeth Fay, who died in 1777, were buried. No mention appears on the stone of the "new wife," Judith Hazelton, whom he had married a month or two before this time.

ELI WHITNEY HOUSE.

son Benj's Family. I made a Business of Seeing and discoursing with y^e Stranger Polly Brown—drank Tea at Forbes's.

10. The Season for getting Hay has been singularly difficult, by reason of so much foul Weather. Yesterday indeed was fair, but today arose a Thunder Storm and poured down heavy Showers. At eve I wrote to Mr. Quincy.

11. Sent my Letter to Mr. Q—by Breck, who hurried me so y^t I was obliged to send him a mere Fragment, without accomplishing my Plan. The Hay Business is attended with great Difficulty, by reason of much Wet Weather. Divers People have many Loads under Water.

12. Still Cloudy and rainy—broken Time for Workmen. Sunshine P. M. They go to ye Hay at ye Swamp between 4 & 5. N. B. Mr. Nathan Kenney's little Lucy (about 4 years old) was scalded by squatting into a Tray of Hot Water. Dr. Hall of Sutton calls here in Return from Boston. Major Peter Harwood of Brookfield came to see my Dauter Baldwin. He leaves us to go to his Grandfather's, Capt. Hubbard of Worcester ye Eve.

13. Parker went to my little Flock in Squire Baker's pasture, got a Lamb, killed it—did not weigh it—it was very small. Breck returned from Boston: but was much overcome by ye Rain and Fatiegue of his Journey—young Henry Pigeon here and dind with us. P. M. Rev. Fitch, his wife and sucking son Elijah—they dind here. Lent Mr. Fitch, Stillingfleet's Origines Sacrae. Mrs. Hawes and her Cousin, Miss Jerusha King, at Tea here.

14. Elias to Northboro, and carrys to Mr. Whitney, Mr. Charles Stearns' Book of ye Art of Speaking.

15. Read Levit. 19 to v. 18, and took v. 12 for my Text to introduce my Exercise on Zech: v. 4 from page 70 to 74. P. M. repeat Sermon on II Peter 1. 10 to y⁰ end of page 8, with omissions of what related to y⁰ Lord's Supper. At evening repeated principal parts of it.

16. Elias shews me his Quarter Bills which are not paid, viz.:

to Feb. 26. 1779 which is — — — —	£ 17. 3. 4	
The 4th Quarter Bill from Feb. 26 to May 28. 1779 is	£ 18. 5. 0	
	———	which
	deduct. 64. 8. 4	buttery
Besides these Mr. Philips Paylons Buttery		bill added
sizing from Nov. 27. 1778 to July 14. 1779 £ 38. 18. 0 not paid.	is £ 103. 6. 4	

N. B. This gave me some Difficulty that these several Bills were unpaid, seeing I gave Elias an Hundred Dollars on March 17, and with a View to his discharging that Bill which was due on Feb. 26 last. Besides which he had more of me at different Times in y⁰ Spring particularly on May 31, 14 Dollars, delivered by Breck; more by Breck again about y⁰ same time £22. 4. 0. (that is 74 Dollars, which with the 14 Dollars on May 31, as aforesaid, made 88 Dollars.)

N. B. The Town met P. M. to see whether they would concur with what the Convention of Worcester have resolved upon as to y⁰ Prices of Things, Lab'. Goods &c. and consented thereto. Chose also a Committee of three to Set a Price on lesser Articles, which y⁰ Convention omitted. They were Dr. Hawes, Mr. Joseph Harrington and Capt. Fisher. N. B. Drury Fairbanks desires to be marryed, tho he has not been 14 days on y⁰ Town Clerk's Book. Mr. Weare & Isaac Forbush came with him, but I refused.

17. I had an Horse of Deacon Wood to go to Minister's Meeting at East Sudbury. Breck being gone to Ashburnham. I delivered to Elias 100 Dollars for ye Steward &c. In riding ye Journey I overtook Mr. Stone, and we remarked ye great Loss of Hay on Sudbury Meadows, by ye late Rains. At Mr. Bridge's were Messrs. Stone, Goss, Whitney, Newell—but Mr. Smith was gone a Journey and was not returned. The same as at last Meeting, was Moderator. Mr. Bridge prayed. After dinner our Subjects were, Mr. Goss' grievances, and ye Dissensions at Marlborough mentioned by Mr. Whitney. I would fain have recommended to have a Concio, or Collections, or some Questions answered y^t we may redeem our Time, and render our associating ye more profitable. When we broke up., I rode to my Son William's and lodged there.

18. Rode from my Son's to Coll. Week's, where my Horse as well as myself was refreshed. The Colonel requested I would visit old Mr. Sam'l Wit, who was very old and weak: and he would go with me. We went—found him in a good Frame. He spoke to the following purpose in a raised, Strong and Solemn Manner. "I had rather have the Glorious God for my Portion, and an interest in ye Merits of Jesus Christ, than to be Lord of ye Whole World." At his Desire I prayed with him. At taking leave, he expressed himself as much obliged to me, glad I would visit him & asked my Prayers still for him. I called a little at Mr. Simon How's, who lent me Mr. Hubbard of Ipswich's Narrative of ye Indian Wars. Isaac Baldwin came from Brookfield to his Mother's great Comfort. Mr. Jacob Foster, late minister of Berwick, came and lodged.

19. My Dauter Baldwin left us, waited on by her son Isaac. Mr. Foster went on his Journey to Canterbury.
20.
21. Winslow Brigham having led an Horse to Ashburnham, for Pamela Coolidge to live with us; but returns without her, to Mrs. Parkman's great disappointment.
22. On Zech: v. 4. to page 73, but used for my Text again Levit. 19. 12. P. M. delivered ye rest of Discourse on II Peter 1. 10. with some additions. At eve read a part of Mr. Culverwells on that Text: entitled The White Stone, which may God bless!
23. Read part of Clark's Lives. Isaac Baldwin and Neddy Parkman came from Brookfield and lodged here.
24. Elias (to whom I delivered 30 Dollars more—see on ye 17th) left us to return to Cambridge and with him Isaac Baldwin. Neddy goes with y^m to bring back ye Horses. Breck has Carpenters at work to raise ye Back Roof of his Store. Mrs. P. is carried to Squire Baker's. At eve she returns with a present of Salt Beef and Six neets Tongues from ye old Gentlewoman.
25. Mr. Hez.^{h} Maynard of Marlboro' here on account of a Draught of a Covenant to be used in their Assembly previous to Baptism: he having brot one that was deficient. I altered and copyed it. Neddy Parkman returned from Cambridge—he brot my Virgil and Tully and some other Books from Elias. Neddy lodges here. The sad news from Penobscot is confirmed.
26. An exceeding rainy time. Neddy cant return to Brookfield. Stephen Maynard here and has brot a Relation.

I read Mr. Fish's reply to Foster of Leicester on Infant Baptism.

27. Neddy goes on his Journey to Brookfield.

My son William came with his Chaise for his Mother to go with him, to Concord (his Wife drawing near ye Time of Travail). He, Capt. Goddard of Sutton, Dr. Stinson now of Marlboro' and Mr. Caleb Harrington dind with us. P. M. Mrs. P. to Concord.

The notorious Thomas Cook[1] came in (he says) on pur-

[1] Tom Cook is one of the picturesque characters of the day, and we wonder, as we hear of his exploits, how he escaped the sad fate of Hugh Henderson and Johnson Green, the latter captured in Westborough and hanged as late as 1786 for breaking into three houses in Shrewsbury one night and stealing, according to his own confession: "From Mr. Baldwin 1 pair of Shoes 1 pair of Silver Buckles 1 furstan jaccot two all woll Do one Shirt cotton and linnen one bottle of New England Rum, two Cakes of Gingerbread 21 coat and jaccot Buttons and four or five shillings in cash—from Mr. Farrar one pair of Shoes, 1 pair of Shoe Buckles silver one Pair of Sizars 20 or 30 Coppers a remnant of black Sattin lasting one linnen pocket handkerchief—from Mr Wyman about fifteen or sixteen shillings in Cash part Silver and part Copper."

Tom Cook, notorious even in Mr. Parkman's day, was supposed by the good people of the town to have been pledged by his mother —the Eunice Forbush who married Cornelius Cook and lived in the old house on the corner of East Main and Lyman streets—to serve the devil, an obligation which he willingly assumed as he grew up, and which he found of great assistance to him in the pursuit of his profession.

He was known as the "honest thief"—although he preferred to be called the "leveller." He figures in many a tale of theft and highway robbery, but he rarely used his ill-gotten gains for himself, but usually bestowed them on some one lacking in this world's

pose to see me. I gave him what Admonition, Instruction and caution I could. I beseech God to give it Force! He leaves me with fair Words—thankful and promising.

28. Lt. Townsend here to get a Dismission for himself and Wife. The Front Wall of ye East yard next ye Road, built out to ye Fence that turns up to ye House. A Barrel of Cyder made at Lieut. Jon. Grout's.

29. I went on with ye Exercises upon Zech: v. 4, but ye goods, He selected his victims thoughtfully, choosing only those who could afford to help their needy neighbors and did not.

He was arrested many times, and once was sentenced to be hanged, but as he informed the Judge, when he heard the awful words, "until you are dead—dead—dead," he was not there "that day—day—day," and he lived to a good old age and is still remembered by a few in our midst.

He is one of our legends now, and we write of him:

> "It was a superstitious age
> When he first saw the light,
> And boldly did his spirit guage
> Its narrow rule of right.
>
> "And because he would not travel
> In the regulation way
> He was thought a son of Belial,
> And beneath Satanic sway.
>
> "He saw no more than we can see,
> Nor felt he more the fact
> That justice means equality,—
> He only dared to act."
>   —Poem read by Dr. Corey on Parkman Day.

He was born in 1738, consequently at this time was forty-one years old. He lived to be nearly ninety, and died on a run-away trip from the home provided for him by the town. His final levelling cost the town forty dollars.

See note on Dana's Tavern, Oct. 4, 1737.

Text was Lev. 19. 12. Read Ex. XX. A. M. Read P. M. Acts 17. took v. 30 for my Text. Delivered both ye Sermons (with some omissions and a few Additions) which I preached almost Ten years ago. Mr. Sumner being gone, sundry Shrewsbury people were at Meeting here. Elmer Cushing & —— Crosby dind here.

30. Breck goes to Boston. I read ye Life of eminently pious Mr. John Janewey, which may God be graciously pleased to bless to my Quickening and eternal Profit!

31. I took a Walk to Mr. Abr.^m Bonds' to visit him and his Wife., under their great Affliction by their son John's continued Lameness. I also went to see and talk with Mrs. Barns being under ye Guilt of Fornication. I solemnly called her to Repentance, and I spent some time with Francis' Wife. Then went to ye Men who were out at plough. When returned Home, I found here Rev. Mr. David Ripley of Abington in Connetic. who dind with me and went on his Way.

SEPTEMBER 1779.

Breck returns from Boston, brings me a joyful Letter from W^m that his Wife was delivered last Saturday morning at 8 A. M. of a Son, baptized John. P. M. My Dauter-in-law Kezia of New Marlboro came from Framingham and lodged here.

2. Kezia was going home to New Marlboro alone. The Difficulty in finding ye Road to Lancaster, engaged me to go with her so far. I went. We dind at Mrs. Wilder's in Lancaster. Thence I went with my Dauter to t'other Side ye Meeting House, and set her in ye Road to her Brother's

in Fitchbourg—I turnd into Mr. Sheriff Greenleaf's thence to Mr. Harrington's,—he not at home, and sat out for home but in Northboro was compelled to go into Deacon Paul Newton's to raising Supper, & lodged there.

3. Broke fast at Mr. Whitney's—borrowed Bp. Hall's Works, folio, and came home, Thanks to God. Col. Cushing and Major Brennan dind here. Four men to be raised from the Town to go to Providence, for two months. A Letter received from Sister Champney at Sutton.

4. Breck to Sutton, but I knew it not in season to write an answer by him. A terrible Storm of Thunder and Lightning, a very violent Crack suddenly and close by us. Afraid we shall hear of Sad effects. The Lord be praised for our Preservation. O ye Power and Goodness of God!

5. Preached A. M. on Zech: v. 5–8. P. M. on Prov. 15. 16, which may God graciously please to bless! Appointed ye Communion and Lecture, but put by ye private Meeting which would otherwise have been at Mr. Tainter's. Mr. Dan'l Forbes has been with me and desires ye next Meeting might be at his House (Tainter agreeing to it) by reason of old Mrs. Stone who lives there.

6. I wrote early to Rev. Mr. Stone of Southboro' to preach my Lecture on ye 8th and sent it by Mr. Adonijah Putnam of Sutton. I wrote to Sister Lydia Champney at Mr. Jonas Bond's in Sutton in reply to hers of Aug. 31. At eve came Nathan Flag from Grafton with a message from one Mrs. Mary Hasham, requesting me to attend ye Funeral of her Husband tomorrow at 2 P. M.

7. I rode to Grafton—dind at Mr. Grosvenor's (He was gone to Conway) I prayed at ye Funeral of Mr. Hasham.—

at Mr. Aaron Willard's, paid him eleven Dollars for mending my Watch. Mr. Simon Willard went with me to Mr. Joseph Brown's and shewed me a Perambulator which he had made and fixed to Mr. Brown's Chaise. Alexander came and lodged here.

8. I received a note from Mr. Stone y^t he could not preach my Lecture. The Town of Southboro' meet today to consider his Salary. I preached my Self. The Text was Romans 15. 13. May God bless my Endeavors! Alexander went to Marlboro' but returned and lodged here. Squire Whipple came in after Lecture, gives but an indifferent Account of ye State of Things in New Braintrey. They go on under Mr. Foster, as if all was right.

9. This morning our neighbor Lamson who has been a long time very miserable was delivered of a fine large Boy, to our great Rejoicing. Blessed be God, ye God of Salvation and may He perfect her Recovery! Alexander and Breck go to Worcester and return. David Fay and Patience Hovey (?) were married. My son Alexander is still here, and lodges here.

10. Alexander leaves us to go to Ashburnham and then home. I thought it my Duty to visit Mrs. Lamson to rejoice with her and stir her up to ye Duty of Dedicating her child to God. P. M. came Mr. Charles Stearns of Leominster & lodged here. N. B. He informs y^t Mr. Whitney of Petersham dyed on Wednesday.

At eve came Mr. John Belknap and Mr. Daniel Forbes— they want that Mr. Dan. Adams should be desired to forbear coming to ye Sacrament. I dont consent without they write and sign it, which they do.

11. Mr. Stearns goes to Mr. Stone's. Mrs. P. came home from Concord with my son W^m. and his little Sophy is with her Father, and after Dinner, they return to Concord. A Letter from aged Mr. Eb^r Hartshorn of Concord. I wrote and sent a note to Mr. D. Adams, concerning his forbearing to come to ye Communion tomorrow.

12. I read Ps: 116. Preached on Ps. 36.7. Administered ye Lord's Supper. Mr. Knight of Boston was at ye Communion. Mrs. Maynard dind here. P. M. delivered ye Latter Sermon on Roms. 15.13. At eve, Mr. Stone came here, having preached at Northboro'. He lodged here.

13. I visited Katy Biglow, ill of a Fever and hysteric Disorders. At her Desire, I prayed there. Had some conversation with Mr. Daniel Adams about his Wife living from him. He tells me he desires she would return and that he would do anything reasonable to obtain it P. M. he came here, shewed me a Copy of a Letter which he had sent to her some time ago, desiring her to let him know what are her Difficultys, and what she would have him do. To which letter she returned him no Answer.

N. B. Dr. Stimson and Miss Nancy Jones of Hopkinton here and dind.

14. Had some Debate with Dr. Hawes about Tim. Bryant's Work for him last year. N. B. Mr. John Thayer from New Haven Coll. came here in his way to Boston, dind here. Received a Letter from Mr. Zebulon Rice of Brookfield concerning Rev. Mr. Buckminster's preparing to answer Mr. Isaac Foster's ordination Sermon, and consulting an Association at Sturbridge thereon.

15. Sent Eph^m. Wheelock with a load of Apples to

Lieut. Grout's to be made into Cyder by him at his Mill. Broke Fast at Capt. Wood's. Had conversation with Dea. Wood and with Mr. Tho. Twitchell about Mr. Adam's Affair with his Wife. Visit and prayed with Katy Biglow.

16. The Day was mainly spent in Retirement—See Natal..[1] but just at eve came to my Sorrow, Mr. Adams and

---

[1] He writes under this date in the small blank book in which, during his long life, he recorded his birthday meditations:—
"Sept. 5. O. S. Westb.
Natalitia,
This Day I separated myself from Worldly Delight, Care and Encumbrances, as my Circumstances w'd allow, and gave myself to religious exercises and Retrospections.
Praising and adoring ye most High, ye g^{rt} Almighty Author of my Being, my merciful Preserver and bountiful Benefactor, who has graciously upheld me through the Revolutions and Tryals of another Year and has vouchsafed me a wonderful measure of Health and Comfort in such advanced Age. I implore ye divine Pity and Pardoning Mercy under so much Guilt and Unworthiness, thro' ye Blood and Merits of my dear Redeemer, and importune ye Gracious Almighty aids and ye sanctifying, comforting and establishing Communications of ye Holy Spirit of Grace. And renewed my Resolutions and Engagements to walk with God and to be faithful to Him.
Beginning another Year still thro ye Lords Long-suffering towards me, I ardently beg His all sufficient and powerful Grace to sustain me under my Decay!—
And O y^t I might obtain clear and well-grounded Evidences of divine Faith and Love and a full Assurance of Hope to the End!—
6. old stile. Rev. Messrs. Reed and Turner of Middleboro' inform me of ye Death of two of my classmates viz:—Mr. Shepherd Fiske and Rev. Mr. Wm. Rand of Kingston. There being now only Four of us surviving, Dr. Chancy, Messrs. Bucknam and Wight —and I.—

with him Lieut. Levi Warrin, who ask (and with some Reluctance) I gave a Copy of Messrs. Belknap and Forbes' Request to me to send to Mr. A. to forbear coming to ye Communion last Lord's Day.

Messrs. Reed of Middleboro' and Turner of same Town, going to ye Ordination of Mr. Reed's son at Warwick, came & lodged here. Mr. Jacob Broaders² was married to young Katharine Fessenden. N. B. The above named ministers prayed before and after ye Covenant.

17. The ministers go on their Journey. A School is kept at ye Grout School-house by Mr. Hazzletine.

18. A no of Theeves who have stole from Mr. Henry Prentice of Grafton, are taken and one of y^m whip'd at Deacon Wood's—ye Chief of ye Money is recovered.

I earnestly beg of God, deeply thoroly, to imprest my Soul herewith that I may be always actually ready for my own Departure!—

² How old Jacob Broaders was at this time, the records say not, but Katharine Fessenden lacked four days of being sixteen. She was the oldest daughter of John Fessenden. A few years after this, he bought the house then vacated by Isaac Davis, and known since his day as the Broaders House. Katharine had three children, and was left a widow at the early age of twenty-three. She was allowed after her husband's death to take of his personal property,—

" An old fine shirt 3/6.
1 pr. Silver Shoe Buckles 14/6.
One pair Silver knee buckles 5/6.
One pair Silver Sleeve Buttons 1s."

His clothing was sold by the "Vendue Master," and show him to have been a well dressed and prosperous man of the day, for he had A great Coat, a velvet waistcoat, and two others besides, a blue coat and a red coat, and a pair of "Red breaches" which Amasa Maynard bought, and "Woolling Stockings."

He was the grandfather of Hiram L. Broaders.

19. On consideration of my beginning a New Year I preached A. M. on Isaiah 46:3.4 and by reason of ye Death of my two classmates, Rev. Mr. William Rand and Mr. Shepherd Fisk, I made up a sermon on Isa: 57.1-2. with proper observations and additions, especially of ye character of Mr. Rand, whom I was much more acquainted with.

I informed ye Congregation of ye Fast, to be God willing, on ye next Thursday, at Mr. Danl Nurse's, on account of his two Sisters.

We had a Contribution for ye Relief of Mr. Artemas Bruce, of New Fane, whose House was lately burnt.

20. The Contribution yesterday was £48./7/. and a Person who was not prepared at ye Time desired 20/ be added for him, which he promised to repay, which was I suppose, done. Bruce was here. I gave him ye Money; he gave me a Receipt and thanks to ye People and to me.

Mrs. Lambson very ill. Visited and prayed with her. N. B. The Town met to see what they would do in Compassion to ye Town of Boston, who are suffering by reason of Market people refraining to go in with ye Necessarys of Life.

21. Wrote to Cousin Briant. At eve call to see Mrs. Lambson. I rode to Mr. Joseph Grout's to see Mrs. Adams who lives there. I dind there, though Mr. Grout and his Wife were gone to Boston. Mrs. Adams seems to be utterly unwilling to go to live with her Husband again.

22. N. B. This morn I sent my Letter to Cousen Briant by Mr. Moses Potter, going to Ipswich: and with it a Bundle containing for Timothy,—Seven yards of White tow cloth &c &c See Memorandum Book. The Widow Fay

dind with us.—Spent ye Afternoon with Mrs. P—and drank Tea. I read in Clark's Lives. Mr. Hugh Broughton's, and several other Parts of that useful Book, was much moved and stimulated by their excellent Examples. N. B. I have received a letter from Mr. John Forbes of Otter Creek, with ye Constitution of ye State of Vermont.

23. Attended a Fast at Miss Lydia and Miss Rebecca Nurse's Mrs. P. with me. I began with Prayer. Mr. Sumner preached a seasonable Sermon, from 3^d Epistle of St. John v. 2 "Beloved I wish above all Things &c" P. M. Mr. Fairbank preached on Matt. VI. 10. latter part "Thy Will be done on Earth &c". I prayed after Sermon. May God be pleased to accept our Humiliation and Supplications, and give His Blessing to ye Word so fitly delivered! N. B. The two Fays, Messrs. Samuel and Jeduthun, Mr. Knight, Mr. Hazzletine (school-master) Mr. Zebulon Rice &c were there. Mr. Z. Rice here in ye evening, with Mr. D. Forbes.

24. more closely applied to my preparations.

25.

26. Read Ps. 44. Took ye first verse for my Text, tho I go on with my subject on Isa: 46. 3–4—P. M. on Isa: 47 1–2, had some Regard to ye Death of Rev. Mr. Whitney of Petersham, which may God Sanctifie to us! After Exercises it rained plentifully, Cousen Saml. (who has lately been graduated at Dartmouth Col.) here at eve and lodges here. In ye Evening Exercise of ye Family, I read A Kempis.

27. Brigham returned to his F. Maynards. Breck goes to Cambridge & Boston. I am reading Mr. Cuthbert Sid-

enham on Hypocrisie, and wish it may be deeply impressed on my own Soul! It is printed very incorrectly, and under much Disadvantage, but contains many useful Things.

28. Catechized at ye Meeting-House A. M. 32 Boys, P. M. 23 Girls. May a Blessing accompany my instructions and Warnings to them of each Sex!

At eve Mr. Brigham brot Master Hazzletine to see me. He borrows Mr. Edwards on Original Sin. Mr. Brigham has 2^d vol. of Montesquieu.

29. Mr. Amos Parker and wife dind here. Capt. Edmund Brigham calls me to visit old Mr. Gale, who lies in a Dying State. I prayed by him. In returning visit old Lieut. Forbush and his Wife. Breck returns from Boston, and brings Sally and her son Sam. A letter from Mr. Moore, says his Negro man Cato is dead.

30. Squire Benj. Whipple from Otter Creek here. Rode to Shrewsbury Lecture—had Deacon Wood's Horse. I dind at Mr. Sumner's, Mr. Whitney there, also several young Students, Stone and Crosby. I preached on Luke 22. 15. not much enlarging on ye Answers to questions 1 & 2. Returned at eve. I marryed Mr. Edward Brigham to Miss Sally Miller, heretofore of ——. The Fee given was 20 Dollars. Old Mr. Abr^m Gale dyed.

OCTOBER 1779

I would thankfully acknowledge ye Goodness of God in preserving me to another month, and pray I spend this to ye divine Glory. I was closely engaged—but Mr. Batherick is urgent to talk with me about ye Affair of Mr. Adams and his Wife.

2. Surprizing Story concerning a negro Family[1] of Natick, whom one Mr. Damon has sold, Surprized and sent off as slaves, they are recovered, and now on ye Road returning to Natick.

Mr. James Bellows of Rutland here, and receives from me a Certificate concerning his Wife Thomasin. Old Mr. Gale was buryed. I attended and prayed at ye Funeral. N. B. had a good deal of conversation with old Mr. John Crawford of North Shrewsbury, who was at ye Funeral.

3. I met with so much interruption this last week, y^t I was obliged both parts of ye Day to improve former preparations—on 2 Thes: 3.1. to page 17. May divine Energy accompany ye Word and render it effectual! Mr. Abijah Gale and his sister Jones dind with us.

4. Mr. Langton and his son returning from Farmington home to York, call here. Capt. John Wood's wife sends for women p. m. & Mrs. P. goes and tarrys.

[1] The historian of Natick and the Boston newspapers of the day do not mention this "surprizing story," but Mrs. Harriet Beecher Stowe uses it in her chapter in Old Town Folks, entitled A Raid on Old Town.

"Wal," says Sam Lawson, "it's Aunt Nancy Prime's children. Last night the kidnappers come to her house an' took her an' every single one of the child'en an' goin' to carry 'em off to York State for slaves." They were rescued and restored to their home through the instrumentality of Ellery Davenport and Sam Lawson.

A letter from a pupil of Prof. Stowe's, who had heard him, and his own parents as well, tell the story, says that: "The family name of the stolen negroes was Boston, and they lived on the other shore of Lake Waban, opposite Wellesley College and in plain sight of the college. The home of the Bostons was in the Wilderness and no neighbors were in sight."

5. Mrs. P. at y⁰ Groaning still. Sally and Sophy, though it is a stormy Day, ride in her chaise to Capt. Maynard's— at night Mrs. P. returned with Joy for y⁰ Deliverance—a Dauter is born. To God be glory and praise!

6. Read Reynolds Gt. Revenge against Murder. Albemare & Clara &c. &c.

7. Elias comes up from Cambridge for money to pay his Quarter Bills to May 28 last, which he says is £64. 8. 4. which gives me some Perplexity, seeing I have given him so much especially last August to pay those Bills. N. B. on August 17 an hundred Dollars and on y⁰ 24 thirty Dollars more. Mr. Jacob Foster has been with us and dind here. He is returning to New Castle. I visit old Neighbor Pratt and his wife, Warren &c.

8. Breck lends me the money I want for Elias viz. 231 Dollars. We are unhappily low in y⁰ Meat Tub: which induced me to go to y⁰ Squires & Deacons, to enquire about Supplys. Drank Tea at y⁰ Groaning House (Capt. Woods) there being both old and young Mrs. Bakers.

9. Elias is up before Day to set off for Cambridge; & I gave him y⁰ whole of y⁰ Money which I borrowed of Breck for him. viz. 231 Dollars, which was to enable him to pay his Quarter Bills.

10. A. M. Read Deut. 32. . In preaching read v. 7 but carried on y⁰ same subject which was begun on Isa. 46. 3-4. The Selectmen were together at noon, & after sermon on 2 Thes. 3. 1 from p. 17 to 22. & administered Baptism. Mr. Gale came up to y⁰ Pulpit to desire me to read y⁰ Congress's Circular Letter, which after y⁰ Blessing, I read part of, and then left y⁰ Congregation to read among

themselves, which I suppose they did. N. B. I read after sermon the votes of Convention concerning Boston, as Dr. Hawes requested. (Dr. Hawes was with me with the vote of the Convention at Concord concerning ye Distresses of many people in Boston, to be read publickly)

11. This day we cutt up, carted home and husked out our Indian Corn. Eph^m Tucker went with my Team and Deacon Wood with his. about nine dind here. There were forty or more of Men and Boys at Eve, and several Neighbors were so generous as to contribute to ye Entertainment. Squire Baker above 50 lbs of Meat, Mr. Eb^r Forbes, Beef & 3 cabbages Lt. Bond, Pork, Mr. Barnabas Newton, a Cheese, Breck, sufficient Rum. Thro ye Goodness of God we had a good crop Sound Corn and ye Joy of Harvest. To Him be all Honor & Glory! We sang latter part of Ps. 65.

12. Breck waits upon Sally and her son Sam to Concord. P. M. I preached at Mr. Daniel Forbes's, especially to old Mrs. Stone, heretofore of Charlestown, a Maiden about 75 years old.

Text was Eph. 1. 14 which may God succeed and prosper!

When I came home to my Surprise found Sister Lydia Champney was here, brot by Mr. Caldwell of Sutton and he was gone before I returned from Meeting.

13. Breck returns from Concord, and dines with us. P. M. He is with ye Officers at Coll. Wheelock's preparing orders to send out Men immediately according to Requisition from Gen'l Washington. Mr. James Dix has been here. He desires me to ask Capt. John Wood, whether he did not write the word [Nov^r.] in a certain Instrument presented before me? My Answer was, Mr. Dix, I am ready and

willing to Serve you in any Matter or Affair which is fit and which is prepared according to Gospel Rule: *This* is not at present.

I directed him to what is written in Proverbs 25 9, & Mat: 18. 15. 16 &c—Luke Baldwin[1] from Brookfield and lodges, a pretty, agreeable, hopeful Lad! May God make him a great Blessing!

14. I was obliged to leave my Study and ride up to Lieut. Johnⁿ. Grout's about some Cyder which Mr. Eli Whitney gives me. I dind at yᵉ Lieut's. Meet with Mr. Joseph Grout there, and he has much to say about yᵉ sad case of his Sister Adams. I advised to have it laid before a few Brethren, and not suffer it to come into yᵉ church. I called at Squire Bakers & found Reason to urge yᵉ Same Thing. Mr. Cushing from Ashburnham. He has led an Horse for Sophy to ride there. He lodges here.

A Letter from Mr. Quincy dated Sept. 23. N. B. Luke Baldwin goes on his Way to Cambridge to wait on his Brother Isaac in going home.

[1] Luke Baldwin was the youngest child of Mr. Parkman's daughter Lucy and Col. Jeduthan Baldwin, and was ten years old, while his brother Isaac was a lad of fifteen.

Col. Jeduthan, whom Mr. Parkman often mentions, was a leading man in Brookfield, and in the army. He was captain in 1755 in an expedition against Crown Point, and served in the Revolution. He was a member of the Provincial Congress, and an original subscriber to the fund for Leicester Academy, giving £100. He died in 1788, and after his death his widow married her brother-in-law, the Rev. Eli Forbes.

Luke was married in 1789 to Polly Avery, of Boston, and settled in West Boylston.

174 DIARY OF REV. EBENEZER PARKMAN.

JUDGE EDMUND QUINCY.

15. Mr. Cushing and Sophy set out early for Ashburnham. At Night arrived the two Baldwins from Cambridge and lodge here.

16. Baldwins to Brookfield.

17. Preached A. M. on Isa: 46. 3 & 4 P. M. on 2 Thes. 3. 1. Mrs. Maynard and Mr. Hazzeltine dind here. N. B. Capt. Fisher after ye Blessing desires ye Company tomorrow morning.

18. A sort of Military Gathering for ye purpose of rais-

ing men to go to ye westward for ye Continental Service, for 3 or 4 men.

I visited Asahel Biglow who is exceeding bad of Inflammation of his Bowels—prayed with him.

19. I rode to Mr. Biglow's at West Sudbury—it being Minister's Meeting. Mr. Stone, Mr. Smith and Mr. Bridge were all that came. Mr. Biglow prayed—no Concio—conversation on ye Difficulties Ministers undergo by ye depreciated Currency. I prayed at ye Close. Mr. Stone and I lodged there, and very agreeably.

20. In ye morning perplexed—Our Horses had left us. I rode Mr. Biglow's Horse in Search after y^m. Found y^m at Mr. Samuel Sherman's in Marlboro. I went on to Mr. Stone's and informed his Son who sent back Mr. Biglow's Horse and his Father's from Mr. Sherman's, so y^t I came home. Elias was come from Cambridge and with him Gen'l Ward's Son (whose Brother led down Breck's Horse for Elias to come up on) and Parkman Bradshaw here likewise—he lodged here and Master Foot, going to Colchester. N. B. Mr. Johnson of Lyn & his Lady had been here while I was absent.

21. I visited and prayed with Asahel Biglow, who is much better On his Horse I rode to Southboro' & preached ye Lecture on Luke 22. 15. which may God graciously own and bless! Returned at eve.

22. Breck is building another small Store. Mr. Jacob Foster and his Lady going to Canterbury, called and dind here. Nigh night came Lydia and Suse Parkman from Concord and lodged here.

23. Sorrowful news from Cambridge of ye Drowning of

a young Student at fresh Pond in Cambridge yesterday. His name was Charles Cutter, a soph-more. The Body not found at nine this morning. May ye Lord sanctifie it to all, especially his own Classmates and Friends. Breck raised his new Store.

24. Preached once more on Isa. 46. 4. nobody dind here. I consulted ye Deacons about having ye Communion notwithstanding the Trouble with some Members, about Mr. Adams. Preached on Prov: 27. 1, occasioned by ye late Disaster at Cambridge. N. B. My son Elias was so far effected by that Providence, that he, by a note, desired Prayers in ye Congregation that God would Sanctifie it to him.

I appointed ye Communion and lecture.

At eve, Breck and Susè, her Brother Elijah &c. were with us and Sang.

25. Breck to Boston. In his way carrys Susè and ye Child to Col. Brigham's. Mr. Francis Whipple of New Braintree makes us a visit. I began to read Mr. Buckminster against Mr. Isaac Foster, which was sent me by ye author, by means of Mr. Maccarty. But was interrupted by ye coming in of Mr. Belknap and after him half a score of ye Brethren of ye Church besides, one after another, to confer about Mr. D. Adams and his Wife. Those that came (besides Mr. Belknap) were Deac. Bond and Deac. Wood, Messrs. Daniel Forbes, Benj. Tainter, Joseph Grout, Jon^n Grout, Levi Warren, Eli Whitney, Joseph Harrington, Jon^n Forbes. They agree upon a small number of them to go to Mr. Adam's tomorrow, to advise him to consent to choosing together with his wife, Referees before whom to try

their Affair, or at least to take Counsel of them in order to Settlement, and Mr. Adams is to be apprized y^t these Brethren request y^t notice be given after ye next Lecture y^t as many of ye Brethren as shall incline to are desired to stop a little for further Conference upon those Matters.—

26. Stephen Fay desires to be Marryed next Thursday, and that the wedding may be at Mr. Andrews', who requests I would go to his House. I am preparing for next Sabbath.

27. Mr. Stone came to my Help. He dind here and preached my Lecture on Rev: 22. 11 former parts "Let him that is unjust" &c. And may God graciously afford His Almighty Blessing! A number of Brethren stopped to confer together about Mr. Daniel Adams' case. A few had been to him to know whether he would join with his Wife to choose some Men to hear and advise y^m, but he refused and did now before ye Brethren y^t were together today. N. B. Dea. Phelps, Mr. Jon^n Twitchell, and Coll. Aaron Perry, all of Holliston were at Mr. Adams' Request with us. But nothing was done Except y^t Mr. Adams in defending his Refusal to do any more, pleaded how much he had done in going to her, to persuade her to return, *taking men with him—writing to her* &c I left y^m. But I was informed when I was come away Mr. Adams warned all of them against entertaining his Wife. At eve, about 8 or 9 Brethren were here at my House, viz. Messrs. Belknap, Dan. Forbes, Batheric, Two Grouts, Eli Whitney, Jon^n Forbes. They agree to have 2 or 3 of them to go to Mr. Adams in some short time, to see what his mind is since his Three Friends advising. Mr. Isaac Parker and his Wife desire to come and join ye Church. N. B. A num-

ber of young Gentlemen, Graduates, were here to see Elias.

28. Elias goes to Worcester in ye Room of Mr. Elijah Brigham to fetch ye Spy in his stead. He brings it, and contains Mr. Danl Adams' Caution[1] to all people not to trust his Wife.

P. M. by desire I rode to Mr. Andrews' and marryed Stephen Fay to Betty Andrews and John Warren to Anna Forbush.

N. B. A great deal of Company and plentiful Entertainment. We Sung part of Ps. 45. N. B. In administering ye Covenant, I made a Mistake in mentioning ye Names of ye Brides.

When I came home, found here my Kinsman Bryant, and her Dauter, Mrs. Pearn Atwell, & her little Girl, Pearn, in a Chaise. Timothy also came to wait on his Mother and Sister. They lodged here.

29. Mrs. Grout (wife of Mr. Joseph) came to ye Door, upon her Reading the Publication in yesterday's Spy. Spoke of ye great Reason her poor Sister has to refuse to live with Adams any more.

30. One John Fletcher, who says he was of Pomfret, but

[1] From the Worcester Spy of Oct. 28, 1779.

"Whereas Perces, the wife of me the subscriber, has absented herself from me and family, and refuses to return to her duty, although often requested by myself and others, and I am apprehensive she may run me in debt. These are therefore to caution all persons against trusting her on my account for I will not discharge any debt she may contract from and after this date.

DANIEL ADAMS.

Westborough, (State of Massachusetts Bay). Oct. 19. 1779."

has been a Prisoner and is come from Halifax Jayl, wants Refreshment, which was given him, but there was Reason to suppose he drinkd too much. Elias brot home Susè from his Father Brigham's. P. M. Breck returned from Cape Ann.

31. I preached again on Ps. 36.7 and dilated on some Instances, particularly Mr. Joseph Alleine, and the Two Janeways, W^m ye Father and John. I administered ye Lord's Supper—a number of Strangers with us. My kinswoman Atwell, member of Mr. Roby's Church at Lynn, partook. Master Hazzletine dind with us—P. M. preached on Isa: 50.10. I received today by Mr. Francis Barns, a proclamation for a Day of Humiliation & Supplication, which I read.

N. B. I baptized Mr. Davis's son Isaac. N. B. I was greatly Spent—insomuch y^t I went down to ye Elder's Seat without praying, but prayed there. At eve, Breck read Mr. Henry's Communication, Comp. Ch. 12 in part.

NOVEMBER 1779

May God grant ye Grace, that as Time is swiftly Spending, I may do with my might what my Hands find to do! I am much concerned about my preparations for ye Day of Solemn Humiliation before us It being unusual, and called in ye Proclamation, neither Fast nor Thanksgiving. I have also much interruption by ye Company which still continue with us: yet they are dear to me.

2. My Kinswoman and her Son and Dauter are prevented journeying by Rain, till it was (they conceived)

too late. Mr. Aaron Crosby[1] of Blandford here, in his way to Boston.

3. It being bright, tho cold, my Cousin Bryant and her children leave us to return to Stoneham N. B. I gave her 14 Dollars for making and mending 3 pair of Shooes by her Son Elias Bryant & to Tim, Leather for a pair of Shooes. Mr. Parkman Bradshaw came from Brookfield, & is going to Stougtonham and thence to Cambridge. He dines here—Seems to be a solid, pious young man, and a Lover of Learning. I engage him to befriend my dear son, that he may continue at College, tho it must be with no small Difficulty, as my Circumstances now are. But I pray my Confidence may be in God alone, who has ever provided for me, and helped me hitherto! D. G!

4. A Day of Humiliation and Prayer with Thanksgiving. I named for my Text A. & P. M. Ps. 51. 17 made a large Introduction, explaining the Proclamation, and then used some former Preparations on that, mentioned passage, with various alterations and additions. I had expected Mr. Crosby to help me, but he came not till near y⁰ Close of y⁰ Exercises. He was with us at eve and then went to his Brother Samuel's. Three Brethren of y⁰ Church, viz. Messrs. Batheric, Gale and Dr. Hawes came here and desired me to give notice to y⁰ other Brethren of y⁰ Church,

---

[1] Aaron Crosby was a son of Samuel Crosby, of Shrewsbury, and brother of Dr. Samuel, who had married Azubah Howe, of Westborough. This Aaron was a missionary to the Indians. Dr. Crosby, whom Aaron goes to see, lived in the southeast part of Shrewsbury, on Boston Hill. He was a surgeon in the Revolution, and practiced in Shrewsbury till 1781.

after ye Exercises of next Sabbath, to tarry and confer a little further upon ye Adams affair.

5. Elias went early to Brookfield for ye rest of my Cattle at Coit Hill. Benj. Grout was here for his pay for making 3 pair of Shooes: and I therefore wrote him a note to Breck, for 63/ old Ten^r of old value.

6. Elias returned with ye Cattle, & had a good Journey. N. B. He paid Landlord Jones[1] of Worcester 2 Dollars for pasturing one yearling. He asked a Dollar per week.

7. I preached A. M. on Ps: 36.7. P M. on Prov. 1.23. for next Thursday has been appointed for ye Execution of David Young. Mr. Moses Brigham & Mrs. Maynard dind here. At eve a Letter received from Mr. Caleb Alexander.

8. I visited and prayed with Asahel Biglow. P. M. Mrs. Dolly Rice here and drank Tea with us. Five Men are requested to go to Mr. Adams & to his Wife to perswade y^m to Reconciliation. They are, Squire Baker, Deac. Wood, Mr. Daniel Forbes, Mr. Gale and Mr. Twitchell.

9. Mr. Levi Warrin here to kill a Cow for me, and informs me that the Said Brethren were together and that Mr. Adams was with them. That they were together till midnight, and then adjourned to next Sennight.

The Cow turns out well. Mr. Warrin dines here, & gives his work. P. M. Mrs. Baker and her sister Bowman of Oxford make us a visit.

10.

[1] Landlord Jones kept the Jones Tavern in New Worcester, on the corner of Leicester and Apricot streets. It would be on Elias' route as he came down from Brookfield.

11. Elias goes to Worcester to ye Execution of Robert Young, who was condemned and hanged for a Rape on Jane Green of Brookfield. At Eve, I went to Capt. Fisher's, who reads part of ye Report of ye Committee for forming a plan of Government. I borrow of him ye new Military Dictionary vol. 2. by T. Simes Esq.

12. Have news of ye poor Criminal's Behaviour yesterday. Mr. Maccarty[1] preached.

13. Mr. Isaac Parker was here and brot his own and his Wife's Relations. He excused the incorrectness of his for want of Time, & took it again.

14. Thro' ye great Goodness of God I am allowed to begin another year of Sabbaths, and would gratefully praise His Glorious Name! I preached A. M. on Deut: 32. 46-47, which may God graciously impress us with! Mr. S. Barrett and his Dauter Nancy with us and dind here. P. M. delivered ye Remainder of sermon on Prov: 1. 28 as being seasonable Warning after ye late Execution. O y^t my own Soul might be deeply impressed!—propounded Isaac & Margery Parker to join with ye Church.

15. Ephraim having rid home on Saturday eve, returned this morning. I visited Capt. Wood's Wife and prayed with her, she being very low. P M. By Mr. Hezekiah Maynard of Marlboro, I sent Mr. Simon How's Book of ye Indian Wars.

16. Visit Mrs. Wood again. Having read I returned to

---

[1] Rev. Thaddeus Maccarty, pastor of the old South Church in Worcester from 1747 to 1784. He was "tall, slender and thin with a black, penetrating eye, which added to his effectiveness in speaking."

Capt. Fisher his Draught of ye Plan of Government: Dind at Squire Baker's. Consult him about paying my Young Man (Parker) and I went to Lt. Joseph Bond's on ye same Affair. Miss Rebecca Nurse here to be examined. Widow Rhoda Maynard here with her.

17. Messrs. Brigham and May lodged here last night. Elias goes to Cambridge and Boston. Mr. Kendal of Southboro' here to look of (Sic) my Sheep. Mr. Isaac Parker with his *Relation*.

18. Read several Lives in Vol. II (B) of Biographical Dictionary. Mrs. Parker (Isaac's Wife) & Miss Anna Parker (Eph^m's Sister) made us a Visit. Deacon Doliber sends me a Present of Fish.

19. Deac. Doliber calls here in his way home — gives me account of the Grants of their Society at Marblehead to their Minister for ye year. P M. Elias returns home from Cambridge, but has not seen the President, tho I wrote him by Elias.

Letters from Ashburnham informing that Mrs. Cushing was delivered of a Son[1] on Wednesday Oct. 27, and it is called Doddridge.

20. Have been and am now much engaged in ye Prophetic Visions of Zechary. May God greatly illuminate my Soul with Truth!

21. On Zech: v. 9-11. And finished my exercises on that chapter. P. M. preached my sermon on Isa. 63. 9-15.

---

[1] Doddridge Cushing, born Oct. 27, 1779, was the son of Mr. Parkman's daughter Sarah and the Rev. John Cushing. He died unmarried in 1866.

I propounded Rebecca Nurse to join in full Communion with ye Church.

Sometimes we have no Singing in ye Family on so much as Sabbath Evenings. But we had this evening. Josiah Brigham is wont to lodge here and assisted in ye Singing

22. Master Elijah goes to Ashburnham, expecting Sophy to return. I wrote by him. I visited Mr. Jonⁿ Tainter's sick Child & prayed therewith. I rode up then to Mr. Eli Whitney's & dind there, and visited Mr. Benj. Wood and his Family (no Kindred between Deac. and him. Some words pass about his son Reuben's living with me. Went in also to Mr. Eben^r Miller's. N. B. At Squire Baker's was assured that Mr. D. Adams did verily sign what was last published[1] in ye Spy: retracting what was published before. Eph^m. Parker comes up this evening to reckon with me for his nine months Work for me: first for six months, and for them asks my biggest Oxen, for which I am told I may have £500, and for ye other three months as ye price is stated. But he would have me ask Advice of my Neighbors.

23. I walked to Mr. Eb^r Forbush, to talk with him, and he not being at home spent some time with his Father and Mother. In returning I made an Opportunity with Mr.

---

[1] "Whereas the subscriber through my own weakness and imperfection, have inadvertently advertised and cried down Perces my wife in the three preceding papers, these are therefore to give public notice, that I am convinced of my imprudence in so doing, am very sorry for my conduct, and for the injury done her, desire her forgiveness and do now recall the former inconsiderate publication.

DANIEL ADAMS."

Elijah Hardy, who tells me that he gave his Young Man for six months, not £250, and Mr. Benj. Fay not more. I next talked with Mr. Barnabas Newton, who will take it into Thought. At eve, speak with Caleb Harrington. But Parker is gone over to his Brother Elisha's.

24. Mr. Brigham returned from Ashburnham and Sophy with him. Left all well there, & Mrs. Winchester is willing to send me her W^m.

25. Mr. Elisha Parker came, and Eph^m and I came to some agreement viz: to give him my Principal Oxen for seven months of his work: and to pay him in Money or Indian Corn for ye two Months of October and November, according to common custom, in ye old way or in proportion as men's wages are for youths'.

26. I had too many anxious Thoughts about ye high Demands of Eph^m.

27. Elisha Parker came when I was about paying Ephraim, but a Controversie arose concerning *What was ye Usual Custom at this time of ye great Alteration of Money within these few weeks.* Eph^m would take no less than £60 for ye Two Months. I was not willing to give any more y^n 55. But I was obliged to borrow ye money of my son Breck, and they all went to ye Shop, where Breck gave Ephraim ye whole Sum he required, viz: £60, and so he went to his brother Elisha's with ye Cattle on ye Cart to carry his Chest and things there, promising to come and make up ye Time, viz. 5 Days y^t yet remains next week & onward.

28. Preached A. & P. M. with new Introduction, Sermons on Heb. 5.9. to p. 12. Mrs. Maynard dind here, as

did Eph^m Parker—p. m. read proclamation for Thanksgiving.

29. Mr. Dan. Matthis of New Braintry was here to consult me about their Troubles with Mr. Foster's Doctrines, but I could not tarry long with him, because I was preparing a line to send to ye Town (of Westb.) who this Day have a Meeting to Consider my Sallery. They met. Mr. Gale was Moderator. I humbly waited upon God most high in ye first place and then sent my Paper, entertaining myself with Judge Hale's Meditation on Contentation. My mind was wrot into a placid Frame; in some Measure resigned to ye Disposals of Providence. At eve, by Lieut Grout I understood y^t ye Town has voted to make up my Sallery £1300, and 40 Cord of Wood. For which G. D.

30. Read Judge Hale of a good Method to entertain unstable & troublesome Times—and of Redeeming Time. In ye Evening unbent a while with reading Mr. de Lange's Journal at Peking.

30. Miss Rebecca Nurse here and gave me her Relation. By reason of a debate about those votes aforesaid by a Friend that came in, Sent to Col. Wheelock, ye Town Clerk, for ye Transactions of ye Town yesterday, relative to me: who wrote that They voted and granted to make up the Rev. Mr. Parkman's Stated yearly Sallery for ye year ensuing £1300.

Voted to get the Rev. Mr. Parkman 40 Cord of Wood the year ensuing. Signed Moses Wheelock. Town Clerk.

My Kinsman Parkman Bradshaw came from Cambridge by ye way of his Father's, and lodges here. I wrote to my old and esteemed Friend, Mr. Quincy, having much Solace in this Correspondence.

Thus ends ye short month of November—An Emblem of this short Life! On Retrospect, how very little has been done of ye Grand Business, with all ye Advantages in my Hands! but how many my Deficiencies, how many and grievous my Miscarriages! May ye blood of Jesus Christ cleanse from all my Guilt and Errors!

DECEMBER 1779

It is of God's great Goodness I am thus indulged to begin another Month. Breck to Boston and Dr. Hawes and his Wife make us a visit and drink Tea.

2. Deac. Wood brings Mr. W^m. Campbell, heretofore of Oxford to see me. He offers to buy my Sheep, but I dont incline to sell part without he takes ye whole. I read Lives of Squire Boyle, Charles Boyle & others.

3. The Doctor brings me a Third Vol. of Biographical Dictionary from Mr. Crauch. Mr. Joseph Grout brot me a Letter from Mrs. Abigail Davis, (heretofore Nichols) who had lived ten years at Mr. Moses Warrin's, bearing testimony concerning ye Harmony between him and his Wife Persis, ye present Mrs. Adams. Mr. Eben^r Maynard came and acquainted me that his mother Winchester Expired last night, at 10 o'clock in her 79th year. The Lord prepare me for my own Decease!

4. Breck returns from Boston, my Relations well there. He brings me a present from my son Samuel, a valuable Silk Handkerchief of Fifty Dollar price, much wanted ; my

son William his Wife and Young Child John, rode here in their Chaise, arrived in yᵉ Evening.

5. Preached A. M. on Zech VI. 1–7. P. M. went on with discourse on Heb: 5. 9—admitted Isaac Parker and Wife, also Rebecca Nurse into Communion. May God accept them and make them Ornaments to Christianity.

6. Was called away to see a young Son of Capt. Jonas Brigham viz. his son William in his 12ᵗʰ year, who was thot to be under extremely dangerous Symptoms. I went, prayed, breakfasted there. P. M. Town Meeting by Adjournment. Capt Morse was here, full of earnest advice & Entreaty that I would send something to yᵉ Town of my Thanks for what they had done lately for me, and my satisfaction in it. I accordingly wrote a paper and sent it by Mr. Joseph Harrington, and he was here at eve to acquaint me how it was accepted, and he believed it was *well*.

7. Mr. Edward Brigham came to acquaint me that his Brother dyed this morning and to desire me to attend yᵉ Funeral on Thursday, at nine A. M. I remonstrated, but it was settled, I suppose.

8. Mr. Samuel Forbush, Mr. Solomon Batheric, & Mr. Nathan Maynard junʳ came with their Teams and brot Wood. The two former two Load, the latter, one.

9. General Thanksgiving thro out the States.

I did not go to Capt. Brigham's, as I was at first desired, Mr. Edward had come yesterday and told me his Father would conform to yᵉ proposal to bring yᵉ Corps to yᵉ Meeting-House. They did so, and I prayed there. After this they proceeded to yᵉ Interment and I went to yᵉ Grave with yᵐ.

We re-entered ye Meeting-House and having prayed already began with singing. Preached on Ps. 68. 26-28. I took to my House a Stranger, one Mr. Joseph Thompson, by Birth, a Philadelphian. At eve we had singing at my House, a number of young Gentlemen came, besides Mr. Elijah Brigham, and Josiah Brigham, Mr. Moses and Mr. Saml Brigham, Mr. May (the two last lodged among us) and Master Hazzletine. This evening also Eleazar Wheelock and Thankful Maynard (Captain's Dauter) were married— such a Variety of Exercises had I in one Day! May God forgive what was amiss, and accept what was (thro Grace) sincere!

10. Breck, Susè and Sophy (by invitation) ride in ye Sleigh to Col. Brigham's. Mr. May goes to Boston. At Mr. Stone's Request I headed a number of Papers of Subscriptions for printing a spirited Letter against Mr. Isaac Foster, Sent one to Mr. Stone, gave to Mr. Simon How, to Mr. Moses Brigham, Mr. Isaac Parker, to Master Sam Brigham, each of them a Paper in Trust to promote Subscribing. The account from Northboro is confirmed that they have there voted Mr. Whitney for this year 3000£. Messrs. Forbush and Batheric bring old Wood, 2 Load apiece. The weather prevented my visiting Mr. Jon^n Childs' sick Dauter. I wrote to Mrs. Winchester of Ashburnham concerning her son Billy to come and live here.

11. Sent to Ashburnham by Harvey Maynard. I cant change with any minister. I there review and make large additions to former preparations, which I humbly hope God will graciously accept through Jesus Christ.

12. Mr. Benj. Wilson jun^r came from ye Widow Eager

of Northboro to desire me to attend y⁶ Funeral of her daughter Cutter tomorrow, (the wife of Ebenezer who is among y⁶ British troops. I preached A & P. M. on 1 Pet. 1. 8. Administered y⁶ Lord's Supper. Master Hazzleton and Mrs. Maynard dind here. May God graciously accept our offerings ! N. B. Cold, stormy, few at Communion.

13. Deacon Wood came with his chaise to go to Mrs. Cutter's Funeral, but it was too stormy for me to venture. Elias rode with him.

14. I sent by Dr. Hawes, Mr. Cranch's 2ᵈ Vol. of Biogr. Also my Watch for a new Crystal. Mr. Elisha Parker brot me several worthy presents, Beef and Tea, 10 lb. of one, ½ lb. t'other.

15. Read part of Biographical Dictionary. The Lives of Confucius &c. Messrs. Sam. Forbush and Sol. Batheric sledding wood from the Minister's Lot. Newspapers from Boston and Worcester. Received a Letter from Bethiah Parmenter, alias Wheeton, dated Hopkinton, Oct. 19, 1779 open & dirty, desiring a Contribution.

16. Went to Deac. Wood to inquire about y⁶ Letter received last evening. Wrote to Mr. Fitch about it & enclosed it. Sent it to Deac. Wood by young Asa Brigham for conveyance. Messrs. Forbush and Batheric more wood. Gave y⁶ former a Receipt for ten cord. He tells me y⁶ Town voted to give 7£ per cord to Four of yᵐ 70£ apiece for 10 cord each. viz. Sam¹ Forbush, Solomon Batheric, Nathan Maynard Junʳ & Jonⁿ Maynard, who have undertaken to bring 40 cords.

17. Breck to Sutton in yᵉ Sleigh to get Paper. Succeeds

but in part. Elias has borrowed a mathematical manuscript which he is transcribing.

18. It is exceeding Stormy, snowing, blowing and very cold, but thro God's great Goodness, we have Shelter, Wood, Bread, Meat, Drink, Cloths but especially Health, Reason, above all ye Day of means of Grace! to His Name be praise and glory! May God commeserate ye exposed, and ye Necessitous!

19. Difficult getting to Meeting, but few there. I was first, preached A. M. on Zech. vi. 8th and from v 9-11. P. M. Went on with and concluded Sermon on Hab. 5.9. which may ye Lord bless to us! At eve read part of Fleming's Confirming Work of Religion.

20. A very cold season, & continues so. I am engaged in Biographical Dictionary. C. Confucius, Cato, Casaubon, Mons. Le Clerk &c.

21. Mr. Wm Chandler of Pomfret in straight for a sled to go to Framingham. I have let him have mine, & he leaves his Waggon here.

22. I am taken up very much with Biography. The Life of Lucius Cary who is Lord Falkland, Dr. Sam'l Clark, old Mr. Calamy, Des Cartes &c.

23. Young Chandler returns and solicits for my sled to go to Pomfret. I yielded to his Importunity and for Mr. Lamson's putting two Guards in front, and for his Journey to Framingham he pays me 10 Dollars and for ye Sled 50 Dollars. P. M. came Mr. Nathan Goddard to desire me to change with him, who is to be in Mr. Sumner's stead, while he is to go to Hubbard's Town to preach for Mr. Parker.

Mr. Peter Whitney here and relates ye Proceedings of his Parish in granting him 3000£.

At eve, Mr. Ruben Puffer and his Brother with a Letter from Fisk concerning ye said Puffer's Examination. I referred him to ye three Ministers which are near to him: viz. Messrs. Bridge, Biglow, and Newell.

24. Breck and Susè, Mr. Brigham and Sophy rode in ye Slay to Mr. Whitney's.

25. I rode up to Shrewsbury— to Mr. Nathan Goddard's who has persuaded me to take this cold ride. Went to Mr. Sumner's who was gone with design to preach tomorrow at Hubbard's Town. I lodged at Mr. Sumner's.

26. Preached at Shrewsbury. A. M. on Ps. 74. 17. P. M. on Ps. 90. 10. which may God graciously own and bless! lodged there again.

27. Breakfast at Sister Cushing's. Visit Mr. Farrar's Wife who is sick, dind at Mr. John Maynard's, called at Mr. Gershom Brigham's[1] and begin to take Thomas's Spy of him—went in to Mr. Saml. Fay's, but neither he nor his Wife at home—arrived safe at home. D. G. Mr. Goddard preached for me yesterday. His text A. & P. M 1 Cor: 23. 24. Dr. Hawes brot me my Watch from Mr. Cranch—the new Chrystal cost 12 Dollars.

This evening came Wm Winchester to live here.

Mr. Nehemiah Maynard came with him. N. B. His father Mr. Nathan Maynard sat by and heard. I told Mr.

---

[1] Mr. Gershom Brigham was the son of Dr. Gershom, of Marlborough, and the father of Dr. Gershom of Westborough, and grandfather of Col. Josiah, whose portrait, with those of his wife and son, hangs in the hall of the Historical Society. The Gershom Brig-

Maynard that I would do what I could conveniently & reasonably in teaching & influencing him in Reading, Writing and Cypering, according as his Business in taking care of y⁰ Cattle, Cutting y⁰ wood &c. would give opportunity and as his Capacity should admit it. This was in answer to what Mr. Maynard delivered me as Mrs. Winchester's Errand to me by him.

ham place was but little out of Mr. Parkman's way as he rode down from Shrewsbury, and the old house still stands. The new house now standing on the opposite side of the road, was built not long before 1810.

GERSHOM BRIGHAM'S HOUSE.

28. Read Biogr. A close time for study, but a great Storm abroad. God be merciful to y^e poor and to all y^e Exposed!

29. A very dismal morning. Storm continues till about noon. Snow-Banks very high one nigh my saddle-house 6 feet high. Roads blocked up. What can have become of poor Mr. Goddard, who proposed to set out with Wife & children &c. on his great Journey to Walpole, has sold at Shrewsbury and would now move.

My son Breck had also designed to go in a double Sleigh to Ashburnham, but no Team nor Sleigh can Stir. How wonderful the Works of ye Great God!

30. I keep close to my Study, tho Mr. Antipas Brigham[1] had requested me to go to Capt. Edmund's to marry him. But nobody disturbs me. Enough to do to keep warm.

31. Jejan.(?) and Prec. Reflections on ye Year past, with praise for Preservation and numberless Benefits. Humiliation and Penitence for Ingrat. Deficiencies and Miscarriages. May a gracious & merciful God remitt through Jesus Christ—So teach me to number my Days y^t I may apply my Heart to true Wisdom! Lt. John Forbes from Otter Creek here and gives me account of ye State of Vermont.

1780.

JANUARY

If I have heretofore had great Cause to bless and praise

---

[1] Antipas Brigham was the son of Capt. Jonas, who lived on his father David's homestead. He married Hepsibath Brigham, the oldest daughter of Dea. Edmund, a distant cousin of his.

See Journal January 24, 1780.

ye Name of God for his Wonderful Mercy & Goodness in my and my Families' Preservation, What have I now! to be permitted to begin a New Year. I would celebrate His Praises, with all Hearty Gratitude. And in Special in so difficult a Season, of so Much cold and Snow & tedious stirring, I am favoured in divine Providence, with ye Necessarys and so many of ye Comforts of Life. But in peculiar for ye protracting ye Day and Means of Grace, and ye blessed Influences of ye Holy Spirit. I would magnifie ye Lord and hope in His Salvation.

People are chiefly employed in making Roads, providing for ye Fires, taking Care of Cattle, &c. But ye Lord pitty ye poor and exposed!

2. Exceeding Difficult getting to Meeting. A. M. I went on with the discourse on ye Everlastingness of God, begun on ye last Year first Sabbath, from Ps. xc. 2. Master Hazzletine dind here. P. M. I repeated part of Disc. on Ps. 39. 4. O that God would awaken us, and teach us to profit hereby! At night, another Snow storm.

3. The storm is very severe, much more snow has fallen. It was higher than ye Red Fence before my House by ye Storm last week: it is now higher, and ye Front Gate is not to be seen.

4. God has his Treasures of Snow and Hail and Wind. POWER belongeth unto GOD! How distressing to ye Poor! Read Biographical Dictionary, Cicero, &c.

5. Thro' Divine Favour this was a bright, pleasant Day. Both my Sons and my Steers join with a number of ye Street Neighbors with Cattle and Shovels to break ye Roads. Tis difficult to compute ye Heighth or Depth of it. I am almost

ready to conclude that there has not been so much Snow upon ye Ground at a Time ever since ye GREAT SNOW[1] in year 1717.

6. The great God has his Treasures of Snow & has supreme Command of all ye Meteors. It is very stormy again, and ye Snow deeper, and tho ye Sun was visible a little while in ye P. M, yet it was soon clouded, & ye Storm rages at night.

7. An astonishing morning — for ye dreadful Storm rather increases. Besides the snowing and blowing with violence the cold is very intense. This is thought to be the most tedious of any that has come hitherto. May God most compassionate pity and relieve me, and also support and provide for ye poor! Who can stand before Thy Cold!

---

[1] The snow of 1717 was a terrible storm, of which Cotton Mather has left a minute description. This storm of 1780 also passed into history. "All the harbors and bays on the Atlantic coast," writes Barbour, "as far south as Virgina were frozen. Loaded sleds passed from New York to Staten Island; Long Island Sound was frozen into a solid highway, where it was several miles iu width. The birds that winter in this climate almost all perished, and in the succeeding spring a few solitary warblers only were heard in our groves. The snow was nearly four feet deep in the northern Atlantic States, for at least three months."

Under date of January 15, Rev. Mr. Hall, of Sutton, writes in his Journal: " Preached last Sabbath in my own House, about 30 hearers; to this day the snow is vastly deep and the weather extravagantly cold. I walked out one day this week about 40 rods to a few neighbors, and was much worried, besides not been from home almost three weeks," and again on January 29: "Extream cold yet attends. I am a poor Creature and the cold is almost too hard for me!"

N. B. All ye Pains taken about breaking Roads, in great Measure frustrated. Very few persons can stir abroad at all.

8. Hardly ever was ye Sun more welcome—but yet ye cold is so Sharp and ye Wind so high, it is very difficult to undergo the Hardships we are called to. But what becomes of ye poor who have not the Favors which through ye great goodness of God I enjoy!—

9. Tho I had prepared an exercise, & it was a long one, yet it not being calculated for ye Season, I did not use it. I was in Doubt whether there would a Meeting. But a few came upon Racketts : and I repeated what remained from last Sabbath's Entertainment upon Ps. 39. 4 A & P. M. for I was obliged for my own Sake and for ye Sake of ye People to be exceeding brief. A number of men came to my kitchen at noon, and I shortened ye Intermission. Mr. D. Forbes is extremely bad, & desires Continuance of Prayers. At eve I read to ye Family part of Mr. Shepherd's Doubting Christian drawn to Christ, in my study ye Life of Susanna, Countess of Suffolk.

10. The Life of Mr. Daniel Forbes is much doubted of, but I cant get to him by reason of ye deep snow, and difficult stirring. I am chiefly reading lives of eminent Persons.

11. Mr. Forbes still alive, but no Horse can go in ye deep snow, but I have no Racketts nor Strength to go far, as to visit him. Send my Love and Sympathy by those who (eight of y^m) draw on an Hand Sled his two Dauters Forbush and Bond to see him before he dies. My Heart is much with him, & to God for him. Mr. Hannaniah Parker returning from him comes in at eve to let me know he is yet alive, tho with signs as they think of Death upon him. May it

please God to be almightily present with him! His Brother Fisk has been on Racketts there.

12. Fair, but too rough and severe for me to go abroad, and therefore cant visit Mr. Forbes, who I hear is yet alive.

Read ye lives of several remarkable persons, particularly in Biogr. ye Life of Oliver Cromwell, & in Clark's Lives, the Life of Rev. Mr. Vine. Elias reads Earl of Chesterfield.

13. A very cold day—we think the severest of any that has come. May God almighty support us thro' these Extremities! but especially ye poor and destitute! P. M. Mr. Elisha Forbes came and informed that his Father was dead! that he expired last evening about 8 o'clock. He was 69 years old last October. It was conceived that his Distemper was bilious: had his senses to ye last, & was calmly resigned to ye Sovereign Will of God. The Funeral proposed to be tomorrow, and he, Elisha, will take effectual Care of my comfortable Transportation.

14. Squire Baker and two or three hands with him, which soon increased to half a dozen, drew me on a sled to ye House of Mourning. It was sharp cold, ye Wind piercing, ye sled goes over ye Tops of Walls & Fences. Tho it was very difficult to get there, yet there were many People—as it is said by y^m that were with him most he dyed happily; so he was buried honourably, & great Respect shown to his Remains. May God graciously Support ye Widow, who solidly mourns ye Loss; may ye Fatherless find Mercy with Him y^t was their Father's God. Mr. Forbes has left, of Children, Grandchildren, and one Great grandchild about 60. His Brother, his Sister, his oldest Son were not could none of y^m be notified & therefore were absent. There were so many Persons

with Snow Shoes y^t there was a good Path and ye Corps was carried on a Bier, on Men's Shoulders. I was drawn by a number of Rackettmen, in a very handsome Sleigh, with ye Widow, Mrs. Abigail Forbush, & his sister, Mrs. Daniel Bond. It was too tedious for me to stay at ye Grave.[1] I came away before the Coffin was let down—by that time I got to Breck's Store, I was nigh overcome, by one means & another. The Mourners, Bearers &c. came to my House, to hear ye Will. Dr. Hawes read it. At request, I in ye Evening wrote a Letter to Mr. Forbes of Gloucester. I wish ardently that I may truly profit by ye Providence! Elias finishes ye first Vol. of Earl of Chesterfield's Letters.

15. It holds an uncommon cold, difficult season.

[1] Daniel Forbes lived on Jackstraw Hill, and he was buried in Memorial Cemetery, back of the Soldier's Monument. Eli Forbes, of Gloucester, was his brother. Mr. Parkman writes in the funeral sermon of January 16: "We, of this church, have fresh reason to take notice of the Holy Providence of God in removing from among us one of the aged and useful members hereof, the late Mr. Daniel Forbes, who, besides his great regard for religion, and forwardness to promote the interest of true piety and godliness among us, was remarkable strenuous in the cause of liberty and for maintaining our just rights and privileges, civil and sacred. He was also much engaged and much employed in reconciling differences. . . . . He had not been long sick of his last illness before he was persuaded that it would prove fatal to him, and accordingly he set himself to improve his short space and set his soul and his house in order, and with so much success, through the grace of God, that he had great serenity and comfort, even in the midst of grievous pains and dying agonies."

His oldest son, Daniel, was living in Brookfield, where he was a wealthy farmer. Mistress Abigail was an unmarried daughter, at this time forty-five years old.

16. Preached A. M. on Zech: 6. 13. P. M. on Ps. 92. 12 and mentioned y⁰ Death of Mr. Daniel Forbes, with some short character of him. N. B. The Widow Forbes, Mr. John Forbes of Otter Creek and Master Hazzletine, dind here; as did Breck and his family: also Mr. Winslow Brigham. May God graciously add his Blessing! Breck &c. attended here in y⁰ Evening.

17. I am reading y⁰ Life & Letters of Philip Dormer Stanhope, Earl of Chesterfield. The Letters to his son Philip Stanhope Esq. Deac. Wood here with a Spare Rib.

18. As no Team of Oxen or Horses can pass, people are obliged to go to Mill with Hand. Sleds. Elias went today with a Bushel of Indian.—

19. Mr. Timothy Parker, his Wife and Child came a while ago in a Sleigh from Templeton, to visit their Friends here, but are not able to go back, except himself, who returns on Racketts. His wife and her sisters Newton and Wheelock visit at Breck's and I was desired to drink Tea with y⁰.

20. Elias goes again to Mill and Breck with him & carry of Rye Indian & Oats, Six Bushel. Mr. Eli Harrington of Alstad (?) makes me a long Visit. He dines here. Discourse of Church Covenant & Church Government &c.

21. Mr. Solomon Batherick & his Brother came and killed my principal Hog, which weighed 190. I read in Capt Bell's and Mr. De Lange's Travels to Ispahan, Peking, Derbeni (?) & Constantinople and finished y⁰ second Vol. of that work.

22. Elias goes on Racketts to Mr. Gershom Brigham's. A newspaper of Dec. 30 is y⁰ Last.

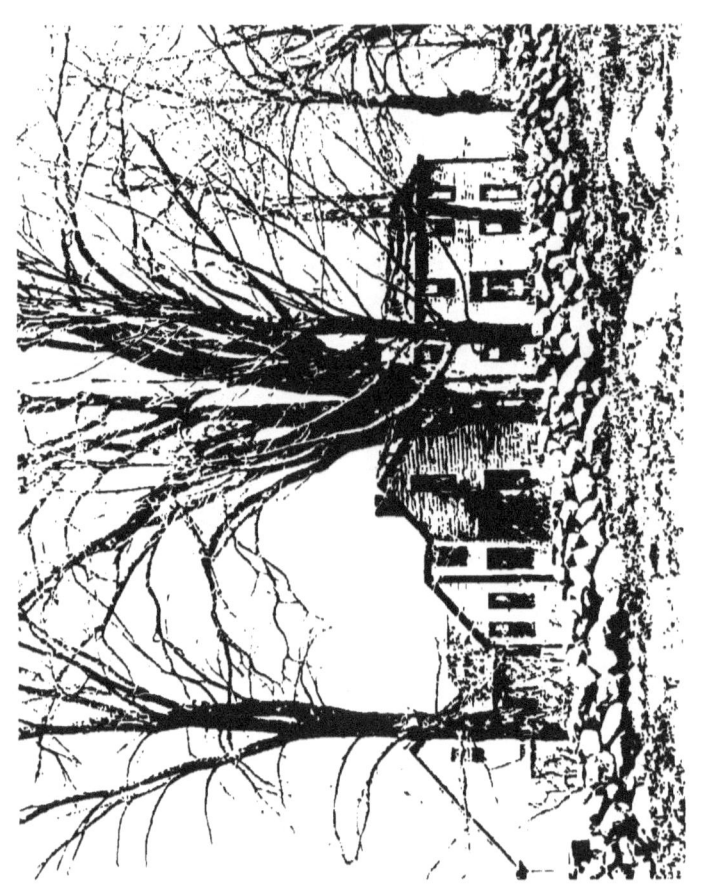

THE HASKELL HOUSE.

23. Preached A. M. on Zech: 6. 13. P. M. on Ps. 92. 13. 14. 15. Ephraim Parker dind here. A considerable Congregation, tho very cold.

24. An urgent message from Mr. Antipas Brigham to go to Capt. Edmund Brigham's, with request to marry him I went, but with great Difficulty, by reason of ye deep snow. My sons Breck and Elias drew me on a light sled as far as Mr. Haskill's,[1] nigh which a number of young men, Brighams accompanied me on foot to ye House, where I performed ye Solemnity. After ye Supper they brot me to Mr. Gale's, who kindly obliged me to lodge there. Mr. G. Andrews there & invites me to dine tomorrow.

24. Mr. Gale & his wife, also Capt. Edmund accompanying me to Mr. Andrews, where I was kindly rec'd and entertained. Capt. Brigham & Mr. Gale went to Deac. Woods, on an Arbitration. The Subject was a Difference between Mr. Pierce & Mr. Joseph Smith, both Blacksmiths, where many are assembled to hear W^m. Stearns of Worcester, Esq. advocate for Smith.

N. B. Mr. Andrews waited upon me home. By ye way visit old Lieut. Forbush.

25. Elias leaves his Studys and helps those who are breaking the Roads with a yoke of Cattle. I read Ld Chesterfield's Letters.

26. Squire Baker is so engaged in breaking Roads that he has got Elias & a yoke of my Cattle, on ye Road again Ephraim Parker being at work for me in dressing Flax for

---

[1] Mr. Haskell's is one of the few houses in town still occupied by the descendants of those living there in Mr. Parkman's day.

me—, brings in a quantity of it on a Pole & hangs it before ye Fire to drie it. I had a good deal of Reluctance at it, remembering that Capt. Gouge's House at Hopkinton was, some years ago, burn't down by Flax taking Fire.

27. As ye Flax aforesaid hung before ye Fire, notwithstanding ye Distance it was placed at, a Coal was snapped out from the Fire, & began immediately to burn in it, which had it occurred last night, while we Slept, what would have been ye Event!

All hearty Thanks to our great Preserver!

Elias is gone again with ye Cattle today to break and shovel ye Road. Mr. Andrews and Mr. Gale, generous to y^m, have got to ye crotch of ye Road, below Mr. W^m. Wood's. The northern Neighbors have tryed to plough their Road today. I read Lord Chesterfield's Letters.

28. The latter part of this was ye most remarkable Cold Day that we have had (as every body is free to allow) and Elias goes again with Squire Baker, and drives two pair of my Steers, to breaking ye Road down to Taplin's in Southboro; The evening and night were so extremely severe that I was much concerned for him till he returned; and did survive though he had been in Danger of being overcome with Cold & Fatigue. N. B. Miss Mary Bradish came P. M and lodged here.

29. The morning was ye most severe and sharp—Elias thinks some of his Limbs are froze, but (God be thanked) he is about with usual Currency.

30. Preached A. M. on Zech: vi. 14. 15. P M. on Joh: 18. 18 with some Alterations and Additions. May God bless

His Word to us! At Eve, read Fleming's Confirming Work of Religion.

31. Read in Fleming & Chesterfield's Letters. Mr. Nathan Maynard borrows several of Mr. Prince's Sermons. Hear that Sue Bimeleck[1] was lately frozen to Death. This whole month has been Cold to admiration. We have scarce ever known its Equal.

The Cold of this Day is to high Degree of Extremity.

May God Almighty sustain and support us, protect and supply us, & extend Compassion to all ye Indigent, the aged and ye Exposed!

February 1780.

I am reading Lord Chesterfield's Letters. I highly prize some of them. They shew him to be a man of very extensive Learning & Sagacity. Read Mr. Isaac Foster's sermon on Luke 2.14 delivered at New Salem June 9 last at ye Ordination of Mr. Joel Foster.—P. M. I went to Mr. B. Newton's—reckoned and paid all by a note to Constable John Harrington, was at Capt. Fisher's, at Mr. Graves & Nichols. Mrs. P. was at Deac. Wood's, where I drank Tea. We walked on ye Top of ye Snow, which was many times as high as ye Top of ye Fence.

2. It was too cold for me to go out. I go on with ye Letters. Elias sits with me in ye Study & reads Vol. 11. of Stanhope.

---

[1] Sue Bimeleck was the daughter of Abimeleck David—a son of old David Munnanaou, mentioned by Mr. Parkman in 1737. She, with her sisters, lived where her father had his wigwam, under the shadow of the old Chestnut Tree near Williams' Pond.

3. I walked over to see old Mrs. Kelly and prayed with her—dind there (at Mr. Beeton's[1]) called at Mr. Eb' Maynard's and at old Mr. Pratt's. At my return here was Lieut. Marble. Mrs. Lambson &c who drank Tea here. N. B. Breck to Boston—gave him 126 Dollars towards an Hatt for Elias. Sent by him a letter to Mr. Quincy to be left at Mr. Pattins for Conveyance.

4. Not very well after my yesterday's Walk. The Calves of my Leggs were sore, & was indisposed in Body.

5. My Indisposition increases. Hear that Mr. David Goodall and his Wife were come from Athol, & passed by to Capt. Maynard's yesterday. He has been to Otter Creek, and relates that Enemies have come upon a Town there (Soby) and destroyed it. He is going to Marlboro', his Father being dyed lately.

6. I was much indisposed still both last night and today. N. B. I was in my preaching A. M. I was very unable to see what I had written in my Notes, by reason of y'' Lines appearing in Rinkles. I carryed no Spectacles—borrowed Deac. Wood's, but to no purpose. I was able to give some

---

[1] Mr. Beeton was living in the old parsonage, on Lyman School Hill. He was a young Scotch blacksmith, who had walked over from Hopkinton with his wife bringing some bags filled with English coin, thirty years before, when he had heard that Mr. Parkman's farm was for sale. The minister firmly refused to consider the matter—he wished to sell only to a man of quality, but the young Scot was canny, and interested Stephen Maynard in his behalf, and Mr. Parkman was only too happy to sell to the wealthy captain, who in turn passed a deed to John Beeton. He proved a good citizen of the town, and Mr. Parkman cordially recognized his worth, and became his good friend.

account of what I had prepared, tho not Verbatim, after a while could see more distinctly, preached on Zech. vi. 15 Breck and his Family dind with us. So did Mrs. Maynard and her son Brigham.

Have heard ye sorrowful news of ye Death of our Brother of ye Association—the Rev. Thomas Goss of Bolton by a Fever. The Lord sanctifie this Providence to me, to the mournful Widow, the bereaved Children, to ye Association of which he was a Member, but especially the Church of which he was Pastor, and to ye whole people of Bolton ! That now they may be directed into methods of Peace, and ye new Church especially may be wholly settled, & edified. P. M. I preach on Ps: 55.22 former part (which I delivered in Oct 1773) now to ye end of page 8. which may God graciously succeed! In ye evening Exercise, Breck read Fleming's Confirming Work.

7. Several young Women, viz. Lucy Maynard and Anna Fay, hired by Mrs. P. to spin, came here for this week, came duly.

P. M. Mr. Jonⁿ Forbes brot a Cheese &c & made me a Visit. At evening Ephraim Parker borrows the History of human Nature &c. Advises concerning ye sowing my Island with Clover &c.

8. Providence further frowns upon us in sending another snowstorm, which covers ye Rackett Tracks & fills ye Roads again. Mr. Elisha Forbes dines here, & spends most of ye Afternoon—will endeavor to provide me some Quantity of Hay seed. I read Chesterfield's Letters.

9. Elias goes with Breck & others to break ye Roads to Southboro. Mr. Daniel Forbes from Brookfield, Mr. Isaac

Pratt of Hardwick. N. B. I am troubled that Elias should so readily leave his Books to join with them whose Gain and Interest prompted to clear ye roads for their Teams to be going again, seeing that he could have no great Inducement, but Benevolence, public Spirit &c. which had been sufficiently served by five times before now, exposing himself in Cold and Dangers by Night and by Day in this work and all of it Gratis. This Sixth Time, when his own Time is so extremely precious in which he has so much to read and write before he can be fit to return to his College Exercises again. And yet this is not ye most trying. he is planning an unseasonable journey to Cambridge to fetch a Table[1] from thence; now at ye very Day when ye Vacancy is finished, and he should go to stay there, the rather because he has been absent from ye Recitations so long, that he ought to be one of ye first that returns at this Term. He proposes also to go and return incog. presuming that ye Vacancy is prolonged by reason of ye difficult stirring & enormous price of wood.

10. The plan for going to Cambridge is so ripened that I can't defeat it. The affair is chiefly Breck's, who loads a a sleigh with Grain &c. & loads up with Rum—has provided two Horses as well as ye Sleigh. And his Brother Josiah Brigham was to go down to Watertown therewith, but Elias is so urgent to undertake it, and has already agreed to go with David Fay, who is going likewise, that this morning to my no small Disquietment, sat out. Master

---

[1] This beautiful old table is still in the possession of Mr. Parkman's descendants, being given now an honored place in Mr. Parkman Denny's library, in Leicester. The slate was broken and has

Hazletine dind with us. P. M. Elias returns, not being able to proceed on his Journey.

11.

12. P. M. Am called from my study to visit old Mrs. Baker. (Mr. Andrews takes me into a double Sleigh with his wife and with Capt. Jonas Brigham's Wife, who are going also to see their Mother). She was very dangerously ill of an Asthma. Discoursed and prayed with her.

been replaced by wood--but the oddly curved frame is still strong and beautiful. No wonder Elias made up his mind that it was a great bargain, for which he was willing to put himself to no little trouble.

ELIAS' TABLE.

13. A. M. on Ps: 92. 15. P. M. used notes on Ps: 55.22 from page 9 to bottom of page 13. After meeting at eve, Squire Baker sent his Sleigh for me. Mrs. P. and I went up to his Mother. Examined and prayed with her. We returned in ye Sleigh safely.

14. Elias rides in a Sleigh to Cambridge. P. M. Mr. Hazeltine makes me a visit and returns Edward's on Original Sin, the three pamphlets he borrowed. He now borrows Bp. Cambray on ye Divine Existence. Breck invites us to Coffee at ye Shop & we complyed. Read Lord Chesterfield.

15. Walked to Mr. Nurse's on various small Affairs.

The air is exceeding thick. P. M. it rains, the snow wastes. I finish Lord Chesterfield's first volume. Many admirable Excellencys in these Letters, and they evidence him a Man of great Understanding, extensive Reading and accurate Taste, & yet too extremely indulgent to his Son's Pleasures —throws him into dangers that it must be a Miracle if he escapes. And what affectionate wise, pious Parent could find in his Heart to take such pains to breed him to be a Man of this World, to ye so shameful neglect and Inattention to another! notwithstanding all ye Care of his Religion devolved upon his Preceptor; who he ought at least to have seconded.

At eve a Storm of Wind and Rain which beat vehemently, yet unexpectedly Elias came home from Cambridge, brot Rum for Breck and a valuable, tho old fashioned chamber Table, with large slate in ye Middle, for himselfe. He got thro ye Storm with great Difficulty.

16. A fine day after such a violent Storm. The Snow is

much sunk, but it is so pervaded by ye Rain that ye Creatures slump very deep, and no Horse can pass ye Road. I begin to read Lord Chesterfield's 2^d Vol. I am called away to visit old Mrs. Baker. Two young men Enoch Greenwood & John Baker draw me on a Sled to ye House. She is very low and in great Distress for want of Breath. She is able to say but very little. I at her request prayed with her. The same young men brot me home. May God prepare me for my own Turn!

17. Mrs. Baker expired last eve a little after I left her. May God grant His Omnipotent Grace to Survivors! Mr. Sam'l Harrington of New Braintree here. Mrs. P. and I dind at Breck's. Our lowest and best well has been, ever since ye great Storm, froze up and filled with Snow that we have not been able to use it, till today, when we got it open.

18. Closely engaged in preparing a Discourse on 1 Thes. 4.13. At eve Squire Baker here and desires me to attend ye Funeral tomorrow.

19. Squire sent a Sleigh for me to go to his House. Mrs. P. Sophy, Susé with her child, and little Susé of Concord rode with me, to ye House of Mourning. I prayed at ye Solemnity. N. B. Breck, Elias, Josiah Brigham, the two Williams (Winchester and Spring) there. Rev. Bowman and his Wife came after prayer. I did not go in to ye Burying place.—I could not *comfortably*, especially stand on ye snow. I came home. Breck and his Family dind with us. P. M. Pursued my preparations.

20. Rev. Mr. Bowman, who attended ye Funeral yesterday, came in the morning to my Assistance. In ye Assem-

bly, I prayed first, Mr. B. preached A. M. on Phil: 4.11. P.
M. he both prayed and preached. His text was Matt: vii.
24-27. At eve, he repeated y⁾ latter sermon, but did not
lodge here, he returned to his spouse at Squire Bakers.
At dinner were poor Deacon Miles and Master Hazzletine. May God graciously awaken and quicken us!

21. Elias went with me in y⁾ Sleigh to visit aged Mr.
James Maynard, who being weak and decaying, desired
Prayers yesterday—found him better and conversible—was
not asked to pray. I went in to Amasa's.[1] N. B. Tho
Amasa has kept House above twenty years, yet had never
lift up his Hand for Minister's Sallery. At eve, came Wil-
liam's brother Jonathan from Ashburnham, & brot him
Shirts and Frock & Shooes and Stockings &c. he lodges
here. Mr. Bowman and his Lady made us an evening Visit.
N. B. His people make very little provision for him.

22. Mr. Winchester went from us intending as far as
Lancaster. N. B. Josiah Brigham is gone for Breck to
Boston in y⁾ Sleigh. But today it is very difficult passing
by reason that y⁾ snow is exceeding soft. It is foul weather
P. M. The rain spoils travelling—.

22. Yesterday and today Chesterfield's Letters.

23. Very bad Travelling. Josiah Brigham with difficulty gets home.

24. Mrs. Lamson (wife of Mr. Thomas) comes to work
on Elias's Cloths. Mr. Hez. Taylor of New Fane makes a
visit and dines with us. Capt. Morse came in to see me.

---

[1] Amasa Maynard lived in the house on the Northborough road,
which has been enlarged into the Wayside Cottage, belonging to
the Lyman School. He was much given to practical jokes.

25. Mr. Buckminster and his Brother Col. William call here.

N. B. Mr. B. owns to me that he is ye Author of ye Letter which is advertised to be printed—he tells me also that in his Paraphase on Romans 10, 4. p. 13 by "another in his Neighborhood" he means Mr. Mellen of Chauxit, in his large Book, on Justification. My Dauter in-law receives a young Cow which her Father Brigham gives her. She is put into my Barn to be kept.

26. Mrs Lamson about 3 P. M. attempts to go home, but the rain prevailed so that she turned back & tarrys with us.

27. A. M. Delivered ye remainder on Ps: 55. 22
P. M. on 1 Thes: 4 13–14 & prepared on ye Occasion of ye Death of Mrs Persis Baker. Mr. Hazeltine & Mrs. Lambson dind here. She went home after Meeting. N. B. My son Breck not well. A Letter from Alix, dated ye 18th, he writes of ye Birth of a little Dauter on Nov. 16 last.

28. Old Mr. Jonah Warren dyed about 10 A. M.
I wrote by Mr. Levi Brigham of Fitz-William to my son Alexander. I read part of Lord Chesterfield. My son Breck grows worse. At eve came Master Hazeltine and lodges here. Anna Fay begins to learn to write.

29. I have spent some time in reading Ld Chesterfield and cant but take notice again that a Father with so much Learning and Sensibility has so little to say to a Son in whom his Soul is so bound up, about Religion and ye Eternal Condition of his immortal part. As much pleasure of mind as I feel for my son Elias's Education & Settlement in ye World or Serviceableness in his Generation, yet I have (I think

quite other Solicitude about his most inestimable Interest, that of his Soul, and his Condition in another, an unchangeable State in another world. And O ye God would grant him, & each of my dear Children His renewing and sanctifying Spirit! Breck removes to lodge here, Susè and ye Children also.

Miss Polly Howard makes us a visit & tarrys with us.

We have now a pritty round Family, of ye whole.

MARCH 1780.

Notwithstanding ye Rain and very difficult travelling, I went A. M. to ye Funeral of old Mr. Jonah Warren, who expired in ye Eighty——year of his age—many people attended. I prayed—ventured to come home on foot. The Snow and Ice made it dangerous to ride. Breck is somewhat better. At night he grew worse. My Family and his united are 14.

The Harvard Vacancy is up today; but ye weather rough and Roads very bad. Elias cannot go to Cambridge.

2. Am engaged in my preparations for ye Sabbath. Breck is recovering D. G.

3. Miss Polly Howard goes to Capt Maynard's. Breck goes to his Shop.

4.

5. On 1 Thes: 4.14, on occasion of ye Death of old Mr. Jonah Warrin. Cousin Maynard, Misses Brigham (as well as Breck and his Family) fill our Dining Board.

P. M. repeated on 2 Tim: 3.7 to page 9 bottom.

Cousin Maynard lodges here. N. B. Rec'd a Letter from Mr. Quincy by Mr. Thomas Whitney, dated Feb. 12.

6. Town Meeting. Mr. Eb^r Maynard and Dr. Hawes came to me with ye Town's Request to go to ye Meeting House and pray with y^m. I went, prayed and add a few words of address to y^m, but no word concerning my own Case. Mrs. Maynard and her son, (Master Samuel) dine with us and at eve a number of young Scholars, Hazletine, Sam'l Brigham.

7. Mrs. Maynard and her son went home.

8. Breck Susè and ye Child moved back to their Home. Read Lord Chesterfield, At night, Pearson on ye Subject I am preparing upon for ye next Lord's Day.

9. Mr. Thad. Warrin came and killed two Piggs for me, both of y^m weighed 226. P. M. at Mr. Stockwell's Desire I rode down to Mr. Tim. Warrin's. Elias went with me to drive ye Sleigh. I marryed Stephen Belknap to Eunice Warrin & supped there. Elias went for me again at evening,—and we returned safely, notwithstanding ye badness of ye way—ye Horse breaking in to ye Snow banks, oftentimes and ye Sleigh tossing uncomfortably, being also in ye Rain.

N. B. A number of Westboro' combine to take again ye Worcester News.

10. I agree with Breck to pay half ye Price of Thursday's Worcester paper. Anna Fay goes home, though the weather is bad.

11. The weather is still so rough and ye Roads so unfit for Travel, Elias remains at home, to my great Regret—but it cant be helped. I desire to resign ye whole matter to ye Divine Providence.

12. Preached again on 1 Thes: 4. 14—" and rose again." P. M. went on with 2 Tim: 3. 7 to ye end of page 16, which may a Divine Blessing accompany! It was so great a

Storm of Snow and Rain that there were but few at meeting—especially in ye afternoon.

13. Adjournment of Town Meeting. N. B. A sad Contest between Mr. Benj. Fay & Col. Wheelock, about a Chestnut Tree, cut down by ye latter in ye Time of ye late Extremity for Wood. Anna Fay again.

14. We are much reduced as to wood, but ye Weather is still too cold to be indifferent about it. No going to ye Ministerial Lot. Elias goes to sundry places, and gets Hay seed to sow ye Fields at ye Island.

15. Elias Sows Hay Seed upon ye Snow. Col. Brigham's Dauters Mindwell and Anna come up in ye morning on ye Snow and lodge here. Elias prepares to go to Cambridge tomorrow.

I wrote to ye president—to Mr. Quincy—to my son William.

16. Elias depended upon Mr. Elisha Parker to go to Boston and in returning to bring up our Horse: but by Parker not going, Elias is disappointed and does not go.

I finished reading Ld Chesterfield's Letters, but ye Miscel. no farther than page 578. We have such another Winter by ye Storm of Snow, which came today as makes us think of ye Value of Wood, and pity such as are destitute.

17. Mr. Nathan Maynard jun^r and Mr. Isaac Parker brot Wood. Two loads apiece. Elias P. M. got Hay Seed at Mr. Batherick's, several Baggs: which William sowed at ye Island.

18. Mr. Moses Nurse brings a load of Wood for Mr Maynard. N. B. The Measuring of Wood has been chiefly performed by Elias, and sometimes by Breck at ye Shop. Mr. Amos Parker here. He relates what occurred last tuesday at North Shrewsbury by ye deliriousness of Mr. Ger-

shom Flagg, who did mischief at Mr. Fairbank's new erected House, but chiefly at y⁵ Meeting House. Mr Parker speaks also of y⁵ Drowning of several men attempting to pass over Merrimack River

19. Preached on 1 Thes: 4.14 & P. M. on 2 Tim:

A PAGE OF A PARKMAN SERMON.

4.7 which may God bless N. B. I read today Zech. 7, P. M. I did not read, but we sung twice, began y^e 119th Psalm.

20. Elias is still disappointed of going to Cambridge. P. M. I rode to Squire Baker's. He gave me (as I understood him) ye Tallow I wanted of him. I was too destitute of common money, & therefore went to ye Treasurer Newton for Supply—but there was none for me: but he offered to lend me an hundred pounds of his own Money. I was at Deacon Wood's—am grieved at its being such a Seat of Lazy Typlers. N. B. I returned by Dr. Hawes, W. R. Cranch's Biog. Univ.

21. N. B. I delivered to Elias Four Hundred Dollars of which one hundred and seventy-six from my own Desk and borrowed 224 Dollars of my Son Breck. Breck goes for Boston. Sent by him to Mr. Quincy and to my kinswoman, Mrs. Eliz. Bradford. Elias on Mr. Elisha Forbes' horse to Cambridge, and by him I sent to ye President, and to my Son William at Concord.

I borrowed 20£ of Money of Mr. Barney Newton, Treasurer, which he must have again from ye Constable when he can gather it of ye People.

22. Gave Mrs. P.— 33 Dollars to pay Miss Lucy Maynard.

Mr. Stone came—dind—preached my Lecture, on Isa: 53. 6, tarried over night. N. B. We read a Narrative of ye Journal[1] and discoverys of two of General Gage's Officers,

---

[1] This was probably the report of Capt. Brown and Ensign D'Berniere, who reconnoitred, in disguise, the roads between Worcester and Boston, and Boston and Concord, in the early part of 1775.

when reconnoitring ye Roads and as far as Worcester—previous to Lexington Fight.

23. Mr. Stone and I walked up to Squire Baker's to ye stones and to see 4 great Oxen, of uncommon Bigness and Fatness. Mr. Stone returned home. Breck returned before night—brot two letters from Mr. Forbes to me. One from Mrs. Rebecca Wetmore at London to Mr. W^m. Spring. One also from Mr. Thomas Barrett of Cambridge to Miss Lydia Champney, which relates ye Death of her Brother, Mr. Samuel Champney, Feb'y 3^d last.

Breck brot also a present of a Barcelona Handkerchief to his Mother from Samuel and another from ye same to Sophy, and another from ye same to Susè. I perceive y^t he gave 50 Dollars apiece for y^m——

24. Breck unhappily brot back ye Letter I wrote to my son William, about Wood for Elias. I wrote another, but know of no conveyance. It is so rugged Weather that I am much afraid Elias will be put to Difficulty, and be obliged to buy at ye excessive Cambridge price.

25. Mr. Nathan Maynard jun^r brot one load of Wood, which my son Breck measured, and says is 77 feet. But inasmuch as (to deal rightly) several loads of late have been of exceeding crooked wood, & this today has such a quantity of small wood I told my son I would be glad to have more allowance made on those accounts.

26. Preached again on 1 Thes. 4. 14. & read ye verses following. I administered ye Lord's Supper. O y^t it might be accepted thro ye Merits and Intercession of Jesus Christ. Old Mrs. Green dind with us. P. M. I went on with the subject from 2 Tim: 3. 7. From page 23 to page 29., which

may God graciously own and bless! In ye eve read part of Mr. Henry on Due Return from ye Lord's Table.

27. Dr. Crosby came in to see me. He is about selling part of his place in Shrewsbury, viz. His Buildings, and about 60 acres of his Land, to old Mr. Rider. W^m. Winchester remains much unwell. I was obliged to get Josiah Brigham to tend my Cattle in ye Morning.

Breck has received two Letters from Mr. Moore.

28. Josiah Brigham goes to Boston. I write and send by him to Mr. Moore and also to Elias at College. John Barrett of Hopkinton came to see me—dines here. His ardency is still to go to College. He is now desirous to go to that at Dartmouth. He borrows two pamphlets of Mr. Hutchinson's Sermons. W^m. Winchester still complains of much Indisposition, yet has been to ye Barn.

29 W^m. grows worse, takes physic of Dr. Stimson, who called to see us and dines here. P. M. Mrs. P— to Harrington's. Suse goes to her Fathers. Breck takes care of ye Cattle for me. Eph. Parker was here at Evening. I try to have him live here, but I cant succeed.

N. B. Mr. Nathan Maynard jun^r & Lieut. Bond, bring so much Wood as compleats (as they, Maynard and Breck say) Maynard's Ten cord, so y^t I gave a Receipt for it.

30. Parker came to work on our Flax, but found it not rotted sufficient, therefore breaks off and returns. Mr. Abr. Holland here and gives me a more perfect Account of Mr. Gershom Flagg's Frenzy. We cant but remark how uncommon ye Cold has been and continued.

31. Dr Stimson came from Sutton and returns to Hopkinton—dines here; he gives W^m. Winchester a Vomit.

which works well, but he remains sick and exercised with Pain, in both Head and Stomach—The months flie apace! may I have a due sense of my own hastening hence!

APRIL.

2. Preached on 2 Thes: 4. 15-16. Mrs Beeton dind with us. P. M. on 2 Tim: 3. 7, & finished ye Discourse except ye Additions. O y^t I might be duly affected myself with what was delivered!—At eve Breck and his attended ye Repetition &c.

3. Went to Mr. Nurse's and Mr. Thad. Warrin's,—to bespeak Spring and Summer Work, but ye Earth is as yet partly covered with snow, and where it is open, is froze.

P. M. Col. Brigham here upon an important errand in behalf of his Son Elijah, with regard to Sophy,—which I gave my Consent to.

4. Preached at Deac. Woods on Eccl. 12. 13. There was a considerable Assembly. Mr. Knight and Mr. ODonald of Boston were there, & I had an Opportunity of conversing with both after Meeting. Col. Baldwin and his son Isaac, also my grandson, Thomas P. A Letter by them from my dear Ebenezer, dated Morris Town State of New York, March 10. 1780, when he was well, tho he had endured Hardships, and suffered by cold, lying on ye Ground. They lodge here and have three Horses.

5. Col. &c leave us to go to Cambridge. My son Breck undertakes a long, circular, difficult Journey, to Bridgewater, Boston &c. Very much perplexed with a flock of Sheep belonging to Dr. Hawes, daily feeding on ye Rye at ye Island. Stephen Maynard who has ye Care of ye Dr's Affairs

here in ye Evening to tell me y^t he could not take Care of ye Dr's Sheep, being in preparation to go to Market.

6. Disappointed of Help to repair my Island Fence., and therefore those Sheep are in again upon my Rye. Young Winchester is poorly—pain in his Hip is his principal Complaint,—but ofttimes in his Head.

7. Mr. Thad. Warrin works for me, mending my Island Fence, and Fences before ye Meeting House. A Letter from my son Alexander. Miss Betsey Taylor of Grafton here—tells me Mr. Grosvenor goes sometimes to hear Mr. Henstick, ye Baptist Minister: and y^t many others do since Mr. G. cannot preach. At eve Capt. Wood and Mr. Jon^n Fay here.

8. Fresh Troubles with ye Doct^r Cattle & Sheep on ye Rye, notwithstanding all ye pains used yesterday to make ye Fence Secure and strong. 4 times today.

Mr. Thomas Stone here, wants ye Association Records for his Father, which I gave him, and a number of Papers belonging to ye Association.

9. At night sent for to visit Lt. Bond's Child—went and prayed there. It was very rainy. A. M. preached again on 1 Thes. 4. 16-17.

P. M. on 2. Cor: 4. 1-3. O y^t we might grow wiser and better by all y^{ese} means.

10. Deac. Wood came to acquaint me y^t there was at his House an Indian in Gentleman's Habit, who was a Scholar and Preacher from Dartmouth Coll. I sent for him—he came—his name was Daniel Simon. The Brigham Scholars were well acquainted with him. His Credentials were (besides his Diploma and his name in ye Catalogue) his recom-

mendation by ye President, Trustees and Tutors, License for preaching by Rev. Grafton—Presbytery—a Letter from president Wheelock to Rev. Mr. John Sargent of Stockbridge, and a Certificat from ye Selectmen of Stockbridge. I also examined him myself.

The Deacon urged he might preach in ye afternoon and he would take care to notifie ye people. Mr. Simon was not forward, but would not deny. I could not refuse. He dind here. At 3 P. M. a Congregation was gathered. He preached on 1 Pet: 2. 7 "To them who believe, he is precious." It was a serious and Methodical Discourse, & delivered decently. I hope it was useful and profitable.

A number of Scholars, who were acquainted with Mr. Simons, came in at eve to see him and he lodged here.

N. B. The people made a Collection and presented him ye Sum of one hundred and twenty-four Dollars

One Ebenezer Crosby came here to let himself and lodged here. N. B. Dr. Hall going to Boston calls here.

11. The Indian Preacher leaves us to go on his Journey to Stockbridge. Mr. Crosby insists for Cloths to pay for His Labour; which I not being able to engage him, he leaves me. I catechized at ye Meeting House. Boys 32. Girls 17. Dr. Hawes has brot me Another Vol. of ye Biographical Dictionary from Mr. Cranch. Vol. 4 Letters D and E.

12. Read Col. Ethan Allen's Narrative of his Captivity & Several Lives in Biography aforesaid. viz. M^ons. and Mme Daciers, John Daillé, author of de User Patrum, John Dee, mathematician, Conjurer &c. De Foe, Demosthenes, Thomas Dempster, noted for his remembering whatever he read, and yet commonly read 14 hours in 24.

13. Mr. John^n Maynard brings — Turns of Wood in all ——. Dr. Hall from Boston. N. B. Genl Hancock exceeding Generous to him. Col. Baldwin & Thomé Parkman, Mr. Eliot, Tutor and Mr. Zechary Hicks here. These 5 last dind here.

Col. Baldwin brot two letters from Elias, one of March 30th ye other April. Am informed y^t Mr. Samuel Williams of Bradford is chose professor instead of ye late Dr. Winthrop—that Rev. Mr. Harrington of Lancaster was married ye night before last, to Mrs. Bridge of Framingham.

14. My kinsman (Elias Parkman of Boston) sent me a Copy of ye Address of the Convention and Plan of Government. P. M. walked (on some special occasions) to Dr. Hawes. Having no man yet and young Winchester lame & infirm, my business is behind. Breck works in ye Garden—plows and hires Mr. Kenney part of the Day to renew and mend up ye Garden Fence. B. sows Peas there.

15. Breck and W^m. Winchester at times in ye Garden. I cannot afford any time to it, nor have I any Inclination. Josiah Brigham returns from an Excursion to purchase Cattle: he has been as far as to Fitz William and has brought two Cows, one has a Calf, t'other with Calf. They are put into my Barn to keep. Breck has now four Creatures there, his Horse and 3 cows besides ye young Calf.

16. A. M. on 1 Thes: 4. 17-18. P. M. on 2. Cor: 4. 3-4 read A. M. Zech 9. Mr. Brigham dind here, as did Cousin Maynard. At eve Breck and his Family (as they have done frequently) came to ye Repetition.

17. A very snowy Morning (Apr. 6. old style anno 1732 was a time of exceeding deep snow). I sent a Letter to Dr.

Hawes who would go to Boston, for Elias, at College. Was at Mr. Newton's about driving young Cattle to pasture at Coi's Hill.

18. Rode to Minister's Meeting at Stow. Met Mr. Stone at Mrs. Speakman's. Borrowed of her Pope's Essay on Man, with Warburton's Notes. We called at Mr. Jon[n] Loring's, and delivered him Beard's Theatre of God's Judgments which I had borrowed of him. At Mr. Newell's were Messrs. Stone, Smith, Bridge, Whitney and Biglow, and occasionally Messrs. Adams of Acton, Stearns and Allen, preachers. Mr. Mellen of Chauxit. Some debate about a Concio, whether if there be not a Concio prepared on purpose, we mayn't have a Sermon for our Christian Edification. Mr. Bridge opposes it. I asked advice about y[e] case of Mr. Daniel Adams & his wife. Answer was to prevent its being heard in y[e] Church till it is heard in y[e] Civil Law, if y[e] Woman's Complaint must be supported by her Oath.

Mr. Allen prayed at y[e] Conclusion of our Meeting.

Next Meeting by divine leave to be at my House. Old Mrs. Gardner (at whose House we were) was not able to sit at Table when we dind Mr. Stone and I rode together to Marlboro'. I visited our Kinsman, Lt. Uriah Brigham,[1] where I lodged.

19. A Storm of Rain and Snow—but I ventured to try for Home. Sat out in ye Morning under another Disad-

---

[1] Uriah Brigham, in 1750, had married Sarah Gott, a niece of Mrs. Parkman's, and sister of Mrs. Stephen Maynard. "He lived in the south part of Marlborough," says the Marlborough Historian, "in the style of the English gentry, receiving the visits of the élite far

vantage, viz., the Horse lame—got to Capt. Edmund Brigham's and dind there. Arrived safe at home about 3 P. M. All Glory to God, my Guardian at home and abroad! Am informed that Dr's Sheep have still been troublesome.

20. Mr. Nathan Kenney here & agrees (if I dont hire a man) to take my North Field to plant to y⁰ halves; and likewise to take another piece of Ground for Flax, in y⁰ like manner.

I read y⁰ Conventions Address to their Constituents, with Declaration of Rights & Form of Government.

21. Was forced to go to Dr. Hawes on y⁰ Account of his Sheep, which were again yesterday upon my Field of Rye, and was at Neighbor Caleb Harrington's, his Hogs having done Mischief several times in my Garden, and mentioned to him my putting out my Chauncey Meadows to y⁰ halves, much interrupted and tossed in spirit by having no man to work for me, when so many different affairs to mind, in looking after my Husbandry at this Season, and Creatures to guard from transgressing.

22. Mr. Eleazar Rider, who saws at y⁰ Whipple sawmill having given me Slabbs &c, Stephen Maynard in Dr. Hawes' Service, goes with my Cart and Steers, & puts in y⁰ Dr's Steers, to y⁰ Saw-Mill, & brings a Load.

23. I have for a great while thought of repeating my Sermons on Mat: 3.10. which were preached above 30 years since. I undertook it today, though with alterations and

and near; he kept an open house, and showed a hospitality without measure or stint." He left quite an estate, but so involved that it took his administrators thirty years to disentangle it. It is said he never did a day's work in his life.

additions. N. B. Have read ye Ch. publickly. At eve read a sermon of Mr. Flavell's England's Duty; on Rev: 3. 20.

24. Mr. Hez. Maynard of Marlboro' here; as was Mr. Simon How, afterwards came Mr. Joseph Mottey, a preacher at Marlboro, with Mr. Elijah Brigham. They dind here. Mrs. P. walked to see her Cousen Maynard and tarried there. N. B. James Hopkins of Mansfield came to let himself, and he lodged here. I have made him ye best Offer I could.

25. Hopkins goes to work—uses my Steers and Deac. Wood's Oxen & Harrow & Ben Wood helps, in harrowing & getting out muck. Mrs. P— returns at evening. I am preparing on Zech 7. 5-7.

26. *General Fast* thro'out ye States. Preached on ye Text above.

In going to Meeting P. M. was informed y^t Mr. Whitney's House of Northboro was burnt down this very noon. I preached on Ps 107. 43 & took occasion frequently to apply it to ye present Occurrence, so surprising and affecting! May ye Lord sanctifie it to ye Sufferers & to us all!—The Brethren by desire was stayed to confer about ye Adams Difficulty. I manifested my Desire to keep it out of ye Church, but they saw cause to appoint a number to go to her. See Church Records.

27. In ye Morning, I rode over to see ye Ruins, & sympathize with those who are bereaved. I found ye sad Cause to be, Mrs. Whitney made a Fire in her Oven, that morning, sat in her Food to be baked for Supper; but ye Fire, while ye People were at Meeting in ye forenoon, kindled in ye Kitchen Chamber, & was discovered by Mr.

Sam¹ Allen in y ͤ time of y ͤ last prayer. Many goods in y ͤ lower rooms, y ͤ Church plate &c were saved, but the Library and Papers, which were of great worth: 4 feather Beds, all their Cloths and Linnen, except what they had on, Corn, Cyder, Sauce, &c. &c. burnt. Mr. Sumner came also and carryed various Things. I went in to see Mr. Jonas Badcock, whose Hair, Face and Hands were much Scorched, Swelled and blistered by y ͤ Flames. I dind at Mrs. Briggs's where Mr. Whitney and his Family had repaired to. Mr. Sumner and Mr. Allen, preacher at Bolton, dind there also. The people meet this afternoon to see what they can do toward assisting. N. B. A great deal has been brot in already. I rode to Mr. Seth Rice's for Flax seed. I there informed Mrs. Adams, of y ͤ Church's Appointment yesterday relative to her. I was at Capt. Maynard's—visit old Mrs. Kelly, drank Tea there. When I came home am informed of y ͤ Conduct and Language of Hopkins.

28. Hopkins desires to go off, and tho it throws me into much perplexity I consent and he goes away, giving in his work and offers to pay the Damage of Disappointment. I went over to Mr. N. Kenney and got him (again) to take my North Field to y ͤ Halves; which he agrees to.

29. Kenny and his Son came to get out muck, and has my Steers and Cart. Mr. Moses Nurse joins with his Horses and waggon. I was obliged to go up to Deac. Wood's and Squire Baker's to forward a Contribution, but neither of y ͫ at home. Deacon came P. M. My son W ͫ, Lydia & W ͫ, from Concord came to tarry over y ͤ Sabbath here.

30. On consideration of y ͤ burning of Mr. Whitney's House, I preached (with alterations repeated) on Lam: 3.

22-23. both A. & P. M. Baptized Capt. Godfry's Twins, Sullivan and Salmon. Appointed ye Communion, but no Lecture Appointed contribution for Rev. Mr. Whitney next Sabbath. At noon conferred with Selectmen as well as Deacons about ye Contribution. At eve in ye Family read Mr. Flavel's Sermon on Gal: 5. 24. See his works p. 254. Vol. 1.

MAY 1780.

The Town met to read ye Address of ye Convention, with the Draught they had made of a Form of Government for this State. I understood that they read it over, and after some debating upon it, they adjourned to this day three weeks. May God ye Fountain of Wisdom, grant them Knowledge and understanding. Wrote a long letter to my son Ebenezer at Morris Town, New Jersey to be ready for Col. Baldwin to carry. Billy and Lydia here yet.

2. Wrote to Mr. Quincy to ye care of Breck, who goes to Boston Sophy to Mr. Whitney's and to ye Fulling Mill[1] at Northboro! I went to Mr. Thad. Warrin's, his wife sick. I was lamed by a slab falling on my right Foot. A very cold damp season. Too cold for Billy and Lydia to go

[1] "About half a mile from the meeting house on the post-road, and on the river Assabet, there is a mill for the fulling of cloth, and works for carrying on the clothiers business in all its branches, where about 7000 yards of cloth are annually dressed and the work is most acceptably performed to the honour and advantage of the town, and the interest of the community. These works are the property of two brothers, Captains Samuel and Abraham Wood: but the business is performed at present by the latter only."
— Peter Whitney in his History of Worcester Co.

home. W^m. Winchester out of Health still: Stomach ache, Lame in his Hips, & can do very little.

3. Sheep more than ordinarily Troublesome., My affairs are much perplexed. W^m. Parkman and his Sister Lydia leave us to go to Concord. Mr. Joseph Harrington has been here, and tells that Providence had prevented the Committee of ye Church that were appointed to go to Mrs. Adams, so y^t y^y went not, for Deac. Bond was too infirm to go, Mr. Davis was very ill, and confined by a Fever, or pleurisie—Mr. Harrington went, to little purpose.

4. While much embarrassed and pritty lame, Stephen Batherick came within Reach, and was very much at Leisure. I hired him for 15 per Day to be paid according to ye old way, and he came and worked ye afternoon.

Breck returns from Boston, brings a Letter from Elias at Cambridge, concerning ye Installment of Mr. Sam'l Williams heretofore of Bradford, Professor of Mathematics & experimental Philosophy—a marvellous time.

At eve came Lieut. Jon^n Grout, Messrs. Eli Whitney & Jon^n Forbes, and are concerned about Brother Adams's coming to Communion. I advised y^m to go and make him a visit, and after that let me know.

5. Old Mr. Hardy came in Warmth & inveighed against ye Contribution for Mr. Whitney, because he has not asked any to be made for him. He is a very rich man, said he, & might take it as an Affront to him, except he desired it. I endeavored to inform him better, & chid him for his Rashness. Mrs. P— visits Mr. Davis and Mr. Thad. Warrin's Wife—both sick.

6. Mr. James Dix came—but I refused to meddle at all with his Quarrells.

7. None of those Brethren about Adams's Matter, make me any Return. preached on Ps: 133. 12-3. Administered y⁰ Lord's Supper. Mr. Adams did not stay to commune or disturb us. Mrs. Maynard dind with us. P. M. repeated sermon on 2 Cor : 8,7. expecting a Contribution, but Messrs. Belknap and Gale inform me, it is very much desired by considerable numbers yᵗ yᵉ Contribution might be deferred to another Sabbath ; for as much as yᵉ Town when together last Monday were so engaged in yᵉ weighty affairs then depending unhappily forgot to mention it, and therefore were not so prepared as might be wished, and may be hoped for, if they might have further time. It was therefore deferred till next Lord's Day—but advised yᵗ the Sermon which had been delivered might be improved as an Excitement and Preparatory thereto. N. B. As to Mr. Adams, I understand that he went away from yᵉ Communion because he was himself offended. Also Capt. John Wood's Wife for some Reasons withdrew.

At evening worship read yᵉ 2ᵈ of Mr. Flavell's Sermons on Rev: 3. 20.

8. William Winchester left us to go to Ashburnham. I wrote by him to his Mother. I gave him 10 Dollars, Mr. Barnard's Sermons to young people and on yᵉ Earthquake, and furnished him with various Things to accomodate him for his Journey. May God grant him Health and Grace! I have now neither Man nor Boy—but Billy Spring to tend Cattle and Sheep. Dr. Hawes, yᵉ Court[1] being Dissolved, is returned ; visits and dines with me.

[1] Dr. Hawes was representative in the General Court for the years 1778–80.

9. Wrote to Mr. Moore. The Referees upon y⁵ Case of Capt. John Wood, versus Benj. Fay, & his Mother-in-law, set here at y⁵ Meeting House. They are Judge Dorr,[1] Tim. Pain[2] & Joseph Wheeler, Esq.[3] The Lawyers are, for Wood, Wᵐ. Stearns, Esq.,[4] & Dan'l Biglow,[5] for the Fays, Mr. Sprague.[6] The latter came to see me. I attended part of y⁵ P. M. A most unhappy Strife! May God pity yᵐ.

10. Attended y⁵ Court, part of y⁵ Day. Mr. Andrews delivers me a Letter from Mr. Whitney, concerning our Contribution for him, manifesting his Satisfaction in our defer-

---

[1] Judge Dorr was Joseph Dorr, of Ward (now Auburn), appointed Judge of the Court of Common Pleas in 1776.

[2] Timothy Paine held a number of important offices in Worcester. He was the father of Dr. William Paine, and of Nathaniel Paine— the Judge of Probate for Worcester County for thirty-five years.

[3] Judge Wheeler, also, was a Worcester man. He was at this time the Register of Probate, being at the time he came to Worcester, a retired clergyman. His house, known as the old "Wheeler Mansion," stood on Main Street, near Lincoln Square, until a few years ago.

[4] William Stevens, was a prominent lawyer in Worcester, from 1776,—when first admitted to the bar,—until his early death, in 1784. "He possessed good sense, respectable bearing, lively wit and much kindness of feeling." He was associated for one year with Daniel Bigelow (afterwards County Attorney), in the publication of the Massachusetts Spy.

[5] Daniel Bigelow was a young man, having been born in Worcester, in 1752--the third of the name. He was a nephew of Col. Timothy Bigelow, of Revolutionary fame, and was himself a distinguished lawyer, senator, counsellor, etc.

[6] Mr. Sprague was probably John Sprague, of Lancaster, first District Attorney of Worcester County, being appointed to that position in 1780. He was succeeded by Daniel Bigelow.

ring it, and how gratefully he will accept of what soever shall be afforded. Mr. Joseph Hardy was here, & was examined in order to his joining with ye Church. Mr. Joseph Smith and his Wife made us a visit. Mr. Smith manifested his Desire of ye Ordinance of Baptism for their Child; but I was in much Suspense about proceeding with him.

11. The Pleading finished last night about 10 o'clock. The Judges are together A. M. & draw up their Determination. P. M. Judge Dorr here. N. B. Send my Letter to Mr. Moore by Master Crosby, going to Boston, to be left at Gill's Office for conveyance. Pamela Cooledge of Ashburnham came to live here. Mrs. Hardy, wife of Mr. Joseph.

12. It is but a Melancholly Time with me. Nothing at all doing in my Husbandry, having neither Man nor Boy to assist me. The weather is indeed cold, & ye season backward.

Mr. Thomas Adams of Medfield came to see me and lodges here.

13. Mr. Adams wants my Volume of Chubb's Tracts in 4to.

He gives me Dr. Brown Languith's Modern Theory and Practice of Physick; Dr. Goodman's Penitent Pardon. Judge Hale's Contemplations, part 3. with his Life, and Mr. Durham on Scandal. Besides Chubb, he has Dennis's Advancement & Reformation of Modern Poetry, and leaves me two Pamphlets, viz: Dr. Cardogan on ye Gout &c. and Mr. S. Webster's two Discourses on Infant Baptism. He promises Dr. Owen on Sp^l Mindedness: for which he takes with him Dr. Bray's Bibliotheca Parochialis. Further I lent him Cornelius Agrippa of ye Vanity of ye Sciences. To be sent to my son Saml Boston. Mrs. Harrington here P. M. Makes Return of their Visit to Mrs. Adams, & gives me a Paper signed by her, & ye Committee.

14. Although I have attempted something in preparation for today's Exercises, yet had so many interruptions and avocations, that I was obliged to lay it by, & preached on Mat: 5. 7. A. & P. M. N. B. After ye forenoon Exercise, I read some parts of Mr. Whitney's Letter to me on ye 8th to ye Congregation. Appointed a Church Meeting to be ye 30th

P. M. *A Contribution for Rev. Peter Whitney.* At eve read Flavel on Rev. 3. 20. Serm. III.

15. Deac. Wood here to count ye Contribution made yesterday. It was in Notes 262£, in Money (including 5 Pistareens, 175 In all to Mr. Whitney 438£. There was also a number of Dollars which were included in a paper directed to ye Selectmen, for the Benefit of ye poor Cripple John Forbes.

16. I rode to Mr. Fessenden to try to put out my Sheep, but in Vain. I dind there. P. M. rode over to Mr. Whitney's and conveyed ye Contribution which we made for him in Money and Notes, & took his Receipt. I delivered him Six Books as my own Contribution viz. Calvin's Harmony, Morning Exercise, Pierce's Sinner inplead, Claggett's Abuse of Grace, Butler's Sermons, Bradbury and Pike on Trinity, went to Mr. Wood's ye Clothier, returned at eve. Stephen Bathcrick works here.

17. I keep Stephen in planting in ye Beeton Field. P. M.

went to Mr. Levi Warrin's, obtained easily of him to bear my Message to Mr. Daniel Adams concerning ye Church Meeting to be next tuesday come Sennight at ye Meeting House 2 P. M. oc.

18. Stephen still works for me in planting various Things, and Mending the fences &c. went with him to ye Island, to shew him what was most necessary—but at night goes home. P. M. Elias came up from Cambridge, with Josiah Brigham. The last brings a Letter from my son Samuel concerning W^m. Parkman of Boston (son of Nat.) his proposal to buy out ye several Heirs to ye Mansion House &c. Cousen Maynard made us a Visit, and drank Tea here. My Friend, Col. Joseph Buckminster[1] of Framingham was buryed.

19. *A very Cloudy Day*.[2] It rained some part of ye Morning, when it held up it not only remained very cloudy, but

[1] Col. Joseph Buckminster was made colonel in 1739, and served in the French and Indian Wars, and in the Revolution. He was selectman for twenty-eight years, town clerk for thirty-two, and representative for nineteen. He lived west of the old cemetery in Framingham. He was the father of Rev. Joseph Buckminster, of Rutland.

[2] The famous "Dark Day" of History.

Mr. Parkman and the people of the town seemed to take it as calmly as Col. Davenport, of Conn., whose common sense and courage have been sung in verse and story. I think this is the only instance in these years of the Journal where Mr. Parkman speaks of enjoying, especially, any article of food.

A different scene was being enacted in the neighboring town of Sutton, as we learn from the Journal of the Rev. Dr. Hall. He writes:—"Y^e Day was so dark as y^t we needed candles at noon day. People came flocking to the meeting-house, and desiring my

from about 10 A. M. it grew very dark—the Obscurity increased by about 11 it was too dark to read unless at ye Window—by 12, I could not read anywhere in ye House— We were forced to dine by Candle Light. It was very awfull and surprising. Thro divine Goodness ye Light gradually returned & I wrote this before two.—Before Night, I find y^t the unusual Darkness has given general Surprise. At eve went to Supper at Breck's, on agreeable Haddock. The Night was exceeding dark, insomuch y^t the Committee which sat at Deac. Woods, on ye Affair of ye Form of Government could not without Difficulty find their way home. Several of y^m did not get home at all.

20. I am concerned for my Neighbor Thad. Warrin, who is so behindhand in his Business. I have offered him my Cattle and plow—and I have said so much to him to persuade him that he uses y^m today.

21. On account of ye late unusual *Phenomenon*, I read A. M. Amos 5. and preach on x. 4.5.6.7.8. Messrs. Brigham and Hazletine dind here. P. M. I went on in Repeating Sermon on Mat. 3.10 from page 9 with some Omissions. at Eve read latter part of Mr. Flavells Third Sermon on Rev. 3. 20, which may God graciously bless to us!

22. Mr. Joseph Hardy here with his Relation, which requires many alterations. Esq. Baker, Mr. Batherick and Mr. Joseph Harrington came to me from ye Town Meeting, to desire me to go with y^m. to pray with y^m & give y^m my Presence. I went and prayed with them, and preached a sermon to y^m Extempore from Joel 2., 1. & part of ye 2^d. 4 & ye people were very attentive. The Lord Sanctifie his Hand and awaken us up to our duty!"

Advice, they being assembled upon ye very important Affair of ye Plan of Government,—went and prayed & joined with y^m in voting. Voted y^e *Bill of Rights:*—Voted y^e *Introduction* of ye first part on Government—voted Article I. then adjourned—Elias studys Anatomy.

23. Mr. Elijah Brigham in Squire Baker's Chaise, waits on Mrs. Parkman to Boston. I wrote to my son Saml my Consent to my Kinsman W^m. Parkman's having, for reasonable price, my Right in that which was my late Honored Mother's House.

24. I met with ye Town on ye Adjournment. N. B. Strenuously insist that the Govr shall not only declare himself of the Christian Religion, but a Protestant. It was obtained to have ye Word Protestant inserted ; ye Vote had two against it., Capt. Fisher and Mr. Hananiah Parker.

25. Mr. Joseph Hardy's Wife here, & have so many Corrections to make, that it was necessary to transcribe it. This I did for her. Elias is reading Chesselden's Anatomy. Mr. Elijah Brigham returns from Boston & Says Mrs. P— had a good Journey. N. B. I found that my son Breck is a *FREE MASON.*[1]

26. I discover also that my son Sam is- that Capt. Elias and y^t. Coll. Baldwin are.

N. B. The *American Academy of Arts and Sciences* formed, constituted And Made a Body politic & Corporate by an act of the General Assembly of this State, at y^{eir} present Ses-

---

[1] Breck Parkman was one of the members of Trinity Lodge, of Lancaster—the first lodge west of Boston. This was founded in 1778. In the early part of the present century he became a charter member of the Northborough Lodge of Free Masons.

sions. The Names of y⁰ Members are published in todays Spy. It is matter of Joy to me! But it was also of Surprise, as I cant trace its Conception nor Author, nor Fantors; (?) the char^rs. Qualifications, Duty, Immunitys, & Emoluments.

27.

28. Read A. M. Zech. x. with some Exposition of it. Preached on Amos 8. 9, P. M. on Mat. 3. 10. read in y⁰ Evening part of Mr. Flavell's 3ᵈ & 4ᵗʰ Sermon on Rev. 3. 20.

29. Rec'd a Letter from Rev. Whitney to request me to dine with him & to attend the Raising a New House¹ for

¹ This new house still stands under the large elms.

PETER WHITNEY'S NEW HOUSE.

him. In riding over there met with Mr. McCarty—he was going to Boston. But turned about and went with me to Northborough. Mr. Stone came also. We dind at Mrs. Briggs, & there Supped. Mr. Maccarty went to Boston. Mr. Stone and I went to the Raising. I prayed and gave ye Psalm (ps. 127). Mr. Stone made ye last prayer. *No Evil occurrence.* Blessed be God! Mr. Elijah Brigham was my Company home. An Excellent Frame, & a great Company;

30. A. M. Assist ye Selectmen in forming their Return to the Convention, with ye Exceptions and Alterations. P. M. Attended ye Church Meeting. Opened it with Prayer. The first Affair was that of Sister Persis Adams, wife of Mr. Daniel Adams who was present; but her Husband, tho notified seasonably by a Messenger, sent on purpose by ye Pastor to him, to acquaint with ye Meeting, *for what, when & where,* did not come. This caused us to defer the Hearing any Complaint against him, till we might have accuser & accused Face to Face! Act: 25. 16. The Church Meeting, as it relates to this Controversie, is adjourned to ye last Monday in August next, at 2 P. M.

The other Matter on which we met, was to choose two Deacons: and chose Dr. James Hawes for one, & Br. Jon^n Child for ye other by 17 Votes—ye rest scattering. The Dr. desired leave to take so weighty a Concern into Consideration. The other denyed and again refused, but he was urged to consider of it, & not be too resolute in Denying.

The Meeting concluded with prayer and ye Blessing.

Mr. Cushing came from Shrewsbury (from Ashburnham

yesterday) and lodged here. Has two Horses, one for Mrs. Cotton to ride upon.

31. I have writ a Letter to Mrs. P.— and Dr. Hawes was to have carryed it, but he went too early this morning for it to reach him. However Mr. Lemuel Grosvenor and his Sister called here in their way to Boston, and took it. We had a cheerful and good Day—praising God for his Goodness to his People in continuing our Liberties and Privileges and Oppt'y ye Day for ye Exercising y^m., and supplicating ye Divine Presence with the People in their Solemn Assembly; & ye Ministers in their Convention.

Elias rode over to Hopkinton to wait upon Mrs. Cotton, but she was not well eno' to come today, Elias brings me from Mr. Barrett's the illustrated Sir Francis Bacon's Advancement of Learning. A Book of Stupendous Fame!—

JUNE.

Mr. Cushing Sets out for Ashburnham. I again go to ye Meeting House to assist ye Towns Men in their making Reply to ye Convention at Boston, and Breck is desired to transcribe it for Capt. Fisher to carry with him. A variety of Company interrupts and discomposes me. I read in Brog'r. Dictionary At Eve. Mr. Elias Harding & Thankful Forbes marryed.

2. Tho it is Friday, I seem obliged to go out and look after my Affairs. My Cattle begin to be unruly. I went to Mr. Isaac Parker's to see what he would do about working for me instead of his Br. Ephraim, some of whose Time remains to be made up, and to make some Agreement with him to take my Young Oxen to keep. Elias goes to Hop-

kinton again with Mr. Cushing's Horse with him for Mrs. Cotton, who comes here at evening. Mr. Hazletine waits on Miss Nabby Martyn and two of Squire Baker's Dauters, & Miss Mindwell Brigham who all (of ye last) drink Tea here. Dr. Gershom Brigham makes me a visit respecting ye Baptism of his new-born Twins.[1] Mrs. Cotton lodges here. I am much prevented studying.

3. Ensign Snow brings his Dismission from Southboro and desires to be admitted into ye Church here. N. B. Frederic Lock who works for me today in moving and setting up a Fence at ye Island to make a Lane from ye Road to my Pasture, meets with a Disappointment by ye unruliness of my Steers, and leaves ye Work undone—which prevents my pasturing my Cows there.

4. Read Zechariah II. Preached A. & P. M. on Luke 16.23 & by divine Help, I accomplished ye whole. I humbly ask ye Grace & Power of God may be magnifyd in ye Awakening of many Souls! In ye eve read part of another Sermon of Mr. Flavell's on Rev. 3.20. N. B. Dr. Hawes has brot. me from my son Samuel, Melmoth's Sublime & beatif. Mr. Ripley of Concord is ye Proprietor.

5. Hear that Mr. Henry Quincy is dead! If so, I heartily sympathize with my old Friend, his Father.

6. Elias setts out on Breck's Horse for Cambridge. I gave him to pay his Quarter bills and other Expenses, to be used with the utmost Prudence, Eight hundred Dollars.

Mr. W^m. Knight of Boston, Chandler made me a Visit,

[1] Joseph and Benjamin Brigham—married Hannah and Lucy Hardy.

so did Mr. Grosvenor of Grafton, whom, to my Joy, I now hear, speak with much Audibleness and plainness. They dine with me. After dinner, I rode with Mr. Knight in his Chaise to Mr. Gale's, and preached there, on Eph. 5.2, those words " As Christ Also hath loved us, & hath given Himself for us." Had to my Grief, but a small Company, but it was chiefly occasioned by his aged Mother's long Confinement.

7. Breck goes to Boston rides with Mr. Gale. I wrote to Mrs. P— by my Son; and by him sent my Watch to Mr. Cranch to be mended.

In much perplexity about my Cattle which are missing; nor have they been seen ever since some time Yesterday; late in ye day they are brot home. Am reading The Sublime & Beautiful of Scripture. Mr. Jon^n Forbes at Eve. His Heart is Friendly toward me under my Suffering by ye depreciations.

8. Tho Things are Dark as to outer Circumstances, yet God is my Refuge. I would beg Grace to hope and trust in Him! Squire Baker came and invites me to the Raising of a Grist Mill[1] and a Saw Mill. I went. The Company was double, but all supped together at Mr. Rider's. No evil Occurrence befell anyone D. G. In ye latter part of ye Day came Mrs. P—— from Boston with various Tidings in her Mouth. First ye joyful y^t Sally was

9. Safely delivered, and had been favoured with a comparatively easy Travel, has a fine fat Dauter, and very like

---

[1] The mill which gave the name to the "Old Mill Road." It was the upper mill site on that road. It was built by Rider, who lived in the old house occupied until lately by Mr. John Johnson. The mill has long since disappeared.

to do well. The praise to God for all His Mercys!—But y'e sorrowful news is from y'e Harbour of Cape Anne, that Mrs. Forbes departed on Monday night last, in Child bed. She had been delivered of a Dead Child about two Hours before. A sad loss to my poor Son-in-law! The Lord sustain him! and pity y'e Motherless Children, for there are pritty many of them—hope they will all find Mercy!—I am informed y't Mr. W'm. Parkman, Grandson of my Brother, lives in y'e Antient Mansion.[1]

10

11. My son Samuel's Chaise being here, Breck rides with me to Northboro' I preached there on II. Cor: 5. 1 —a Building of God &c. P. M. on Col: 3. 1–2 " Sett your Affections &c" Mr. Whitney here on being saved by Hope.

N. B. The Congregation sung without Reading *lineally*. I baptized Mary, an infant of W'm. & — Brigham.

We each of us returned home at evening. Coll. Cushing has been here to raise Recruits here for y'e Army at New York.

[1] The "Antient Mansion" was on Battery Street, a large, square, wooden house, with the door in the middle. It remained in the possession of W'm. Parkman, and his son, grandson and great-grandson of the same name until about thirty years ago. Then it was sold, and made into a store. For more than a hundred years after the Rev. Ebenezer called it ancient, it stood as it did in his day—with the front door opening at the side on the yard, and the shingles growing blacker, but never putting on the modern fashion of paint. Only five years ago Battery Street was widened, and Mr. Parkman's early home and the home of his "honored mother" gave way to the spirit of improvement.

12. Visited Mr. Simeon Bellows, (who was prayed for yesterday,) being confined by various Disorders. I dind there, prayed with them. Visited at eight of ye houses of that Corner, as far as to Mr. Belknaps.

Mr. Elijah Brigham and Sophy rid in Sam's Chaise to Hopkinton, Visiting Dr. Stimson. They returned here at night.

13. Wrote to my son Ebenezer at Head Quarters, Morris Town New Jersie. Was at Deac. Woods. N. B. We discoursed of ye late Deac. Tainter's Legacy of fifty pounds[1] old tenor, to this Church.

14. I should have depended upon Mr. Grosvenor to preach for me today, but it was too foul weather. I preached myself on Ps: 63. 8 to page 5 and part of ye Additions at ye bottom continued for several Pages. By Desire of ye Deacons ye church Stopd: The Business was to Consider of Mr. B. Tainter's Note of Hand, by which he is bound, to

---

[1] Dea. Simon Tainter died in April of 1767, and left by will "unto the First Church of Christ in Westboro' aforesaid, of which I am a member, the sum of Six pounds, thirteen shillings and fourpence." I know of no other Dea. Tainter to whom Mr. Parkman could refer. His son Benjamin was unfortunate financially, selling the farm which his father had deeded to him, a little while before his death, for Continental money, which proved of little value. He went to Vermont, as Mr. Parkman records on the 20th, where he died in 1810.

He was taken prisoner by the Indians in 1746, and had many strange experiences among them. "In person he was tall, straight and robust and was rough with the Indians, who liked him the more for it—and during his captivity he became a great favorite with them."

pay ye Legacy his Father left. Deacon Bond put it to vote, whether they would do anything about that Note? It went negatively, for there was no Hand lifted up that I saw.

15. No certain news yet that Charlestown, South Carolina, is taken, but reasons to fear it is, are greatly increased. Sad accounts from ye West on Mohawk River. May it please God to extend Pity and Compassion to them, as their case may be & fit us in these parts, for His Sovereign Will! Finish reading Courtney Melmoth's Sublime and beautiful of Scripture.

16. Mr. Abr^m. Holland and Miss Crosby visit here. I purchase of him Lord Somers on Government entitled The Judgment of Kins and Nations concerning the Rights &c. of Kings and ye Rights &c. of ye People." I gave Mr. Holland for this eminent Book, Mr. Prince's Compendium Logical and 3 Pamphlets besides. Mrs. Snow and Mrs. (wife of W^m) Johnson. The former desires to be propounded for admission &c. Susé goes to her Father's with a view *to Wean her child*. Further Alarms—more men called for.

17. Capt. Fisher returns from Boston; informs y^t two thirds of ye people of this State appear to accept of ye Plan & Form of Government which ye Convention had drawn up & recommended: That ye Convention is Dissolved; and y^t some very important letters from Congress and from Gen'l Washington had arrived; & recommended most immediate & vigorous Exertions in raising *men and furnishing Provisions for ye Army.*

He also brings a Letter from Elias, who writes that as the Conclusion of all Collegiate Exercises was at 3 o'clock ye afternoon of ye 13th, and no public Performances to be on y^e

21th as was expected, by reason of ye immense Expense of necessarys there, so there is nothing to hinder his returning home on Monday next &c.

18. Read Ps: 63 preached on Ps: 63. 8. Administered ye Lord's Supper—Mrs. Maynard and Mrs. Davis dind here. P. M. on Ps: 133. 3.

19. Dr. Hawes rides down to Court designing (as I suppose) that Elias shall ride up from Cambridge on his Horse.

20. The Association was at my House, but we were only Three. Mr. Stone and Mr. Whitney. They would maintain Order and therefore had a Moderator, who prayed and gave an abstract of an Exercise on Ps. 133. N. B. While we were dining came in Elias from Cambridge. The reason of Mr. Smith's absence was his very low afflicted State of Body. Perhaps for the same reason his son Bridge, is absent. Mr. Newel Raises an House today, and Mr. Whitney makes Haste back to Northboro' to carry Nails for his. Mr. Saml Thurston here and was examined. Mr. Benj. Tainter & Sons. with their Wives & Children, Goods &c. move from Westboro' and try to go towards New Fane.

21. Took an Opportunity to reckon with Elias, as to his Expenses. I found there was so great Alteration of Times, Customs & Charges as was very astonishing — especially considering that no alteration was made by ye Constable, or ye Town as to what is paid to me.

Read ye Life of ye Celebrated Erasmus in Biogr. Dictionary. Reced a letter from my Son Forbes dated ye 6th containing an account of his Wife's Death. I undertook to write him an answer to it—Great Difficulty in raising Men for ye War. Twelve are called for, but 9 obtained; & yet (I hear) Orders are immediately for twelve more.

22. My wife and Susé ride to her Father's and to Capt. Jones's. They bring home little Hannah, who was been *Weaning*. I walked to visit several Neighbours,—was at Mr. Newton's, Parker's, Warrins, Isaac Parkers, (where I drank Tea) Davis's, old Mr. Pratt's. My Kinsman Lovering here from ye Hamlet, & lodged here.

23. N. B. have been in uncommon Surprise at Elias's wanting so large a Sum of Money as was called for to pay his Buttery Bill, which amounts to £321.6. I gave him 300 Dollars of my own, borrowed of Breck 620, and am obliged to send money for the Degree which must be 30 hard Money, which at 60 for one (as now ye Custom is) comes to 300 Dollars. These I receive of Breck, and offer him 5 Milled Dollars. So y^t I now give Elias 1220 Dollars, & he goes to Cambridge to clear off and finish there. Lovering goes on his journey to Westfield.

N. B. He gives strange account of several Praeternatural Births lately, & of ye Worms destroying ye Trees, in his Neighborhood.

24. My son Elias returned home from Cambridge, having now finished at College, taken up my Bond which I gave to Stewart Hastings, on Oct. 1. 1776.

25. Read Zech 12. Preached on Luke 16, last v. P. M. read Luke 17. repeated and preached on esp : X. 32. which may God graciously bless! By Request of Selectmen and commanding Officers, I warned the Company of Soldiers to meet tomorrow morning at 7 o'clock. Mr. Elijah Brigham and Mrs. Susan Snow propounded.

26. The Town met, and ye two Companys of Soldiers to raise men to go into the war — 15 to be compleated for six months, and there are orders for 14 for three months. Master Sam. Brigham and Winslow Maynard (son of ye late James Jr. deceased) dind here.

N. B. Mr. Gale takes account of ye Acres I own in Westboro' viz. ab't 66.

27. Sophy rides to Boston in her Brother Saml's Chaise. Josiah Brigham goes with her and carrys Susé Parkman to her Father's. N. B. Sent by Sophy a letter to Mr. Forbes, Gloucester. Another to Mr. Thos. Adams[1] at Medfield, also to Mr. Ripley, his Melmoth on Sublime and Beautiful of Script. Rev. Mr. Ebenezer Sparhawk of Templeton here, and dines with us. P. M. came Mrs. Sarah Thurston to be examined in order to her joining with ye Church. Mr. Josiah Bowker and his Wife, with Deac. Wood's Wife, make us a Visit, & drink Tea here.

28. The Companys meet again to raise Men. Mr. Thad. Warrin mows part of my Square — but is catched in ye Rain. Two of ye Selectmen, viz. Mr. Eb^r Maynard & Mr. Tim Warrin here, to inform me that they are going to call a Town Meeting, and they ask me whether I would have any Thing put in, relative to my Circumstances. I consented that they should. Master Sam Brigham lodges here.

[1] Mr. Thomas Adams was remarkable for his literary proclivities. He was the father of Hannah Adams the authoress, "the pioneer of feminine culture in America." He was born in 1725 and died in 1812. He kept a Diary of minute events from 1750 till his death, and altogether must have been a very congenial friend to Mr. Parkman.

29. I have ye Comfort to have my square Piece of Grass mowed and the mower, Mr. Warrin dind with us. But ye people are in trouble for they cant raise the men that are called for. Viz: 15 for Six months & 14 for three months. They meet again this afternoon. Old Mr. David Maynard & Deac. Wood here.

30. Josiah Brigham returns from Boston & Concord, with little Susé.

Thus we finish this month, but with very gloomy and doubtful Apprehensions concerning the Events of the Next. But may a good God Support us!

JULY 1780

The chief Conversation is about ye Men who are to be raised for Six Months, and those which are for three Months. P. M. Mr. Huntington Porter, a young Preacher, was here in his Way from Ward, where he has been preaching, to Hopkinton where he is expected to preach tomorrow.

2. Read Zech. 13. I delivered ye latter part of Sermon on Luke 17. 32 Mr. Elijah Brigham dind here. P. M. read Ps. 92 and preached on Luke 16 ult. At eve read part of Mr. Flavell's 4th Sermon on Rev: 3. 20.

3. Much hindered by both ye old and ye young Bees swarming. Went to Mr. Warren's to see his Wife, & request him to come and mow my Grass which is dying, but could not succeed.

Mr. Z. Hicks does not come for Sister Champney as she expected.

4. Notwithstanding it was very rainy, I went to Private Meeting at Mrs. Newton's and preached on Isa: 64. 9, occa-

sioned by these unhappy Times. I have writ to my Daughter Baldwin.

5. Breck is gone to Boston. I read Warburton's Notes, on Pope's Essay on Man. Mr. Thos. Kendal who has been Preaching at Kittery, is returning there again; but tarrys today, while he is here Mr. Sam Brigham commissioned to be a Lieutenant to those that are ye Militia, and for three months, Desires prayers & a Sermon. in behalf of not only himself. but others that go with him. Old Mr. Danl Hardy, who went to Brookfield yesterday A. M. returns from there today about three P. M. By him came news not only from My Dauter Baldwin, but that she has had Letters of June 15 from her Husband & Br. Eb^r.

Mr. Zech. Hicks came for his aunt Champney,—lodged here.

6. Sister Lydia Champney removes from hence to Sutton, both herself and her Goods,—by ye Assistance of Mr. Zech. Hicks, tho this parting from us is with no small Regret.

At eve I was miserably dull & unfit for any Thing. The little Sleep and Multitude of heavy Cares & Trouble have made me very soggy and incapable of laudable Exertion.

7. But this morning am (thro God's Goodness) in tolerable Plight—had an Opportunity to discourse with Ensign James Miller, who being commonly an Opposer of ye Town's Adding to my Salery, I enquired of him the Reasons, & endeavored to obviate them.

A. M. Breck returned from Boston. P. M. Ensign Snow & Wife. She brot her Relation.

8. Four Men came kindly to give a Morning Jobb, & cut

down ye English & Clover Grass in my West Field. They were Messrs. Thad. Warrin, Paul Lamson, Jon^n Pierce & Eb^r Force. They worked till nine o'clock A. M. Mr. Brigham brot home Cloth from Clothier Woods, Northboro.

9. Read Zech. 14. Preach A. M. on Gal: 6. 7-8. Mr. Bridge of Worcester, Mr. Jon^n Fay, and Lieut. Sam Brigham din'd here. P. M. preached on Deut.—— and addressed ye Soldiers who sat by themselves. Mr. Brigham and Mrs. Snow were admitted into ye Church. So was her Husband, who removed from Southboro'.

At eve in ye Family read Flavell on Rev. 3. 20.

10. Town Meet Early to compleat ye Number of Soldiers, but they are so unhappy that they cannot do it.

Mr. Jon^n Pierce and Isaac Ruggles came to work for me. Elias had spoke to them. They finished ye Mowing of ye West Field, & P. M. went to the Island. Ruggles lodges here.

11. The foresaid Men work here and Mr. Pierce all day at ye Interval. Mrs. P—— rode over to Capt. Wood's to Enquire into ye Cause of spoiling a piece of black Cloth. She had no Recompense. Mr. Sam Thurston here about his joining to ye Church.

12. P. M. Came Mrs. Thurston and her Mother Harrington with her to assist her in her Examination.

N. B. Mr. Brigham sat out for Boston and going thro Marlboro. I sent Mrs. Speakman's Pope's Essay on Man. A Piece well worth Reading—At eve I visit Capt. John Wood's Wife being in deep Grief for ye Loss of their Babe. The mowers here yet. But Elias towards night gives up is sick and goes to bed.

13. Elias lies by wholly: but y[e] hired Men attend to my Work, mowing Raking and Carting—they bring home one Load of Hay.

14. Elias is better, and though feeble he Carts Hay. 3 Loads.

Mr. Brigham returns with Sophy, from Boston, late at night.

15. Mr. Pierce does not come to work, but Ruggles comes for the forenoon only. Two load more from the Interval.

At ev'g came Mr. Daniel Adams with a Paper which is addressed to y[e] Church, he complains of hard Usage: & is in some warmth with me. I told him I could not lay it before y[e] Church tomorrow, because there were various things to be done &c.

16. Read Malachi, Chap. I. & forenoon Exercise was upon y[e] beginning of it. N. B. *Mr. Brigham and Sophy were published*. Capt. Fisher, with leave, read to y[e] Congregation, after y[e] Blessing, his very urgent Orders for raising Soldiers. Mrs. Maynard dind.

P. M. I preached on Gal VI. 7-8. On account of y[e] Harvest. At evening I read further Mr. Flavell on Rev. 3. 20.

17. The Militia Soldiers 14. under Lieut. Brigham marched.

Mr. Corn. Biglow came to reap my Island Field of Rye. I had conference with Mr. Han. Parker. Elias does not work, but waits upon Miss Lois Burnet, who is here at work on his Coat which is made of y[e] Cloth which Mr. Wood of Northboro had dyed black & fulled. lately for us.

Town Meet, partly to see whether they will do anything

in regard to my Salary. I sent them a Paper, which was read I hear that they voted thirteen Hundred to make up the Deficiency of ye last year. I thank God for thus much. May I have grace to improve it!

18. Am sadly disappointed of ye Work which I hoped for. Elias, being not well, can do nothing; tho everything is pressing and urgent: only he went up the street to speak to Mr. Joseph Smith, who had told me once and again that he would work for me: but is now engaged to Deac. Wood, & Elias fetched me ye Paper (which the Col. as Town Clerk has) which I sent ye Town yesterday—and he copy'd it.

19. Many Interruptions and Avocations from my Studys, so that I can but imperfectly prepare for ye Solemnity approaching, but would humbly commit myself, my Way, my Work to God.

Elias has been so out of health, that he has not been able for Several days to work. But today he went a while to ye Interval & there being part of a Load of Hay in Cock there, he mowes 3 or 4 Cocks, and with my Team he brot it home: and P. M. he went to ye Island, where Mr. Biglow is reaping, and (Mr. Biglow pitching it) Elias brot home a Load of Rye of 12 Shock and 1 Sheaf. N. B. Miss Lois Burnet at work here and part of P. M. her Kinswoman Henrietta with her. Miss Patty Fisk here and dines with us. We are under ye Holy Frowns of Heaven, by parching Heat and Dryness. May the God of infinite Pity and Mercy send Relief to us!

20. *A Day of Humiliation, FASTING and Prayer*, on account of the uncommon Distress. Preached A. M. on 1. Kings 20.28 last clause and tho I wrote much, and was long

in ye Exercise, yet could not be so particular in Application as I designed, & very much desired. P. M. I delivered some parts of Discourse on Eccl. 8. 11 and added Applications, Reproofs, Exhortations & Cautions. When we returned, found my Grandson Isaac Baldwin from Cambridge here, going home. He lodged here with us.

21. Was forced to go out and look up Workmen. Capt. Fisher is gone to mowe for me at *Middle Meadow*, (or my Interval). Mr. Biglow again reaps, & Elias part of ye forenoon. P. M. goes to ye Interval, to look after ye Hay there. When he returns he goes up to ye Flock of Sheep. N. B. A Fire prevailed a while in ye Hill Nigh Wood's Field, but did not much Dammage, tho a dry Time and somewhat Windy.

Mrs. Hannah (wife of Mr. Thomas) Andrews here & passes Examination freely, as to knowledge and hopeful Experience. D. G.

Paul Biglow comes with Joshua Twitchell & Fortunatus Miller.[1] The two latter being Deserters: to see Gen'l Washington's Proclamation of Pardon to such: And P. Biglow would for a large Reward, go in Miller's stead.

22. Three men are mowing at ye Interval, viz: Capt. Fisher, Mr. Elijah Force (who goes for Mr. Joseph Smith, & he is instead of Mr. Isaac Parker, who will work for Smith instead of it.) Mr. Thad. Warrin also works A. M, but no longer. Elias brings home a Load of Hay at noon. At Night another, but too late.

[1] Fortunatus Miller, about a year after this, married Ebenezer Forbush's daughter Patty.

23. Read part of II. Chron. 6 & preached on 6 to 31. on Consideration of ye uncommon Dryness of ye Weather. P. M. on Gal. 6. 8 former part. N. B. The Church was stayed and I read Mr. Adams' Paper dated July 21. 1780 & signed Daniel Adams. The consideration of it was deferred to ye Adjournment of ye Church Meeting, which is to ye last Monday in August next (God willing.)

N. B. Mr. Brigham & Sophy were published ye last Time. At eve Read part of Mr. Flavell's 5th Sermon on Rev. 3. 20.

24. Mr. Biglow comes again to reap. Capt. Fisher works at the Interval partly for me, helping Elias in getting the Hay there ready, and Elias brings home one Load,—having Deac. Wood's Oxen added to our Team: & Elias carrys one Load of ye Interval Hay to Capt. Fisher, and at eve he fetches home one Load of Rye.

Miss Lois Burnet and her Kinswoman (Henrietta) at work here again on making Cloths for Elias.

25. Mr. Bigelow reaps. Elias with our own Team only, brings home two Load from ye Interval. Capt. F. helps him somewhat (but his chief work was at Lieut. Bond's). Miss Lois and Henrietta finish for ye present.

26. Elias went with our Team, and Breck went with him to load and tho it was but a small Jagg, it was ye last from ye Interval. In all thirteen times, ye Team has gone for me, & once for Capt. Fisher. P. M. Elias goes to reaping, for Mr. Biglow reaps but slowly. Mr. Beriah Ware[1] here, and

---

[1] Beriah Ware's name appears only once in the History of Westborough—as living in 1789 in the Sixth School Squadron, the same one to which Capt. Maynard belonged. Who he was or what he did,

was in great, singular and distressful trouble, but not so much upon spiritual as temporal accounts. Remarkable uneasiness by reason of a Disappointment &c. &c. This was y ͤ more noticeable as y ͤ Man is well towards 40 years of age.

27. My Affairs are in a very uncomfortable situation. Mr. Biglow reaps, is too old and feeble to do much—there is a great part of y ͤ Field of Rye yet remaining. No body offers to assist, though divers talked of it. The late Grant of the Town was *for my present Necessity* but y ͤ Money cant be raised and paid & a Man or Men provided till y ͤ Grain & Grass are lost. The Newton Meadow is untouched & no help provided. In this critical Juncture, Elias would fain break off from work and rest himself, intending tomorrow to go to Brookfield and then to Springfield: tho there is no man that can by any means possibly be obtained: When Mr. Biglow finishes y ͤ Reaping, there can be nobody to cart it home. Elias reaped part of y ͤ Day. I walked up to Mr. Warrin's & acquainted him with my present State. He sent his son John. I went to Mr. Kenney, who sent his son Joel —those Boys reaped P. M. Capt. Morse came in to see me. No Hope from him of any Help. Capt. Fisher agrees to go & cut my new Swamp, & he is to allow me as he finds is just. The Drought is become very intense. The Corn suffers very much, & all Vegetables. An holy Frown of God ! May we be suitably affected with it, & prepared for y ͤ Divine Will! Elias carted home about 11 Shock of Rye at evening.

we know not, only that four years later his distressed heart found peace, and he and Hannah Hardy " were Joyned in Marriage " by James Hawes. He lived in Westborough until his death, in 1832.

28. Mr. Bigelow reaps A. M. Elias also. — Breck took a morn-spell at it. Deac. Wood has ye Oxen part of A. M. Breck has them P. M. He sends them down to meet a Teemer, who is bringing up a Load from Boston. P. M. About a quarter after two o'clock, God was pleased to remember us in Mercy and sent Rain, together with Thunder and Lightning. To His Name be Glory! Mr. Biglow went home about 4 P. M, & Elias to reaping again.

At eve heard that Mr. Abra^m Bond's Barn was burnt by ye Lightning.

29. Went in ye Morning to see ye sorrowful Desolations, & sympathise with ye Sufferers May ye Lord sanctifie ye sad Loss to y^m!

Elias goes again to Squire Baker's Pasture to look for ye Lamb which he sought for before, but returns empty.

30. I preached on I. Cor: 11–29. Administered. ye Lord's Supper: before which Saml Thurston and Sarah his wife were admitted into ye Church. Mrs. Maynard and Mr. Hazletine dind here. P. M. on Gal: 6.8. At eve read (Breck, his wife &c. attending with us as usual) another part of Mr. Flavell on Rev: 3.20. May God graciously accept!

31. *My son Elias left us to go to Springfield*, to keep School there. Carrys principal Classicks, expecting to teach Grammer.

I wrote a letter to Brother Breck. It is an article which much Affects me. May God Almighty bless him, & make him a Blessing! Delivered him 170 Dollars.

August 1780.

A Message by Mr. Elijah Brigham from Mr. Sumner, to preach his Lecture—borrowed Mr. Ware's Mare to ride there,—made several short Visits in ye Street—dind at Squire Baker's, but he came not home as was expected. N. B. The Private Meeting was, according to Custom, to have been at his House today, but it was put off because of ye Busyness of ye Season, & few Hands to do it.

2. Rode to Shrewsbury. Mr. Fairbank came here and was my Company to Mr. Sumner's: where I dind. Preached his Lecture to an extremely thin Auditory. Text Rev: 14, 6-7. After Lecture came Mr. Whitney to Mr. Sumner's House. N. B. Col. Symmes' Widow there also. At eve arose a Thunder Storm. I lodged at Dr. Crosby's.

3. In returning called to see Mr. Joseph Knowlton's Wife, who relapses somewhat to her old state; visit Mr. Gershom Brigham's Wife, who languishes. I went in to Mr. Saml Fay's, his wife having been lately much indisposed — but he treated me with *roughness*. At Deac. Wood's I saw one Mrs. Abigail Giles, Dauter of Mr. W^m. Jenison, that was of Salem, & widow of Mr. Sam'l Giles., greatly reduced & lame. P. M. Mrs. Hawes, Squire's Dauter, Polly Wood at Tea.

N. B. In Biog'r. Dict. Variety in Human Life.—Eginhard's Wife, (Dauter of Charles the Great) carry'd him on her Back from her Apartment thro ye Snow, y^t the prents of his Feet might not be discovered; yet her Father saw them from his Window. Queen Elizabeth's Life notable for her Wit and Learning, affected Grandeur & power, Magnificent

Dress, Entertainment, Amours,—but a secret reason is given by Mezeray why she would not Marry. — Equatius (John-Baptist). This great Man had almost a divine Memory: whatever he had read or heard, he could relate by Heart, & in a very agreeable manner. He was born at Venice 1473.

4. Have writ to Mr. Quincy and to Mr. Moore, and committ ye Letters to Mr. Elijah Brigham, who is going to Boston.

5. I was much interrupted by being obliged to go to the Island to mend Fence, that the Cows might not break in upon Mr. Andrews. Mr. Abr^m. Bond was here with his Petition for a Contribution. Mrs. Fay (Mr. John Fay's Wife) came to be examined, but I could spend but a little Time with her.

6. I had partly prepared on Malachi First, but was obliged to lay it aside, and went on considering ye Harvest Season, with my Repetitions, with additions and alterations of Sermon on Gal. 6. 7-8. A & P. M. and finished ye Subject. May God be pleased to add his special Blessing! I read Bond's Petition for Contribution. Mrs. Maynard dind here. At eve read in Mr. Flavell on Rev: 3.20

7. Was anxious about Breck's Horse, which Elias rode to Springfield, and is not come back: but before noon came young Joshua Johnson of Bolton, who returning from his 3 years Warfare rode Horse from Springfield hither, thereby saving Charge, and brot a Letter from Elias, who has taken ye School there, for a year upon settled pay to his Satisfaction. Thanks be to God for ye Favour.

8. Mr. Saml Crosby (young preacher) dind here.

P. M.   Mrs. Giles spent y⁶ P. M. here & drank Tea with us.

At eve, Eben⁷ Chamberlain jun⁷ full of earnest Conversation about Sallery.

9. Extracts from Biog'r. Dict^ry.

10. Messrs. Motlay, Ezek Savage, preachers, and one Mr. Pearson of Newbury, made me a Visit, dind &c.

11. Mrs. Mehitable Fay (wife of John) here with her Relation, which I corrected and copy'd. *Josiah Brigham came to Breck* again to live with him. They clear y⁶ lower Well.

12. Mr. John Fay was examined—left a Relation to be corrected & transcribed. He dines here.

13. Preached on Malachi: Ch. I. V 6-9. P. M. previous to a Contribution for Mr. Abr^m. Bond,[1] I preached again on John, 4.10. At eve read Flavell on Rev. 3.20. Serm. 6.

14. Rode over to Mr. Beeton's to visit old Mrs. Kelly and prayed with her, of which she said she missed but little. Her Conversation generally sp^l. and savoury. John Beeton's Wife is greatly recovered from her Lameness.

15. Tho it was a very hot Day, I rode to Southboro, hoping to meet ye other Brethren who would associate there —but no other Members came. We nevertheless improved ye Opportunity in Prayer & attendance on a Discourse Mr. Stone read on Gal, and I read an Extract from Cicero on Old Age. Ch: XIX.

[1] "A contribution for Mr. Abraham Bond, when were gathered 593¼ Dollars, and thirteen notes of Grain, Labour and other things necessary and usefull. His Barn was burned by Lightning Friday July 28th last."—*Church Records*.

Mr. Stone has lately been exercised with the Gravel, and particularly last Lord's Day. P. M. did not go to Meeting, but is somewhat better.

I returned at eve. Mr. Elijah here *de die in diem*. His Brother Josiah is gone to Medway in order to Miss Eliz. Beal's Return to Westboro' again.

16. Benj. Wood and his Brother John came here to be set to work. I employed Benj. in mowing in my Newton Meadow. John hoed a little with Billy Spring in Beeton Field—It was but of trifling Value.

P. M. Ben mowed a while, and ye lesser Boy reaped and cocked—but they were all beat off by Rain, Thunder & Lightening.

17. Sent by Breck to Mr. Stone's for Notes y^t I inadvertently left there. Breck goes before Day, designing for Boston.

18. Mrs. P. out of Health. Dr. Hawes to see her.

19. Breck returned from Boston—he brot me a large letter from Mr. Quincy, who since ye Death of his Son Henry is moved to Boston, and for ye present lives with his Dauter-in-law, who (with her children) dwells in William's Court.[1] This Week was filled with Encumbrance.

20. Read A. M. ye Latter part of Joh. 4, and repeated ye latter part of Discourse on V. 16. At noon, Breck and his Family, Mr. Brigham and his Sister Anna, Mrs. Maynard, Isaac and Luke Baldwin (who came from Shrewsbury this

[1] Williams Court still appears on the maps of Boston under the same name, although familiarly known as Pie Alley. It is not the place that the Quincys would now select for their home. It is usually crowded with hungry newsboys, seeking a five-cent dinner, with an

morn) dind with us. P. M. did not read before it but preached on Isa: 55. 10-11 p. 191 to ye bot. of p 202. N. B. baptized Six Children of Mr. Sam'l Thurston. At eve read in my Family part of Mr. Flavell's sixth Sermon on Rev: 3. 20. Rec'd a Letter from Mr. Forbes of Gloucester. Mrs. P. is so indisposed that she has been but little at Meeting for a great while: could not go today: is sick, faint, and weak. The Child also has been not well, for some days.

21. My young Baldwins take leave for Cambridge & Byfield.

22. A very dry hot Season. After a great deal of Pains and Trouble, Benj. Woods, who tho but a Youth, works well and with ye Help of Josiah Brigham, a few Hours, they get in ye last of my Newton Meadow Hay. I have been employed in making Extracts from the Biog'r. Dict.

23. I am too much taken up with my Farm Affairs, particularly to have my Fences repaired, that my Cattle may have Feed, and cant attend much to my Studys. Mr. John Fay and Mr. Thad Warrin are employed.

24. Mrs. Nabby Martyn is at work here for Susé. I attended ye Burial of Mr. Abijah Gale's Child, Sarah, of more than four months, it dyed somewhat suddenly. I called to see Mr. Eben^r Forbes, who (and his Wife) had

occasional hungry lawyer hurrying through their midst for a more expensive lunch at Young's.

It is entered now, as in Mr. Quincy's day, under an archway on Washington Street, between School and Court streets.

In the first quarter of this century a residence in Williams Court was considered much more aristocratic than on Beacon Street, which was too far out in the country.

been sick. Visit also ye old Folks. Mr. John Fay, with his Relation here, and signs it.

25. Mrs. Persis Adams here and prays ye Church Meeting (to be otherwise next Monday) may be adjourned to some future time, inasmuch as she cannot get ready.

N. B. Breck & Susé with little Hannah go to Col. Brigham's, at eve, to lodge there, in their way to Ashburnham & Marlboro'.

26. Breck and Susé, leaving their little Girl, at Northboro' proceed on their Journey. Mr. Daniel Adams came here to enquire whether any Complaint against him, was lodged here. There was none.

27. Read Ps. 104. preached on Mal. 1. 9. 10. 11. and P. M. on Isa. 55. V. 11 "So shall my Word be" &c. Three persons taken into ye Church. The Church Meeting was adjourned. At eve, I read further in Mr. Flavells, England's Duty on Rev. 3. 20.

28. On Deac. Wood's Horse I rode to Mr. Gershom Brigham's to see his Wife, who is dangerously ill. The State of her Soul deplorable as well as her Body. She was very sorry y^t she had neglected ye Lord's Supper. She was in much Confusion. I prayed with her and ye Family. I dind there. Thence went to visit ye North West Corner of ye Town, Messrs. Gleason's, John Maynard's, & Saml Riders, Mr. Thomas Lamson's (on Edmund Rice's place) old Mr. James Maynard, & his son Amasa's.

29. An uncommonly burning Season, hot Sun & drying Winds—so y^t ye Droughth is much increased.

30. Exceedingly taken up with ye Creatures breaches for

want of Feed—especially my Oxen—Mr. Belknap and his wife here.

P. M. Mr. David Andrews of Northboro' here to request me to visit his little son extremely bad (Mr. Whitney being gone to Northboro') I went, prayed &c —

31. Mr. Gershom Brigham brings his Wife's Earnest Desire y^t I would visit her again & preach a Sermon there today. I complyed—delivered a short Discourse (as I could) from several passages in Isa. 55. "hear and your Soul shall live." May God bless what was delivered! Mrs. Br. is brot very low. At eve found Sophy ill. She has taken physick: Mr. Elijah Brigham with her.

September 1780

Breck and Susè return home having been to visit their Brothers Cushing, Levi Brigham & Alexander.

Capt. Goddard of Sutton calls at Breck's Shop & relates, That ye Scholars at College (from whence he was come) had so generally signed a petition y^t. Pres. Langdon might be dismissed, that he himself had asked a Dismission and that it was granted him. Whence this has arisen, I know not.

2. Sophy has been poorly several days.

3. Read P's. 105. preached on Isa: 55. 12. Mrs. Maynard dind here. P. M. preached on Exodus 18.21 on Consideration of ye Election of ye Morrow: and therefore added a new introduction and application, to what I heretofore prepared on that text. But it being rainy there were but few to hear it. At eve, Mr. Flavell on Rev. 3. 20. Breck read. Mr. Brigham here

4. Deacon Wood in no small Trouble on account of his

Wife's Difference with his son John and his Wife, who have had grievous Contentions and Threatening to complain to ye Grand Jury tomorrow.

P. M. Y^e Grand Meeting of ye Town to choose a Governor, Lt. Governor, & Senators; Mr. Batherick & Lieut. Grout came with a Message from ye Town to desire me to go and open ye Meeting with *Prayer*—went and prayed— the Chairman of ye Selectmen prevented my going out by asking me to tarry and sit with ym. The hon. Mr. John Hancock was elected Governor by sixty-one votes. There was one vote only besides, which was (mine) for Mr. James Bowdoin.[1] Votes for Lieut. Governor were for Hon. James Warrin, out of 55, 50. I voted for Mr. Bowdoin The meeting was adjourned to Wednesday, 4 P M.

5. By Deac. Wood's Desire, I went in ye Morning to his House, with Capt. Joseph Wood of Hopkinton & Mr. Thos. Wood of Brookfield. Deacon's Wife asked me to go alone with her, and manifested a penitent Frame: desired me to go into her son's Room, and talk with him and his Wife, which I did. then met together and through ye Goodness of God, we brot each of ye Partys to Condescentions, mutual acknowledgment, and asking forgiveness & promises

---

[1] Hancock was the son-in-law of Mr. Parkman's old friend, Mr. Quincy. James Bowdoin had been very forward during the Revolutionary disturbances in opposition to the royal governor, he had been president in 1775 of the council of Government and also president of the convention assembled for the formation of a constitution. He succeeded Hancock as governor of Massachusetts. Bowdoin College was named for him, by his son who gave lavishly to it. It was not founded until after James Bowdoin's death, who left a legacy to Harvard College.

of Reformation. The Deacon desired me to pray and give thanks to God. Whereupon we all parted in Peace and Joy. Glory be to God alone! Josiah Brigham goes to Boston.

Mr. Gleason came and informed y^t Mr. Gershom Brigham's Wife dyed this morning; and ye Survivors desire me to attend ye Funeral next Thursday.

6. Mr. Grosvenor came, dind and preached. Text was Gal: 6,7, latter clause. His voice not only audible, but sonorous, but especially ye Matter good, and ye Manner agreeable. After Meeting ye Church stopped to receive the Answer of ye two elected Deacons. The Doctor delivered a paper in which he acquiesced in ye Choice if there was no Objection, & if ye Choice was unanimous; otherwise he refused. The vote was then tried (though ye members present were but few) upon which there was every Hand, and he was declared a Deacon of this Church. Mr. Child's answer was verbal, and still refused and ye Meeting ended.

Then came on ye Town Meeting by adjournment, and they elected five Counsellors for this County.

My son Alexander and his Wife and young Child came & lodged here. Mr. Elijah Brigham privately spoke to me of his joining in Trade with Breck & would be glad to live here this winter. But I could not determine.

7. I rode one of Alexander's Horses to ye Funeral of Mrs. Brigham (wife of Mr. Gershom) & prayed there. When I returned, here was Mr. W^m. Spring from Brimfield. He brot a suit of Clothes for his son Billy. He dind with us, as did Mr. Elijah Brigham (who keeps Shop for Breck). Sister Cushing and Mr. Daniel Goddard's wife dind here also, but

she rode to Col. Brigham's and lodged there; ye rest here.

8. Mr. Spring changes his volume of Royal Magazines, viz: Some parts of Vol. I and Vol. II. bound together, but many numbers missing for Osterval's Causes of ye present Corruption.

Mrs. Cushing, Alix and his Wife, dine with us, but P. M. they all leave us, & Billy Spring goes home for a while with his Father.

9. My Circumstances are somewhat singular—the Difficultys thence arising, not a few. I made some preparations, but did not near perfect them—and I have entered upon such Repetitions as I think I had best go on with—correcting and amending as I review them.

10. It being Sacrament Day, I (after reading Ps. 106 former part to verse 25) went on with my Discourse on 1. Cor: 11. 27-29 first part. I administered ye Ordinance—the new Deacon Hawes officiating, without any special Ceremony as to his Induction. N. B. Deacon Dolliber of Marblehead, Mrs. Barrett & Mr. Stephen Stimson of Hopkinton were present. Mr. Barrett and his Wife dind here. P. M. preached on Isa: 55. 12 to ye End of page 225.

At eve read part of Mr. Flavell's seventh Sermon on Rev: 3. 20.

11. This Day begins ye 44th year since my Marriage with Mrs. P——. May God be praised for His great Goodness! May all our Sins throughout all these Years, espepecially ye last, be freely forgiven! May we both of us be sp'ly Espoused, & mystically united to Jesus Christ, and

may God grant us Grace to discharge y⁶ Dutys incumbent on us in the Conjugal Connexion!—

I dind at Mr. Graves's with Deacon Dolliber, Alexander and his Wife, with their Child, from Framingham and lodge here. [Note in pencil. Married Sept. 11. 1737, he being 34 years old, minus 5 days—see next page.]

12. Sent a Letter to Mr. Buckminster of Medway by Sq⁽ʳ⁾ Singleterry[1] of Sutton. My son Alex. wife and child P. M. undertake their Journey home. Messrs. Elijah and Moses Brigham dind here. P. M. Mr. Sumner came to see us,

13. Rode to Mr. Abr⁽ᵐ⁾. Bond's: gave him a book, as my Contribution to him under y⁶ Frown of Heaven. N. B. A number of Neighbors are at work in framing a Barn for him.

I visited other Neighbours thereabout, and dind at Mr. Frost's. P. M. at Mr. Hananiah Parker's.

[1] Squire Singleterry, from whom the pond in Sutton derived its name, was the first male child born in Sutton. He never attended school, but through his own persistent improvement of every opportunity which came to him, he became one of Sutton's most prominent men, and served for many years in the Legislature, besides holding other important offices. An anecdote is related of him which shows his character, by Rev. Geo. Allen, of Worcester, who knew him well. "During a season of revival in the north parish, Mr. Samuel Waters, a manufacturer of hoes in what is now Millbury, being under concern of mind, and seeing Mr. Singleterry approaching, rushed out of his shop and called out, 'O Squire! O Squire! What shall I do to be saved?' The Squire scarcely stopped the horse he was riding as he replied, 'Put more steel in your hoes!'"

14. With some difficulty as to an Horse I rode to Grafton and dind at Mr. Grosvenor's, and preached his Lecture in his House on Mat: 17.4. May God grant His Blessing! I returned home safe at eve. N. B. A. Mellancholy story is current of Gen[l] Gates being defeated in y[e] South. The particulars are not yet known. N. B. One Sibly is sent to Jayl at Worcester under Suspicion of Murthering an Infant.

15. On Consideration of my finishing my seventy-seventh year, I was much employed in Retrospections, Humiliations, and Supplications. May y[e] Lord graciously accept of my imperfect Petitions, pardoning &c. thro' Jesus Christ. Mr. Peter Whitney here and Mr. Daniel Adams jun[rs] Wife also is examined.

16. This Day I begin my 78th year. Thanks be to God, who hath sustained me! I still continue a Monument of his sparing Mercy and Goodness. To His Name be all Praise and Glory! See Natilitia[1]—Mrs. P being very much out of Health rode to Dr. Crosby's At eve came my Dauter Cushing from Ashburnham. Mr. Fitch, wife and Dauter from Connecticut, & P. M. Mrs. Dolly Rice.

[1] "1780

Sept. 5. O. S. Westb.
pro Natalitiias.
I have passed such a year as I never saw before. The aspects in Divine Providence have been very changing. Several times exceeding gloomy, particularly on account of the Successes of the british Forces especially in taking Charlestown in South Caroline and y[e] Ravages of y[e] Salvages in y[e] Western and Northwestern Parts. Besides which this year has been very remarkable with me and my Family on y[e] Acct. of Labour on My Grounds, inasmuch

17. Read Ps. 23 & 24, and on Consideration of my beginning a new year of my Life, I preached on Ps. 23.6, and P. M. on Isa: 55.12 and may yᵉ great End and Design hereof be answered.

At eve read again in Mr. Flavell- Neither my Wife nor Dauter Cushing were well enough to go to Meeting, either part of yᵉ Day.

18. Wrote to Dr. Crosby, by his son John. My Wife being no better. At eve came my son Forbes, but from Dedham, where he had preached yesterday—.brot with one of his Sons-in-law, Joseph Saunders, about 8 years old. They lodge.

19. Mr. Forbes and little Boy left us to go to Brookfield. Dr. Crosby here to see Mrs. P——. P. M. She grows very

as not hiring a man to work statedly for me, I was forced to forego many Benefits, from yᵉ Produce of my Land, and was obliged to run into Debt for yᵉ unavoidable Work done. But God has upheld and preserved me and mine nevertheless unto this Day. For which I would heartily praise and bless His glorious Name;, and desire still to commit Myself and Mine to Him for Subsistence, Protection and Supplys. But in peculiar implore divine Grace to furnish me for Christian and ministerial Duty and assist me in yᵉ right discharge of it.

Will God be graciously pleased to remember my dear son Ebenezer under all yᵉ Hardships and Tryals of his Warfare; and provide for his Family in his Absence! Make him useful in his place at Fish Kill and grant him in due time a Safe Return!—

May God mercifully regard yᵉ severall states and conditions of yᵉ rest of my Children particularly Alexander at his distance and under his difficulties; and Elias in his Youth and Setting-out in the world yᵗ God might be his Guardian & quicken him to yᵉ due improvement of his Time and Talents!"

sick, but it may be owing to some Pills which ye Doctor gave her. At eve, she continues ill and goes to bed.

Mr. Cushing comes from ye Cape, having been to see his Sister Stone at Yarmouth, & came back thro Rochester, Wrentham, & Sherbourn.

20. Mr. Cushing last evening brot me from Mr. Moore, Shuckford's Condition vol. 1. He also, having been with various Gentlemen in his Journey, discovers to me some of ye probable Reasons of ye Dismission of Pres Langdon.

Mrs. P. somewhat better—Thanks to God for ye Favour of Heaven to us! P. M. Mrs. Fisk of Brookfield & her son (who belongs to College) dind here. My son W^m. his Wife and Child John, came up from Concord unexpectedly. Afterwards my Son Sam[1] and his Wife with their Baby, Sukey, came from Boston. They all lodged here.

N. B. Mr. Brigham asked me whether it would suit me to have the Marriage of my Dauter to him to be tomorrow? I asked him, where he intended to live? he replyed "Here, if I should like it." I answered that I was willing to do what was in my Power for him. Sent my Complements to his Father and Mother, & Request they would come—likewise his Brothers and Sisters. He acquainted me with his Desire to wait on Squire Baker and his Lady with his Invitations to ye Wedding, also ye two eldest Dauters. To which I consented. My Dauter Cushing rode to Capt. Maynard's to invite him and his Wife. The Return was that Mrs. Maynard was confined with illness.

21. Mrs. P. I hope is better. Sophy has unhappily a good deal of a cough. I had a most agreeable sight of my children & their Consorts at Dinner, viz: W^m and Lydia,

Mr. Cushing and Sarah, Breck and Suse, Sam¹ and Sally, & Mr. Brigham with Sophy. To God be Praise and Glory!

ELIJAH BRIGHAM.

Towards evening according to Invitation, Joseph Baker Esq. and Lady, Mr. Winslow Brigham and Miss Alice Cushing of Shrewsbury, Mr. Hazzletine and Miss Mindwell Brigham, Master Fisk and Miss Anna Brigham, and Mr. Josiah Brigham came to wait on yᵉ Solemnity of the Marriage of Mr. Elijah Brigham to my Dauter Anna Sophia, which was performed, and after ye Covenant, Mr. Cushing prayed. Mrs. P. was not able to attend with us.

N. B. I began to write Mr. Quincy.

22. My son W^m. and his Wife sat out early for Concord. Mr. Cushing and his Wife when ye Day got up, for Shrewsbury.

Dr. Crosby to see Mrs. P. P. M. Sam and Breck with their Wives wait on ye Bridegroom and Bride, to Coll. Brighams.

Mrs. P. has had a poor Day. At eve came Mr. Forbes and his little Boy, Jo Saunders.

Mr. F. delivers me a letter from Col. Baldwin to his wife, containing an account of General Gates's Defeat. An extract from it I send to Mr. Quincy

Mr. Forbes goes to see his Sister, ye Widow of his Brother Daniel. N. B. My Flax is spread—a large piece.

23. My son Saml and his Wife & Child left us. Sent my Letter by him to Mr. Quincy. Mr. Forbes came and I delivered him his first volume of Robinson's Hist. of Scotland. He and his Joseph Saunders left us to go to Concord.

At eve came Mr. Grosvenor, requesting & expecting I would preach for him tomorrow, But I had engaged to preach at Northboro. He lodged here.

N. B. Mrs. Persis Adams was here to acquaint me that she could not be ready for ye Church Meeting next tuesday & prays it may be further adjourned to ye 2^d Thursday in November.

24. Mr. Grosvenor to Northboro'. I rode to Grafton and preached on 1 Chron. 29. 15. A & P. M. Returned home at eve. Mr. Whitney preached here on Roms. 3. 7. 8.

A & P. M. At Dinner were Doct. Crosby, & Mrs. Maynard. N. B. Mr. Whitney read to ye Church a paper from me acquainting ye Brethern with Mrs. Adams' Request: and there was no Objection, so that ye Meeting of ye Church was adjourned to ye time she desired.

25. Breck is roused by an Information that one Williams who is Debtor to him in a considerable sum is seized and put into Jail. My son is gone to his House in N. Shrewsbury.

I read Shuckford's Connection Vol. 1. But I am sorry to see my Husbandry fast asleep, no body at work for me, though my apples are rotting and wasting, and Flax seed on stry,(?) unwinnowed on ye Barn Floor.

Mr. Dan'l Adams, Ben. Tainter, Levi Warrin complain of ye adjournment: came here, but nothing could be done. Mrs. P. something more comfortable. D. Gratis!

26. Am obliged to go frequently to Mr. Thad. Warrin's for Help, and today in particular, he left his own Business and came to mine.

27. I obtained of My Neighbor Newton to send his Boys, John and Stephen to pick Apples and carry a Load, with Barrells to make Cyder at Mr. Frost's Mill.

P M. Mr. Zebulon Rice and his Wife of Brookfield came to see us: and drank Tea here.

28. Dr. Crosby came to desire me to befriend Mr. David Brigham of Shrewsbury, and attend ye Funeral of his little son David who dyed suddenly of Worms .E^s 3.

I went with ye Doctor and dind at his House. P. M. to Mr. Brigham's and prayed and discoursed with ye Assembly: but I went not up to ye Interment. In returning I went into Mr. Coas's & Sibley's—at Mr. Noah Hardy's (where I was regaled with Tea &c. went to Mr. Isaac Parkers &c. Mrs. P— somewhat better.

Breck to Boston. N. B. The Dr. brot me No's 1 to 4 of ye Rise & Progress of ye American War.

29. Wrote to My Dauter Baldwin with my returning her Husband's Letter concerning Gen'l Gates' Defeat & Flight. Sent y^m by Lt. Joseph Bond. Mr. Daniel Adams jr. here with his Wife's Relation : but carryed it back again.

30. Mrs. Adams herself with her Relation tran-and subscribed. Mrs. P.— is exercised still with her distressed stomach, but not in so terrible a Degree.

Mr. Thad Warrin very kind in coming to take Care about getting home my Cyder from Mr. Thos. Frost's. When his son John brot it, Josiah Brigham unloaded, and got it down to place in ye Cellar.

October 1780

Did not read publickly. preached on Mal. 1. 11. P M. repeat Sermon on Isaiah 55. 13. Admitted Mrs. El. Adams. At eve read Mr. Flavell's Serm. 7 on Rev. 3.20.

N. B. To my sorrow, my Oxen have been breachy at Mr. Isaac Parker's and let in Cattle with y^m, into his Cornfield.

2. I rode to a number of Familys in ye South viz. Capt. Morse's : Lieut. and Ensign Warrin's : Mr. Elisha Forbes, where I dind, and he was very generous in a number of presents. I went also to ye Widow Forbes's, where I had opportunity to see old Miss Stone, was also at Mr. Phin. Hardy's, but could find no Body there.

N. B. Lt. Warrin kindly sent his young Man at eve, for two of my Calves to pasture y^m till weaned.

3. I preached at Squire Baker's on Ezek. 20. 11. May it please God to accompany it with His Special Blessing! May we have Grace to keep God's Statutes & Judgments, which we ought to be thankful God has given us. Since if a man do y^m he shall even live in them. Squire got home from Boston at abt 3. yet sat out at Charlestown 25 minutes after 9 A. M.

4. Mr. Nathan Maynard came with a yoke of Oxen, Dr. Hawes' Oxen & my own, having Squire's Plough, & Mr. Joseph Harrington's Lad, namely Aaron Miller & Capt. Wood's son Benj. to drive and they plowed part of my West Field & left it in a broken condition.

5. A Storm of Rain. Read Rise and Progress of War.

6. Dauter Baldwin sends me a packet of Letters—one from Col. to her: 3 of Eben^r to her, which show him to have been in a distressed, disconsolate and now in a sick and weak Condition. I wrote a Letter to him. though I am not sure how I shall send it. I am much perplexed and disappointed about getting my West Field (ye rest of what I proposed) plowed.

7. Intended to have gone to Shrewsbury, but rec'd a Line from Mr. Sumner neg. & recommending tomorrow come sennight. I took great pains to get another Day's plowing done, but it was all in vain, neither could I find time to prepare any New Discourse for tomorrow.

8. Went on with reading in ye Psalms—read Ps. 106 to 24. And I proceeded in Repetition of Sermon on Isa. 55. 13 A & P. M to page 251. which may God bless to our Highest Good!

Rec'd a Letter from Master Nathan Fisk jun[r] of H. C. and another from Mr. Quincy. At eve Breck &c. came, and he read another part of Mr. Flavell on Rev. 3. 20.

9. Jon[n] Frost with my Oxen, Oliver Death with two yoke of Oxen from Squire Baker's, and Joel Kenney to help to driving, plowed in y[e] West Field.

10. Hear much of *Bears*—One is killed by Capt. Jonas Brigham, & others.—weighed 300. I dind at Capt. Brigham's, I visit at Col. Brigham's. P. M. Mr. Eb[r] Forbush conducted me to y[e] thick Swamp, where is y[e] hideous Dwelling of Jacob Garfield,[1] and I went in, tho with Difficulty, to see it. Garfield himself led my Horse out, & I visited at Mr. Tim. Warrin's—but my principal visit was to Mr. Daniel Stockwell's young Child, which was sick—I prayed with it—and then went to y[e] poor at y[e] Work House:

At my return home was informed that Mr. Fitch of Hopkinton had been here, & brot home Dr. Stillingfleet's Orig, Sacrae.

11. I am obliged to take unspeakable Pains to get a very little work done—have obtained Mr. Thad. Warrin to thrash a little Rye to Sowe, and he winnows it—2 bushels &. Mr. Langton called here.

12. In y[e] Morning, Mr. Brigham and Sophy sat out for Rochester. I have writ by them to Mr. Moore, to Mr. Fitch and to Mr. Thos. Adams. Catechized at y[e] Meeting House., had but 28 Boys. P. M had 34 Girls. And may God graciously accompany y[e] Influence and Warning with His special Blessing!

---

[1] There is an island in the swamp still known as Garfield's Island, and a cellar-hole marks the site of this "hideous dwelling."

Mr. Thos. Lamson here, to thrash today, but cannot obtain any more.

13. I attended ye Funeral of Mr. Stockwell's Infant & prayed. The Town met to choose a Representative for ye first Assembly of ye New Government. Mr. John Harrington at eve, & pays all he was to collect.

14. Mr. Eb^r Maynard very kind in sowing & harrowing, both yesterday till afternoon and today A. M. with his son and yoke of Oxen. He did it gratis.

Deac. Wood is in a sad Contest with one Chafey, who with his Wife & Child, boarded several months there, but refuses to pay him for it. I rode to Mr. Sumner's and lodged.

15. I preached at Shrewbury. A. M. on Jer: 8. 20—P M on Job. 31. 24 young Mr. Crosby prayed publickly. P. M. I appointed ye Communion and Lecture there, and returned home at evening. Mr. Sumner rode to Westboro' in ye Morning. Preached for me A. & P. M on 1 Pet: 2. 21. last clause—"left us an example &c." He baptized two Children, viz: Polly and Saml Hall of Danl Jr. and Elizabeth Adams.

Mr. Sumner returned at eve. Col. Wheelock is come home.

16. Mr. Kenney refuses to husk my Corn, tho I conceived he took my Field to ye halves as Dr. Hawes did, who took ye whole care of husking ye Corn, & carrying it into the Corn Barn. However, we came to an agreement. I told him he should ask ye Neighbors to assist, in an afternoon, and tho I would not make an Entertainment, yet I would give y^m some Drink.

17. I rode to East Sudbury to Minister's Meeting, at Mr. Smiths. (So it is called, tho at Mr. Bridge's House). Only Mr. Whitney absent. Mr. Smith very full of pain &c and P—— was Moderator & prayed. A Committee from Marlborough, about a Fast there, Another Committee from Bolton, with new Difficulties there. Before we broke up, Mr. Newell prayed.

Next Meeting to be next April at ye same place.

I went to my son William's where all was well, and I lodged there in comfort and Health D. G.

18. I payd W^m. an hundred Dollars for so much sent to Elias, last Winter, & he paid me Six Silver Dollars which I lent him some time ago. I returned to Westboro. On my way, dind at Col. Weeks' in Marlboro. Proceeded to Mr. Elizur Holyoke's, a joiner at Col. W^{ms}—Col. Brigham's, & at Mr. Francis Barns's.

19. Mr. Kenney brot from ye North Field my part of ye Corn, and a number of Neighbors husked it out. Breck was very generous in treating ye Huskers with Liquor.

Mr. Stephen Johnson and his Wife, from Lyne and their son Eliot of Watertown, with his new Wife, Mr. Johnson's Dauter, all lodged here.

20. The Company leave us expecting to meet a number of Watertown people at Westown to dine there.

Mr. Saml Crosby preached my Lecture on Luke 2. 11.12. After Lecture, Messrs. Hazletine and Fisk here at Tea &c.

21.

22. I preached A. M. on Mat. 26. 21-22 to p. 3. Administered ye Sacrament. Mrs. Maynard at dinner. P M. on

Rev. 5.5. At eve Mr. Brigham read another part of Mr. Flavell's Sermon 7 on Rev. 3. 20.

23. The Widow Hill's little Son, Silas, of about 4 years old, very bad. I visited and prayed with him. After much Anxiety and Trouble, Capt. Wood's two sons work for me in my small Ingathering, Apples and Potatoes.

24. They come again and finish Beeton field and Orchard.

Rev. Mr. Lamson, returning from Connecticut, calls here & Ben Wood goes with my few Apples & Barrells at evening to Mr. Frost's. Breck cut his Foot with an Ax.

25. We esteem this ye Day of ye Commencement of ye honorable Revolution. *The New Constitution of Government now begins The Election of Governor &c.*

It is exceedingly to be desired and prayed for, y^t ye minds of ye People were properly affected with the great Importance of this so unexampled Time! direct ye weighty Affairs of it and grant an happy Issue to His Glory and ye Public Weal! —

26. I have been so much disappointed by those I have spoke to to work for me y^t I am forced to improve Capt. Woods' two Boys

27. to plow for me. We try the new Horse my son Alexander sent me, & with my Oxen I have a sufficient Team for splitting —— (?) and harrowing in Rye. Mr. Brigham has returned I visit and prayed with little Silas.

28. Lieut. Levi Warrin brot me a Barrell of Cyder. P. M. I rode to Hopkinton & Mr. Fitch came here, tho very rainy.

29. I preached at Hopkinton on Prov. 18. 10. May God grant Success to my own Soul especially. At eve, I

went to Mr. Barrett's and lodged there! Mr. Fitch returned from Westboro. & tells me y⁰ sick little Boy (Silas) dyed last night. N. B. Ye Sad News from y⁰ North West is confirmed. Mischief done at Royalton, Schoharie &c.

30. I took some time in viewing Mr. Barrett's Books, dind at home & Mr. Sam Crosby with me. P. M. attended yᵉ Funeral of Silas Hill. a very large Company there.

31. Breck and Brigham have a drove of Oxen brought to sell. I read. Mr. Thos. Hunter's Reflections on Ld Chesterfield, very just and most elegant.

NOVEMBER.

The Month comes in with a Violent Storm. In some part of yᵉ Day rained hard; but it soon turned to snow, and the continuance of it brings on a very winter prospect. Thro' divine Favour, we have Wood, Shelter and Clothing.

2. Wintry Scenes. Earth covered with Snow. Cold & tedious.

Mr. Cushing & Mrs. Cotton from Ashburnham, came this Morning from Shrewsbury, and dind here. Mr. Cushing P. M. returned to Shrewsbury. Mrs. Cotton lodged here. N. B. Sent Hunter's Reflections on Ld Chesterfield's Letters to Dr. Crosby p Mr. Cushing.

3. Mr. Brigham waited on Mrs. Cotton to Hopkinton. Sent Mrs. Abbé Vol. 2 of De Foe by Mrs. Cotton. N. B. It was brot me by Dr. Stimson some time agoe.

As night came on, Elias with Letters from Br. Breck from Springfield. He brings home five young Cattle from Coi's Hill. The two largest Steers have been taken out of Pasture by Alexander some time ago.

Breck sent Mr. Th. Lamson, who cutts wood for me at ye Door.

4. Elias goes and fetches my 12 Sheep from Sq. Baker's Pasture. N. B. The principal Weather is missing, and a strange one is brot in his stead.

5. Preached A. M. on Rev. 5. 6. Mr. Fisk and Cousen Maynard dind here. P. M. on John 10.11. I stayed ye Church and read ye Letter from Bolton, requesting our Help in Council. When proposed to ye Church there was no vote. There were but few Members, but there were but 4 Hands. In ye eve, Mr. Brigham read Mr. Flavell on Rev. 3. 20. Sermon 8.

6. *The Town Meeting.* Granted my Wood and Capt. Maynard to cut and bring it. But as to Sallery, I dont perceive y^t they have voted anything, but ye naked Sum with ye Courts Depreciation.

Rev. Johnson & Lady call here in their returning home.

7. Mr. Gale was at eve thrown by his Horse and much hurt, but after a while returned home. Susè and Sophy ride to their Father Brigham's. Had some Converse with Capt. Fisher about ye Town's Transactions yesterday. My grandchildren Isaac and Betsy Baldwin from Shrewsbury this morning came to see us. Isaac leads an Horse, besides one in his Surkey: these (with Elias's, Breck's and my own) make six Horses which are kept here this Night. Mr. Jon^n Forbes here at eve.—talks of ye Doings of ye Town yesterday with great concern,—he speaks also of Mr. Benj. Fay[1] & Mrs. Th. Whitney's contests.

[1] Benj. Fay seems to be always quarrelling with some one. March 13. Mr. Parkman has recorded his sad contest with Col. Wheelock,

8. The adjournment of ye Town Meeting. By Advice I sent a written Message y^t if they would grant me the Same Allowance of Depreciation which I was required by every one to pay for every Article, I would submit myself to be taxed. Thereupon ye Town chose a Committee to treat with me, viz. Capt. Maynard, Capt. Morse and Capt. Fisher.

9. The Council at Bolton met. I had told ye Church I did not incline to go. See ye Result at ye end of this Book.

The Church met by adjournment to consider Mrs. Adams' Case. The Woman was present but y^e *Man*, though warned was not, and therewith Mr. Adams' paper dated July 23 last. As to ye Former, Mrs. Adams pleaded that she had not got her Evidences ready, but she would have spoke to her Husband, before ye Church—but he was not there: which was to our Surprise, Since he knew that at this Meeting *his own paper* was expected to be read & considered. It was declared that he was at ye public Meeting when Rev. Mr. Whitney read my paper of Adjournment, (which was consented to by ye Brethren) and he had reason to expect y^t the Meeting upon these affairs would be now dissolved: The Pastor has also repeatedly told him he was not debarred from Church Meetings but was desired and expected to come. But since he was now absent, nothing

about the chestnut tree. It was his affair with Capt. John Wood, upon which the foremost citizens and lawyers of Worcester had held their two days' sitting in the old church in May, and now he seems to be in another contest.

In the French and Indian War he was captain of a company, later he is called lieutenant, he was selectman for eleven years and town treasurer for five.

more could be done about his Paper, than to read it and then ye Letter sent to him which he was disturbed by, but which had nothing of grievous Nature in it: which being done, and nobody there to Sustain ye Said paper, nor make Reply to ye Exceptions made against ye palpable mistakes it was founded upon, it was voted to be dropped :—and seeing that Mrs. Adams was now supposed to be trying for Relief in ye Civil Law, the Meeting was dissolved, upon which I prayed and gave ye Blessing. At eve, Col. Silas Bailey here, returning from Rhode Island, his son Timothy dyd there & is buryd.

10. Capt. John Wood was here upon ye Affair of his son Ben's living with me, and he wants that John shall live with my son Breck. Elias has set out early this morning for Boston.

11. The Winter Weather continues. Elias returns from Boston between six and seven o'clock. He brings me from Saml No 2 to 6 (5 Books) of ye American War. I have read 4. He brot also Dr. Evans which Saml had to read, but now returns.

12. Preached again on John 10. 11. P. M. on Mal. 1. 11. Cousen Maynard dind here. At eve Mr. Brigham read Flavell on Rev: 3. 20 part of Serm 8.

13. A committee from ye Town came to treat with me about my Sallery. They were Capt. Maynard and Capt. Morse, but Capt. Fisher, who was the third (I think) was not with them. Their errand was to know what I apprehended my Sallery should be. I answered y^t the Covenant was 55£ Lawful Money, *to be made good to its then Value*. And as to what was now due, the Depreciation which now

I have actually paid, and am required to pay is partly *an hundred and eight:* to some an hundred, & to others 90. If the Town would allow me the Medium, that is, an hundred, then out of Pity to ye People in this Day of their Trouble, I will deduct my Proportion to bear so much of ye Charge of ye War, for ye present year. My grandson, Isaac Baldwin came this evening from his Tour to Newbury, Dummer School &c.

14. The Town meet by adjournment The Committee carry my Answer (as above) to y^m. After meeting, two of the Comittee come, (Captns Maynard & Morse) and acquaint me y^t the Town had granted me for this year the sum of £4000, which though it was 1500 short of my just due) I accepted on consideration of their Distresses: & thanked y^m (Y^e Committee) for their Pains in ye Affair. Capt. Fisher came in when ye rest were going away: but he stayed not.

15 My Baldwins (Isaac and Betsey) leave us to return home. I wrote by y^m to their mother. Capt. John Woods moves and his Wife & Children except Ben who is to live with me. Capt. Wood gave me a Barrell, almost full of Cyder.

N. B. Ben is to live with me for ye sake of getting Learning.—to Satisfie me,, for Instruction, Board, Washing & Lodging, he must tend my Cattle, & cut wood, needful chores, go of Errands &c. & he must tarry with me till next April.

At eve had a message from one Mrs. Mary Nottingham, who lies sick at Deac. Wood's, to make her a visit. I went accordingly and discoursed with her & prayed with her as one extremely bad, & in a Dangerous Condition.

16. I went to Coll. Wheelock's, Capt. Fisher's, Squire's —called to see Mrs. Nottingham, who is no better. Mr. Harrington with my Team fetches me a Cedar Pole for my West Stanchells. Mr. James Gibson here to buy my young Oxen. Thad. Wait was marryed to Sally Morse.

17. Mrs. Eunice Hill of Douglass here; I sent by her to Col. Caleb Hill of Douglass (who married Mrs. Ruth Hicks) to remember their aunt Champney. At eve, Mr. Beriah Ware in Trouble.

18. Joel and Gardner,[1] Sons of Mr. Isaac Parker, have brot home a Calf, which their Father has kept a great while for me.

19. Heavy rain, few at Meeting. I preached on Mal. 1. 12-13. Mrs. Maynard dind here. P. M. I preached on Prov: 18.10. At eve, Mr. Brigham read in Flavell's Works —Rev: 3 20.

20. Elias setts out for Springfield. I wrote by him to

---

[1] Gardner Parker, born March 14, 1772, a boy at this time, kept his name alive in Westborough by starting a mill at the place we now call Parker's Folly, and building a large dam there. He was a clockmaker by profession, having studied with the Willards of Grafton. In 1809 he built an organ into the old meeting-house. His brother Joel, two years older, was more or less prominent in local politics. Isaac Parker lived in the Sixth School Squadron as it was divided in 1789—the same as Beriah Ware, Gershom Brigham, Capt. Maynard and John Fessenden. Joel owned the mill on the old mill road, the raising of which Mr. Parkman attended in June of this year. It is spoken of now by our older citizens as Parker's Mill.

Br. Breck.¹ The Town meets again by adjournment to settle their Accounts. I visited Mrs. Nottingham again. Master Fisk here at eve & lodges here.

21. Mr. David Kellogg, preacher at Framingham dind here, but I was obliged to leave him to Mr. Brigham, who was his acquaintance. P. M. I preached at Mr. Jon^n Childs, to ye Widow Smith, on Ps: 73. 26, which may God bless! Rec'd Letter from Mr. Moore of ye 9th inst.

22. Very stormy, or I should have visited Mr. Abijah Gale, who has not got well from his Lameness. Read Hist. of ye American War, No 5.

23. Mrs. Nabby Martyn has my Horse to ride to Bolton.

---

[1] Rev. Robert Breck, of Springfield, was the oldest son of Rev. Robert Breck, of Marlborough, and next older in age to Mrs. Parkman, being three years her senior. He was settled in Springfield after a bitter controversy as to his soundness, which was started by a sentence in a sermon he had preached at New London.

"What," he asked, "will become of the heathen who never heard of the Gospel? I do not pretend to say, but I cannot but indulge a hope that God, in his boundless benevolence will find out a way whereby those heathen who act up to the light they have, may be saved."

This was considered alarming, and his former life was thoroughly sifted for further evidence of unsoundness in character or doctrine. He was finally ordained in 1736, after the intervention of various councils, courts and even of the legislature itself.

The historian of Springfield, in speaking of this combat between Breck and Jonathan Edwards, says: "Scholars have since bowed down to the genius of Edwards, but the people live the principles of Breck."

The Brecks evidently lived in some little style in Springfield, for Mrs. Breck's fame rests on her having owned the first carpet in the town.

Mrs. P. employs Mrs. Garfield to spin for her from Day to Day. & Pamela helps her. Ben follows his writing &c.

24. Mr. Jon^n Childs brings and gives a Barrell of Cyder & a Bag of Apples. Mr. Hezekiah Maynard of Marlboro came and had two Bushels of Rye for ye two Bushel of Malt which I had of him last Spring. I wrote by him to Mr. Elizur Holyoke.

25. A great Storm of Rain, Wind &c. Towards night it held up: and Miss Nabby Martyn returned on my Horse from Bolton.

26. I have been so many ways interrupted, & my mind discomposed that I could make but slender preparations, & therefore I went on with ye last Sabbath subject both A & P. M. but took those words for my Text, in Prov. 21. 31, last clause; with new Introduction.

Mr. Fisk & Mrs. Maynard dind with us. At eve, Mr. Brigham, read ye rest of Mr. Flavell's 8th Sermon on Rev: 3. 20. God forgive my Dullness and unprofitableness.

27. Robert Wightman came to thrash for me. Mr. Hazletine wants Henry's Exposition. Mr. Cornelius Waters came—is with Mr. Brigham, lodges here.

28. Mr. Waters and Mr. Brigham go to Boston. Wrote to Mr. Moore. N. B. Wightman was in ye Burgoine Army at Saratoga.

Mr. Jonas Bond and his Wife here in their way to Cambridge. Coll. Brigham and Wife make a visit to both Houses. Mrs. Baker very generous, visiting and bringing with an open Hand. I was called to Mr. Barker's, his Dauter Betsey being very ill. I went; & prayed with her.

Visit Mrs. Nottingham & prayed there.

29. Wightman here. Mr. Thad. Warrin and his son John came at almost ten o'clock A. M & carted Muck.

30. Was at Neighbor Newton's where was his Br. Timothy of Hardwick, who gave me a sorrowful account of his son & son-in-law's Captivation[1] by ye Indians last August from Barnard's Town, & their wives pregnant, exposed to ye woods, destitute: but now at Hardwick. Mr. Brigham returned from Boston in ye Night.

December 1780

Rob. Wightman is so successful in his getting out and cleaning ye Rye that in these few Days he has thrashed and winnowed (as he has counted) 40 Bushels besides that he plowed for me half a Day, which he gave in; & he carrys away 4 Bushels for his wages.

I was called away to see Betty Barker, as being near her End. I went—found her very bad, of bilious Fever. She was too delirious to converse much. I prayed with her, and a number more. Called to see Mrs. Nottingham, who seems to be in more hopeful state.

2. I find it a very difficult thing to write Sermons now in my old Age from what I did formerly; and cannot thro Dimness and Trembling, make Despatch as then. As my outward Man decays, I ought to labour to have my inner man to be renewed Day by Day.

---

[1] John Newton "was taken prisoner by the Indians Aug. 9, 1780, and carried to Canada where he was detained until the next Spring, when he escaped and returned to his family after suffering great hardship."—*History of Hardwick.*

Mr. Jonas Bond and his Wife returned home, but I saw y^m not.

3. A very cold stormy tedious Day; and it was doubtful whether we could attend ye Solemnities proposed: yet the Snow which fell was not very deep. I attempted, and God was pleased to carry me through. A. M. on Mal: 1. 13 "And they brot that which was torn" &c. Administered ye Lord's Supper to ye few which came. Mrs. Maynard dind with us. P. M. on Rev: 3. 2. 1. May God graciously forgive, accept & bless! At eve, Brigham, Flavell on Rev. 3. 20 Sermon 9 former part.

4. A great Disappointment arose by means of nine young Cattle of Squire's which broke in upon and destroyed a great part of my Straw which was designed for several uses: Harrington lays up a part of it on ye Hovel and Cart Shed—but, ye Cattle very troublesome, and a sad interruption to me after they had been driven away,

5. Mr. Corn. Waters and Miss Sarah Shepherd going from Newtown to Sutton call & dine here. Mr. Corn. Biglow came for his Rye, to pay him for his reaping. He requires 4 Bushels and half, but releases a peck.

6. Deacon Hawes brings me from Mr. Cranch another volume (ye 5th) of Biog. Dict. Letters F. & G.

7. *Thanksgiving.* Preached on Jer: 3. 23 last clause, which may God graciously prosper! Betsey Barker is dead. Mr. Elisha Livermore was marry'd to Miss Lucy Maynard.

8. A cold and Hoarseness increased to such a Degree upon me that (it being also a Wet Day) I did not go to ye Burial of Betsey Barker, who dy'd on Wednesday morning, and Mr. Barker sent for me to-day: but I had no audible

Voice. May God graciously teach and comfort y^m and ye surviving Children!

9. In compliance with Mr. Corn. Waters Request, I being somewhat better & recovering my voice in some measure, I rode to Southboro' and Mr. Stone to Framingham. I went also to ye Widow Wood's, on an affair of my Wife's to bespeak some weaving. Lodged at Mr. Stone's.

10. A wet Day but (thro divine Goodness) I felt so well that I went to Meeting and preached (at Southboro') A. & P. M. on Ps. 124 Several verses, using with some variations, part of ye Introduction to ye late Thanksgiving Sermon. May God grant Success! Mr. Stone returned at eve. It was too rainy for me, and they urging, I stayed there.

11. In my way home called at Mr. Gale's, Got home safe D. G. Understand that Mr. Grosvenor preached for me: & on Rev. 3. 2. Capt. Wood dind here. I visited at Mr. Barker's, under their Bereavement, and went to Squire Baker's.

12. Mr. Brigham goes to Boston. Wrote by him to Mr. Thos Adams. Ben Wood at his Father's Desire, goes to Worcester to attend at Court, as a Witness.

13. My Hovel, overloaded with straw, in ye late Storm of Rain, broke down: Mr. Lamson and Stephen Maynard kindly came and repaired it. They dind here. I read in Biog. Dict. Vol. 5. F. G.

14. Mr. Brigham returned in ye Night from Boston and he

15. delivers me a letter from Mr. Quincy of ye 6th. Rev. Mr. Israel Evans, a Chaplain to Genl Poor's Brigade, recommended to me by Mr. Grosvenor, came and lodged here.

He relates how Genl Washington was in Arnold's plot, was designed to be Surprised and taken, at Col. Beverly Robertson's House in Philip's Manor, over against West Point.

16. Mr. Evans left us to go to Concord. N. B. He presented me his Sermon delivered at Easton Oct. 17, 1779 to ye Officers & Soldiers of ye Western Army, after their Return from an Expedition against ye five Nations of hostile Indians, published at ye particular Request of ye General (Sullivan) & ye Field Officers of y^c Army, printed at Philadelphia

17. A. M. on Rev. 1. 3. Mrs. Maynard dind. P. M. on 1 Cor: 10. 4 Mr. Silas Brigham dismissed. Mr. Brigham read Mr. Flavell at Even.

18. I attended y^e Funeral of old Mr. Isaac Woods.

P. M. was a Town Meeting to raise Men for y^e Continental Army—to provide Beef for y$^"$ Army. &c.

19. Mr. Beeton has made a Crane for our West Room Chimney, which I have put up.

Breck & Susè and little Hannah are gone, tho it is a lowery Day, to Col. Brigham's. Breck designing to go to Boston. Constable Maynard now first paid me any peny of y^e Grant made last July, paid £701.16.

20. Took a walk among my Neighbors to reckon with y^m, that I might pay them for their Work for me, last Season, this being ye first time that I have had any Money to do it. I went to Mr. Kenny's, dind at Mr. N. Maynard's, was at Mr. Thad. Warrin's. Visit Mrs. Nottingham, who is yet ill and prayed with her. Two Letters from Camp from Eben^r and from Col. Baldwin of Nov. 14, with Genl Orders.

21. Mr. George Morey of Norton preaches here and

dines with us. He informs me that there is a Fast at Marlboro', in order to their Calling a Minister. Mr. Eben^r Grosvenor being there at present.

22. Mr. Danl Miller of Fitz-William dind here. Mr. Brigham returned from Boston, & says Mr. Ripley recovers.

Town Meeting by Adjournment to endeavor to raise Recruits for ye Continental Army; also Quota of Beef & to purchase Corn for ye payment of 3 months' men. At eve Mr. Fisk who keeps ye East School, here.

Capt. Edmund Brigham here, on his Humiliation.

23.

24. Dark weather again. A. M. Mal: 1. 13. last part and 14. former part. Mrs. Maynard dind with us. P. M. on 1 Cor: 10. 4. "And that Rock was Christ."

Mr. Brigham at eve still reads in Flavell on Rev. 3. 20. I read after Exercise, Pierce's Vindic. of Dissent.

25. In morning Family Exercise read Luke 1. 25 to ye End & Ch. 2. divers parts, which peculiarly respect ye Nativity of our B. L. and give *Thanks* therefor. Breck and his Family dind with us. O that we might uprightly and most gratefully join with all true Christians, and with all our Souls magnifie ye Lord, rejoicing forever in God our Saviour!—

26. Winter cold, Sharp, Frost: difficult stirring, it is so rough. icy, with ye Snow that has covered ye Ground; but we are favoured with Health, Food, Raiment, Fuel & Habitation, &c. D. G. Read Biogr. Dict. F.

27. Am forced to keep House by reason of ye Sharp Air. Mr. Brigham brot Mrs. Jotham Bush to dine with us. I read, as yesterday, Biogr. Dictionary, now part of G.

28. Several Neighbours came & killed my largest Hog. They were Messrs. Thad Warrin, Sol Batherick & Caleb Harrington. They would not stay to dine with us. The Hog weighed 316 pounds. At eve, Master Fisk here. N. B. Breck brings in a Letter from Eben^r at Fishkill.
29.
30.
31. I preached A. M. on Mal: 1.14 the latter part, & P. M. on Eccl. 12.13. It is deeply to be regretted that those great and Serious Subjects have so slender Effect upon our Minds, Since they do so nearly, so inf.ly concern us![1]

I have great Reason to be astonished at myself, that I am so far below what I ought to be! I beseech God most graciously to awaken me to a proportionable Exertion!

At eve Mr. Brigham read Mr. Flavell on Rev. 3. 20.

O y^t I might have a Frame of Spirit suited to ye Close of ye Year, & that I might have a lively Apprehension of ye Close of Life, y^t I may be found ready for it.

We know of no later volume of the Journal.

The last entry in any book that we have was written by Mr. Parkman under the date of Sept. 5, O. S. 1782 in the Natalitia—

"I have still fresh Cause to praise and extol ye name of ye most High who endures me and permits me to live in His World, to enjoy innumerable Advantages and especially to enjoy both ye Day

[1] These last sermons on this last day of the year were preached from the texts:—

"For I am a great King, saith the Lord of Hosts, and my name is dreadful among the heathen"— and in the afternoon—

"Let us hear the conclusion of the whole matter; Fear God and keep his commandments; for this is the whole duty of man."

& ye Means of Grace—would therefore offer up a sacrifice of Praise and Thanks to His glorious Name!

That my Senses have been continued in such a Measure; and particularly That my Light has not been utterly taken away—but that I can in such a Measure both read & write; that especially the Day and Means of Grace are continued, that I am yet permitted to Serve in ye Sanctuary and have my Furneture & Ability for it (May I myself savingly profit thereby!)

But while I have been thus highly indulged, O what Ingratitude & Unworthiness I have been chargeable with.

Therefore "———

As he turned the page he found he had written some items on the other side—there was no more room in the book. He commenced on its first page in 1727—he had now—an old man—reached the last.

He lived but a short time after this birthday, dying on the 9th of December.

An article in the Worcester Spy reads:—

"Westborough Dec. 16. 1782.

"On Monday evening the 9th inst. departed this Life that aged and venerable man of God, the Reverend Ebenezer Parkman, pastor of the Church of Christ in this place, in the 80th year of his age and the 59th of his ministry, and this day his remains were decently and honorably interred. He was a gentleman and a scholar, a good divine and real christian. He was a lover of religion and of learning: a lover of the college in Cambridge (where he had his education) and an honour to it; a lover of good men & given to hospitality. He loved his brethren in the ministry, & was an ornament to the order. He was a friend to his country, and to these churches and a firm supporter of their order & constitution, & opposed all attempts to subvert the same. By nature, education & grace, he had much done for him to furnish him for the various services of the pastoral office; and he was diligent & eminently faithful in improving all his gifts for the glory of God & the good of his people. He had a singular talent in private conversation;

his communications were always edifying & ministered grace to the hearers.

"He took heed to himself and unto his doctrine and continued therein to the very last; and we believe (through grace) has saved himself and many who heard him. Having obtained help of God, he continued his ministerial labor for more than thirty of the last years of his life, without any intermission, through bodily infirmities, until Six Sabbaths before his death.

"His widow and children with a beloved flock, and an extensive acquaintance mourn his departure; But sorrow not as they who have no hope, for they believe he has gone to rest: which rest remaining for the people of God was the subject of his last discourse to his people. The great head of the church has said, Be thou faithful unto death and I will give thee a crown of glory."

THE PARKMAN GRAVES.

Mr. Parkman's grave—the only one in Memorial Cemetery with a horizontal slab, has been protected in recent years by an iron fence. For many years it was used by the boys of Westborough as a convenient table for their games, or for a seat in the rare moments when they sat. The Inscription reads;—

" Here lies deposited
the mortal part of that man of God
the Revd Ebenezer Parkman A. M.
who was born Sepr. 5. 1703;
ordained the first Bishop of the Church
in Westborough, October 28th 1724;
and died on the ninth of December 1782
having completed the 79th year of his age
on Septr. 16th & the 58 year of his ministry
on November 8th preceding.

He was formed by nature and education to
be an able minister of the New Testament,
and obtained grace to be eminently faithful
in the work of the Lord:
He was a firm friend to the faith, order and
Constitution of the New England Churches.
He was a learned pious good man
full of the Holy Ghost, & faith unfeigned;—
and answered St. Paul's description
of a Scripture Bishop, being "blameless
Vigilant,'Sober, of good behaviour,
given to hospitality, APT TO TEACH."

Be thou faithful unto death,
And I will give thee a Crown of life
           Says Christ.

APPENDIX.

An Inventory of the Goods & Chattels, Rights & Credits of Ebenezer Parkman, late of Westborough, Clerk, deceased——

	£.	S.	D.
His Library, including as well single Sermons and pamphlets as bound Books, - - - -	80.	0.	0
His wearing Apparel, given to his Son Ebenezer in his last Will and Testament, including a Golden Ring, Sleeve Buttons and Shoe Buckles	14.	6.	0
Pewter lb 60 weight - - - - - -	4.	10.	0
A brass Kittle 36/ two small do 6/ - -	2.	2.	0
A brass Skillet 6/ brass Skimmer 1/ - - -	0.	7.	0
Standing Candle Stick 24/ two brass Candle Sticks 2/6	1.	6.	6
Five iron Candle Sticks 2/ three pair Snuffers 2/ -	0.	4.	0
Tin Tunnel /4 two tin Dippers /4 Canister 1/6 - -	0.	2.	2
A Spit 2/ Gridiron 2/8 A Baster /8 - - -	0.	5.	4
A dripping Pan 4/ Toasting Iron 1/6 Skewer /6 -	0.	6.	0
A large Iron Pot 5/ Small do 2/ Iron Kittle 3/6 -	0.	10.	6
Small iron Kittle 2/ Iron Skillet 2/ - - -	0.	4.	0
Warming Pan 7/ Six Pattie Pans 2/ - - -	0.	9.	0
Tea Kittle 5/ flesh Fork /6 Bellows 1/ - - -	0.	6.	6
Hand Irons fire, Shovel & Tongs in ye Kitchen -	0.	12.	4
Earthen Ware 10/ Coffee Pot 1/ Pepper Box /2 -	0.	11.	2
Pair Pincers 1/ two Gimblets /6 Awls /8 -	0.	2.	2
Knives and Forks 3/, Dish Cover 2/6 Cullender 1/6	0.	7.	0
Three Silver table Spoons 9/ Seven tea Do 8/ -	0.	17.	0
A Silver Cup 5/ 1 sett china Cups & Saucers 6/ -	2.	11.	0
3 Cream coloured Bowls 3/ cream cup /3 - -	0.	3.	3
A Shugar Bowl /4, three delf Plates 1/6 Mugg 1/	0.	2.	10
Block tin tea pot 2/ Table Linnen 45/ - - -	2.	7.	0
1 great Chair 3/ Six lath baskt Chairs 24/ - -	1.	7.	0
9 black Chairs 15/ five leather bottomed Do 20/ -	1.	15.	0

APPENDIX.

	£	S.	D.
6 low back Do 18/ Six Kitchen Do 9/	1.	7.	0
2 Pails 2/ a Mortar & Pestle 2/	0.	4.	2
Best Bed, Bedding, bedstead & Cord	8.	0.	0
Best Bedding & Bedstead in the front Chamber	3.	10.	0
Best Bedding, Bedstead & Cord in back Do	4.	0.	0
Best Bedding, Bedstead & Cord in the Bedroom	3.	0.	9
Trundle Bed & Bolster 18/	0.	18.	0
55 Maps and Pictures together with Atlas (so called)	3.	0.	0

(This "Atlas so-called" is now in the possession of Mr. Henry D. Staples, of Westborough.)

	£	S.	D.
Study Chamber 1 Desk large 18/ Do small 8/ Bookcase 15/	2.	1.	0
1 Press /6 Sett Shelves 6/ Cabinet 12/ one Table 2/	1.	0.	6
Pair Bellows 3/6 Prospect Glass 6/ Slate 2/	0.	11.	6
2 Pair Hand Irons 4/ Tobacco Tongs 3/6	0.	7.	6
Shovell & Tongs 2/6 Gun & Accoutrements 16/	0.	18.	6
West Great Chair & Cushing 6/ Table large 14/	1.	0.	0
Room Tea Table 6/ looking Glass 28/	1.	14.	0
Bedroom. Wooden Chair & round stand 2/ Square table 4/	0.	6.	0
Round Table 2/ Steelyards 12/ Shovell & Tongs 4/	0.	18.	0
Carried over.	148.	10.	9

	£.	S.	D.
Brot over	148.	10.	9
Small looking glass 2/ old Chest with Drawers 8/	0.	10.	0
Part of a Suit of Curtains 8/	0.	8.	0
Five pair old Sheets 18/ Seven good Sheets 70/	4.	8.	0
5 Pair Pillow Cases 8/ Knapkins 13/	1.	1.	0
Back Sole leather & Calf Skin 16/	0.	16.	0
Chamber. Saddler's Tools 2/ Raisors 1/ Bdls 2/8	0.	5.	8
One large Wheel 2/8 two foot Wheels 6/	0.	8.	8
A Meal Sieve /6 Bread Trough /8	0.	1.	2
Cider Barrels, Meat Tubs & old Casks	1.	5.	0

APPENDIX.

	£	S.	D.
2 Doz. Glass Bottles 12/ nine Square Do 9/	1.	1.	0
1 Square Table 12/ A Flute 2/ a Jack 4/	0.	18.	0
A Meal Chest & Churn	0.	6.	0
Tramels & Hooks in ye Kitchen	0.	4.	0
Three Axes 7/ Beetle & Wedges 4/	0.	11.	0
Seven old Scythes, Snath & Tackling	0.	8.	0
Pick Ax and Hatchet 1/6 Garden Hoe 1/6	0.	2.	6
Cart & Wheel 80/ Wheel Barrow /6	4.	2.	6
Iron Bar 8/ Plough Irons 6/	0.	14.	0
Old Iron 5/ Scythe Snath /8	0.	5.	8
Curtain Rods 6/ Hand Irons (Dogs) 2/	0.	8.	0
A Draught Chain 5/	0.	5.	0
Rye Meal & Indian Corn	1.	12.	0
A Horse £7.10 Sadle & Stirrups 18/	8.	8.	0
1 four year old Stear 80/ 1 pair 3 year old Do 90/	8.	10.	0
1 Cow 100/ Young Do 9/ 1 Heifer 45/	11.	15.	0
One Silver Watch	3.	0.	0
	200.	4.	11

The Mansion House, Barn, Corn Barn and other small Buildings together with fifteen acres of land nigh ye Same	300. 0. 0
Eight Acres of Interval (so-called)	80.
The Island (so-called) & 4 acres adjoining	50.
The Newton Meadow (so called)	6.
Pine Lot (so called)	34.
About 5 acres of Swamp—	8.
About 7 acres Cedar Swamp—	7.
	$685. 4. 11

Westborough, June 20, 1783
 James Crosby ⎫
 Joseph Baker ⎬ Apprizers.
 Stephen Maynard ⎭

LIST OF ILLUSTRATIONS.

	PAGE
PARKMAN COAT-OF-ARMS.	*Frontispiece*
FLAGGON AND BAPTISM BASON,	VII
DEA. TAINTER'S HOUSE,	12
OLD COOK HOUSE,	16
SAM'L FORBUSH HOUSE,	17
HANNAH BRECK'S WEDDING SLIPPERS,	22
WIGWAM TREE,	24
HOUSE OF REV. ISAAC BURR,	31
PAUL DUDLEY,	33
HUGH HENDERSON, BROADSIDE,	46
THE PARSONAGE,	50
THE ARCADE,	53
HARVARD COLLEGE,	56
BRECK PARKMAN,	60
BRECK PARKMAN'S SHOP,	61
STEPHEN MAYNARD HOUSE,	63
STEPHEN MAYNARD CHIMNEY,	65
GALE TAVERN,	69
LIEUT. FORBUSH HOUSE,	73
FORBES HOMESTEAD,	87
JOSEPH SUMNER,	88
PETER WHITNEY,	90
SUMNER HOUSES,	95
SAM'L PARKMAN,	100

LIST OF ILLUSTRATIONS.

	PAGE
First Davis House,	112
Madam Hannah Parkman,	142
Thos. Whitney House,	153
Eli Whitney House,	154
Judge Edmund Quincy,	174
Gershom Brigham House,	193
Haskell House,	202
Elias' Table,	209
A Parkman Sermon,	217
Peter Whitney's House,	238
Elijah Brigham,	272
Parkman Graves,	296

INDEX.

Abercrombie, Robert, 56.
Abington, 161.
Acock, Wm., 79.
Adams, Daniel, 135, 163, 164, 165, 166, 176, 177, 178, 184, 225, 230, 235, 239, 252, 255, 263, 274, 283.
Adams, Daniel, Jr., 269, 275, 278.
Adams, Eliphalet, 92.
Adams, Elizabeth, 277, 278.
Adams, Hannah, 248.
Adams, Persis, 167, 173, 187, 230, 234, 239, 263, 273, 283.
Adams, Peter, 92.
Adams, Polly, 278.
Adams, Sam. H., 278.
Adams, Thos., 137, 140, 147, 233, 248, 277, 291.
Alexander, Caleb, 113, 114, 181.
Allen, Eben'r, 149.
Amsden, Abrm., 28.
Amsden, Joseph, 28.
Andover, 115.
Andrews, Benj., 84.
Andrews, Betty, 178.
Andrews, David, 264.
Andrews, G., 203.
Andrews, Hannah, 254.
Andrews, Thos., 72, 144, 145.
Arcade, 43, 51, 53, 103.
Ashburnham, 39, 125, 134, 157, 158, 163, 173, 174, 183, 184, 185, 189, 212, 231, 233, 239, 240, 263, 269, 281.
Assabet, 229.
Atwell, Mrs. Pearn, 178.

INDEX.

Auburn, 232.
Avery, Polly, 173.
Badcock, Jonas, 228.
Badcock, Lemuel, 52, 72, 84, 86, 87, 94, 97.
Baily, Benj., 117, 118.
Baily, Silas, 118, 284.
Baily, Tim., 284.
Baker, Lieut. Edw., 43, 65.
Baker, John, 65, 115, 211.
Baker, Joseph, 43, 65, 77, 97, 107, 109, 124, 131, 155, 158, 172, 173, 181, 198, 203, 210, 218, 219, 228, 236, 241, 242, 257, 258, 271, 272, 276, 277, 288.
Baker, Persis, 43, 83, 209, 211.
Baker, Hon. Sam'l, 107.
Baldwin, Betty, 282, 285.
Baldwin, Isaac, 76, 123, 128, 148, 150, 157, 158, 173, 174, 221, 254, 261, 282, 285.
Baldwin, Col. Jeduthan, 82, 105, 109, 116, 128, 173, 221, 224, 229, 237, 273.
Baldwin, Lucy Parkman, 99, 116, 150, 158, 250, 275, 276.
Baldwin, Luke, 173, 174, 261.
Ball, Mary, 130.
Ball, Nathan, 42.
Ball, Dr. Stephen, 130.
Bancroft, Benj., 126, 127, 128.
Barker, Betsey, 288, 289, 290.
Barnardston, 289.
Barns, Francis, 179, 279.
Barrett, John, 220, 240.
Barrett, Nancy, 182.
Barrett, Sam'l, 133, 152, 182.
Barrett, Thos., 219.
Bartlett, Frank V., 20.
Batheric, Solomon, 188, 189, 190, 200, 294.
Batherick, John'n, 113, 131.
Batherick, Stephen, 234.

Battery Street, 243.
Baverick, David, 13, 27.
Beals, Eliza, 131.
Beals, Elizabeth, 261.
Beeman Family, 14.
Beeman, Eben'r, 42.
Beeman, Major Ezra, 126.
Beeton, John, 206, 292.
Beeton, Nanny, 58, 59.
Beeton, Mrs. John, 260.
Belcher, Alethina, 57.
Belknap, John, 131, 132, 133, 144, 163.
Belknap, Stephen, 215.
Bellows, James, 170.
Bellows, Ithamar, 128, 133.
Bellows, Simeon, 244.
Bellows, Thos., 126.
Bennington, Vt., 15.
Berwick, 157.
Bigelow, Dan'l, 232.
Biglo, Thos., 98.
Biglow, Asahel, 175, 181.
Biglow, Corn., 252, 253, 255, 257, 290.
Biglow, Katy, 164, 165.
Biglow, Paul, 254.
Biglow, Rev. (of Sudbury), 129, 175, 192, 225.
Bimeleck, Sue, 205.
Blandford, 180.
Bolton, 70, 114, 117, 127, 129, 135, 136, 151, 207, 228, 259, 279, 283, 287.
Bond, Abraham, 161, 257, 259, 260, 268.
Bond, Mrs. Daniel, 199.
Bond, Hannah, 36.
Bond, John, 132, 161.
Bond, Dea., 151, 176, 245.
Bond, Jonas, 67, 137, 143, 162, 288, 290.

Bond, Joseph, 115, 183, 220, 275.
Boston, 17, 25, 29, 83, 84, 103, 106, 117, 120, 123, 126, 128, 134, 137, 149, 161, 167, 176, 180, 183, 187, 189, 190, 206, 212, 216, 218, 221, 229, 235, 237, 240, 248, 249, 250, 251, 261, 276, 284, 289, 293.
Boston Hill, 180.
Bowdoin, James, 265.
Bowker, Josiah, 248.
Bowman, Rev. 211, 212.
Bowman, James, 13.
Bradford, 224.
Bradford, Elizabeth, 218.
Bradish, Jonas, 52, 55, 131, 132.
Bradish, Mary, 204.
Bradshaw, Benj., 68, 80, 86, 92, 99.
Bradshaw, Nathan., 86.
Bradshaw, Parkman, 68, 69, 115, 180, 186.
Bradshaw, Wm., 94.
Braintree, New, 70, 131.
Breck, Hannah, 17, 21, 25, 29.
Breck, Rev. Robert, 21.
Breck, Robert, Jr., 257, 281, 287.
Bridge, Eben'r, 67.
Bridge, Rev. Josiah, 66, 68, 129, 157, 175, 192, 225, 279.
Bridgewater, 221.
Brigham, Anna, 66, 216, 261, 272.
Brigham, Anne, 62.
Brigham, Antipas, 194, 203.
Brigham, Asa, 190.
Brigham, Benaj., 80.
Brigham, Benj., 241.
Brigham, David, 14, 25, 37, 38, 42, 274.
Brigham, Edmund, 169, 194, 203, 226, 293.
Brigham, Edward, 169, 188.
Brigham, Eli, 138.
Brigham, Elijah, 61, 65, 66, 68, 70, 92, 97, 106, 108, 113, 115, 117, 122, 127, 128, 136, 176, 178, 183, 184, 189, 192, 221, 224, 237, 239, 244, 247, 249, 251, 252, 255, 258, 259, 264, 266, 268, 271, 272, 277, 288.

INDEX.   307

Brigham, Elizabeth, 78.
Brigham, Gershom, 192, 200, 241.
Brigham, Mrs. Gershom, 258, 263, 264, 266.
Brigham, Hepsibath, 194.
Brigham, Capt. Jonas, 83, 122, 131, 188, 194, 209, 277.
Brigham, Joseph, 241.
Brigham, Josiah, 77, 105, 184, 189, 208, 211, 212, 220, 224, 235, 248,
    249, 261, 262, 264, 272, 275.
Brigham, Col. Levi, 59, 65, 66, 122, 179, 189, 216, 221, 263, 277, 279,
    282, 288, 292.
Brigham, Levi, Jr., 264.
Brigham, Mary, 243.
Brigham, Mindwell, 66, 77, 216, 241, 272.
Brigham, Moses, 87, 97, 106, 110, 115, 181, 268.
Brigham, Nathan, 28, 51.
Brigham, Phineas, 98.
Brigham, Dr. Samuel, 62, 130, 168, 215.
Brigham, Samuel, 189, 248, 250, 251, 252.
Brigham, Silas, 26, 292.
Brigham, Timothy, 42.
Brigham, Uriah, 225.
Brigham, Wm., 188, 243.
Brigham, Mrs. Wm., 133, 243.
Brigham, Winslow, 66, 158, 200, 272.
Brimfield, 266.
Broaders, Hiram L., 112, 166.
Broaders, Jacob, 133, 166.
Brookfield, 68, 69, 80, 82, 86, 94, 99, 105, 107, 109, 115, 116, 123, 124,
    126, 148, 150, 155, 157, 173, 174, 181, 199, 207, 250, 265, 270, 274.
Brookfield, North, 83.
Brookline, 10, 35, 122.
Brown, Mrs. Elizabeth, 122, 124.
Brown, Rev. Joseph, 132.
Brown, Joseph, 105, 136, 163.
Brown, Polly, 155.
Bryant, Lieut. Daniel, 120.

Bryant, Elias, 113, 180.
Bryant, John, 113.
Bryant, Timothy, 134, 164. 178, 180.
Bruce, Artemas, 167.
Buckminster, Col. Wm., 213.
Buckminster, Rev. Joseph, 75, 213.
Buckley, Capt. Joseph, 9.
Bumpso, Sam'l, 13.
Burnett, Henrietta, 253, 255.
Burnett, Lois, 252, 253, 255.
Burr, Aaron, 58.
Burr, Rev. Isaac, 31, 37, 39, 40, 44, 45.
Burr, Thaddeus, 58.
Burroughs, Mrs. Richard, 39, 41.
Burying Ground, 43, 51, 78, 100, 110, 128, 153, 154, 199, 297.
Burying Ground in N'boro', 133.
Bush, Mrs. Jotham, 293.
Byfield, 76, 109, 128, 262.
Byles, Capt., 25, 37, 38, 39.
Cambridge, 9, 16, 35, 43, 68, 70, 72, 80, 82, 93, 124, 126, 148, 149, 158, 168, 171, 175, 180, 183, 208, 210, 218, 230, 241, 246, 262.
Camlet, 80.
Campbell, Wm., 187.
Canterbury, 175.
Cape Ann, 98.
Castle, the, 35, 36.
Chamberlain, Daniel, 126, 129.
Chamberlain, Eben'r, 260.
Chamberlain, Eben'r, Jr., 113, 128.
Chamberlain, Nat., 127.
Champney, Mary, 9.
Champney, Lydia, 9, 18, 29, 67, 71, 109, 134, 137, 162, 172, 219, 249, 250.
Champney, Ruth, 14.
Champney, Sam'l, 9, 16, 17, 18, 35, 219.
Chandler, Wm., 191.

Chandler, Coll., 21.
Charlton, 109.
Charlestown, 124, 172.
Chauncey Pond, 38, 40.
Chauxit, 59, 213, 225.
Cherry Valley, 77.
Child, Jonathan, 67, 287, 288.
Chubb, Eben'r, 43.
Clark, David, 125.
Clark, Capt. Isaac, 19.
Clung, John, 30, 37.
Common, the, 48.
Concord, 9, 39, 45, 62, 122, 134, 139, 172, 175, 211, 218, 241, 249, 271, 273, 292.
Contention Road, 126.
Cooledge, Pamela, 158, 233.
Cook, Cornelius, 16, 55, 72, 120, 159.
Cook, Molly, 16,
Cook, Robert, 120.
Cook, Stephen, 120.
Cook, Tom, 16, 35, 72, 120, 159.
Corey, Dr. F. E., 160.
Coi's Hill, 92, 181, 225, 281.
Crawford, John, 170.
Crookes, J., 83.
Crosby, Aaron, 180.
Crosby, Ebenezer, 223.
Crosby, Master John, 233, 270.
Crosby, Sally, 118.
Crosby, Sam'l, 180, 220, 259, 269, 270, 274, 278, 279, 281.
Curtis, Dr. Wm., 51.
Cushing, Alice, 272.
Cushing, Doddridge, 183.
Cushing, Madam, 152, 192.
Cushing, Col. Job, 40, 82, 96, 126, 135, 162.
Cushing, Rev. Job, 37, 39, 40, 45.

Cushing, John, 85, 120, 128, 135.
Cushing, Rev. John, 40, 120, 173, 183, 239, 240, 271, 273, 281.
Cushing, Sarah Parkman, 81, 82, 148, 271, 183, 269, 271, 273.
Cutter, Charles, 176.
Dana's Tavern, 35.
Dalrymple, Sam., 108.
Danforth, Thos., 9.
Dark Day, 235.
Dartmouth College, 66, 127, 168, 222.
David, Abimelech, 205.
Davis, Abigail, 187.
Davis, Isaac, 62, 111, 152, 166, 179, 247.
Davis, Gov. John, 62, 111.
Davis, Joseph, 111.
Davis, Phineas, 111.
Deadman, Wm., 120.
Death, Martha, 65.
Death, Oliver, 277.
Denny, Parkman T., 208.
Derby, Elias Hasket, 103.
Dix, James, 172, 230.
Dolliber, Deac., 183.
Dorr, Joseph, 232, 233.
Dudley, Paul, 32, 46.
Dummer School, 76, 123, 285.
Eager, Capt. James, 30, 39, 42, 43.
Electrical Machine, 105, 136.
Evans, Israel, 291.
Executions, 48, 182.
Fairbank, Drury, 150, 156.
Fairbank, Eleazar, 148.
Fairbank, Eph., 118.
Fairbanks, Isaiah, 136.
Fairfield, 58.
Faneuil Hall, 103.
Faneuil, Peter, 103.

Farrar, Joseph, 67.
Fay, Anna, 207, 213, 216.
Fay, Benj., 137, 153, 185, 216, 232, 282.
Fay, David, 163, 208.
Fay, Elizabeth, 154.
Fay, Ensign, 121.
Fay, Gershom, 42.
Fay, Jeduthun, 168.
Fay, James, 13, 38.
Fay, John, 81, 259, 260, 263.
Fay, Jonathan, 124, 138, 251.
Fay, Mehitable, 260.
Fay, Rebecca, 121.
Fay, Sam'l, 154, 168, 192, 258.
Fay, Stephen, 11, 14, 15, 22, 177, 178.
Fessenden, John, 111, 134, 166, 234.
Fessenden, Katharine, 166.
Fisher, Capt. Nathan, 89, 125, 151, 156, 174, 182, 205, 237, 240, 245, 252, 254, 255, 256, 283.
Fishkill, 78, 133, 145, 270, 294.
Fisk, Master Elisha, 76, 81, 82, 85, 95, 97, 105, 108, 287.
Fisk, Nathan, 80, 277.
Fisk, Patty, 76, 119, 253.
Fiske, Shepherd, 165, 167.
Fitch, Rev. Elijah, 139, 146, 151, 155, 190, 280, 281.
Fitch, Elijah, Jr., 155.
Fitchburg, 162.
Fitzpatrick, Dennis, 69.
Fitz-William, 293.
Flagg, Gershom, 217, 220.
Flag, Nathan, 162.
Flanders Road, 126.
Fletcher, John, 178.
Forbes, Daniel, 72, 82, 90, 107, 135, 138, 162, 168, 172, 177, 181, 197, 199.
Forbes, Mrs. Dan., 273, 275.

Forbes, Daniel, Jr., 86, 199, 207.
Forbes, Ebenezer, 172.
Forbes, Eli, 82, 97, 98, 107, 124, 126, 131, 137, 139, 151, 199, 219, 243, 248, 262, 270, 273.
Forbes, Elisha, 75, 77, 79, 81, 131, 134, 137, 148, 154, 155, 198, 207, 218, 275.
Forbes, John, 86, 116, 128, 130, 168, 200.
Forbes, Jonathan, 38, 72, 87, 110, 116, 176, 177, 207, 230, 242, 282.
Forbes, Mary Parkman, 39.
Forbes, Patience, 32.
Forbes, Thankful, 240.
Forbush, Abigail, 199.
Forbush, Anna, 178.
Forbush, Dan, 12.
Forbush, Eben'r, 72, 184, 262, 277.
Forbush, Hannah, 72.
Forbush, Isaac, 156.
Forbush, Patty, 72, 79, 80, 254.
Forbush, Rebecca, 38.
Forbush, Sam'l, 16, 36, 40, 131, 135, 190.
Forbush, Thos., 127, 144, 169, 203.
Foster, Edmund, 134.
Foster, Isaac, 131.
Foster, Jacob, 157, 171, 175.
Framingham, 19, 61, 106, 161, 191, 224, 235, 268, 287.
Frisbie, Levi, 69, 76.
Frost, Amariah, 57.
Frost, John, 275, 277.
Frost, Thos., 274, 275.
Gale, Abijah, 69, 115, 170, 171, 181, 186, 203, 242, 248, 262, 282, 287, 291.
Gale, Abraham, 169.
Garfield, Jacob, 277.
Garfield, Lydia, 146.
Gibson, James, 286.
Giles, Abigail, 258.
Giles, Sam'l, 258.

INDEX. 313

Gloucester, 107.
Goddard, Benj., 38.
Goddard, Daniel, 266.
Goddard, Edw., 38.
Goddard, Nathan, 192.
Godfry, Ruth, 52, 135.
Gookin, Daniel, 40.
Goodell, David, 78, 79, 99, 105, 136, 206.
Goss, Rev., 68, 129, 137, 151, 207.
Goss, Thos., 129.
Gott, Auna, 62.
Gott, Benj., 21, 29, 42, 62.
Gott, Sarah, 225.
Grafton, 13, 26, 41, 61, 92, 93, 105, 114, 138, 145, 151, 162, 222, 242, 269, 273.
Greenwood, Enoch, 211.
Grosvenor, Dan., 13, 86, 93, 105, 121, 123, 136, 138, 162, 222, 242, 266, 269, 273, 291.
Grosvenor, Eben'r, 293.
Grosvenor, Lemuel, 240.
Grosvenor, Nathan, 93.
Grout, Benj., 78, 181.
Grout, Daniel, 92.
Grout, Jonathan, 78, 160, 165, 173, 176, 186, 230, 265.
Grout, Joseph, 78, 80, 105, 145, 167, 173, 176, 178, 187.
Grout, Joseph, Jr., 111.
Grout, Mehitable, 87.
Grout, Moses, 78.
Grout, Wm., 78.
Green, Jane, 182.
Green, Joseph, 80, 92.
Greenleaf, Sheriff, 112, 162.
Guildford, New, 92.
Hall, Rev. David, 48, 85, 121, 155, 196, 223, 224, 235.
Hall, John'n, 147.
Hamilton, John, 30.

Hancock, John, 58, 91, 265.
Hardy, Constantine, 26, 83.
Hardy, Daniel, 12, 71, 250.
Hardy, Elijah, 105, 114, 136, 185.
Hardy, Hannah, 241, 256.
Hardy, Joseph, 154, 233, 236.
Hardy, Lucy, 241.
Hardy, Noah, 127, 275.
Hardy, Phineas, 135, 275.
Harding, Elias, 240.
Hardwick, 115, 208, 289.
Harvard College, 56, 58, 82, 265.
Harrington, Caleb, 70, 79, 115, 159, 185, 226, 294.
Harrington, Eli, 200.
Harrington, John, 123, 205, 278.
Harrington, Joseph, 69, 79, 135, 138, 150, 156, 176, 188, 230, 236, 276.
Harrington, Joshua, 43.
Harrington, Molly, 75.
Harrington, Sam'l, 211.
Harrington, Thos., 78.
Hartshorn, Eben'r, 164.
Harwood, Peter, 155.
Hasham, Mary, 162.
Hastings, Stewart, 247.
Hawes, James, 55, 82, 84, 94, 114, 117, 137, 143, 156, 164, 172, 180, 187, 190, 192, 215, 221, 223, 226, 231, 239, 240, 241, 246, 256, 261, 266, 276, 290.
Hawes, Mrs. James, 155, 258.
Hayward, Daniel, 45.
Hazelton, Judith, 154.
Hazeltine, Master, 166, 168, 169, 174, 179, 189, 190, 195, 200, 209, 211, 213, 236, 241, 257, 272, 279.
Henderson, Hugh, 20, 31, 37, 40, 41, 44, 46, 48.
Henstick, Rev., 136.
Hicks, John, 9, 30, 43.
Hicks, Ruth, 286.

Hicks, Zechary, 224, 249, 250.
Hill, Caleb, 286.
Hill, Silas, 280, 281.
Hitchcock, David, 107, 109.
Hobby, John'n, 139.
Holbrook, Dan., 127.
Holland, Abr'm, 117, 220, 245.
Holyoke, Elizur, 279, 288.
Hopkins, James, 227, 228.
Hopkinton, 98, 133, 146, 147, 152, 164, 204, 206, 220, 240, 244, 249, 265, 277, 280.
Houghton, Ezra, 55.
Hovey, Patience, 163.
How, Ben, 28, 67, 128.
How, Daniel, 111, 117, 128, 130, 133.
How, Eleazar, 21.
How, Oliver, 109.
How, Simon, 157, 189, 227.
Howe, Azubah, 180.
Howard, Polly, 119, 148.
Howell, Benj., 80.
Hubbard, Capt., 155.
Hubbardston, 192.
Hutchinson, Aaron, 13.
Hutchinson, Aaron, Jr., 113, 114.
Hystop, Mehitable, 122.
Indian Harvest, 25.
Indians, 20, 25, 144.
Ipswich, 76, 167.
Jackstraw, 75, 199.
Jarvis, John, 16.
Jenison, Wm., 258.
Johnson, Edw., 129.
Johnson, Elliot, 279.
Johnson, John, 242.
Johnson, Joshua, 70.

Johnson, Stephen, 279.
Johnson, Susannah, 57.
Johnson, Wm., 144.
Johnson, Mrs. Wm., 245.
Jones, Landlord, 181.
Jones, Nancy, 164.
Jones, Sam'l, 117.
Kelley, John, 120.
Kelly, Mrs., 59, 111, 128, 206, 228.
Kellogg, David, 287.
Kendal, Thos., 60, 250.
Kenney, Joel, 256, 277.
Kenney, Nathan, 155, 226, 228, 278.
Keyes, Justice, 14.
King, Jerusha, 155.
Kittery, 250.
Knight, Wm., 241.
Knowlton, Mrs. Joseph, 258.
Lambert, Julia, 91.
Lamson, Paul, 251.
Lamson, Thos., 263, 278, 282.
Lamson, Mrs., 149, 163, 212, 213.
Lancaster, 161, 224.
Langdon, Pres., 113.
Lawson, Sam., 150.
Lee, Joseph, 125.
Leominster, 163.
Lewis, Mary, 79.
Littleton, 113.
Livermore, Elisha, 290.
Lock, Frederic, 241.
Loring, Father, 117, 122, 124.
Loring, Jonathan, 105.
Lynde, Benj., 46.
Maccarty, Rev. Thaddeus, 176, 182, 239.
McTaggart, James, 78.

Mallet, Mrs., 122, 125, 127.
Mansfield, 124, 227.
Marble, Henry, 68, 70.
Marblehead, 79, 129, 183.
Marlborough, 9, 16, 18, 21, 25, 28, 42, 100, 109, 111, 113, 129, 134, 136, 157, 163, 175, 182, 206, 225, 263, 279, 293.
Martha's Vineyard, 30, 149.
May, Wm., 124, 125, 139.
Maynard, Amasa, 83, 212, 263.
Maynard, David, 151, 249.
Maynard, Eben'r, 57, 59, 70, 110, 187, 206, 215, 248, 278.
Maynard, Eben'r, Jr., 104.
Maynard, Harvey, 189.
Maynard, Hezekiah, 158, 182, 227, 288.
Maynard, James, 83, 212, 263.
Maynard, James, Jr., 248.
Maynard, John, 51, 119, 192.
Maynard, Jon'n, 93, 190, 224, 263.
Maynard, Lucy, 207, 218, 290.
Maynard, Nathan, 65, 67, 80, 83, 151, 192, 205, 219, 276.
Maynard, Nathan, Jr., 79, 92, 98, 188, 190, 216, 220.
Maynard, Neh'h, 81, 82, 192.
Maynard, Rhoda, 183.
Maynard, Stephen, 62, 63, 79, 83, 84, 111, 119, 122, 123, 130, 137, 168, 171, 206, 214, 221, 228, 271, 283, 284.
Maynard, Mrs. Stephen, 71, 76, 78, 81, 85, 99, 106, 111, 113, 117, 121, 127, 133, 135, 139, 149, 150, 164, 174, 181, 185, 190, 215, 225, 227, 231, 246, 252, 257, 259, 261, 271, 274, 279, 282, 286, 288, 290, 293.
Maynard, Stephen, Jr., 84, 97, 121, 130, 158, 226, 291.
Maynard, Thankful, 189.
Maynard, Winslow, 248.
Martyn, Nabby, 76, 241, 262, 287, 288.
Mather, Rev. Sam'l, 18.
Mathias, Dan, 186.
Medfield, 112, 140, 147, 233.
Mendon, 134.

Messenger, Esther, 57.
Milford, 57.
Miller, Aaron, 276.
Miller, Dan'l, 293.
Miller, Eben'r, 184.
Miller, Fortunatus, 72, 254.
Miller, Isaac, 107, 127.
Miller, James, 250.
Miller, Sarah, 130, 169.
Monanaow, David, 25, 205.
Montague, 125.
Moore, Rev. John'n, 94, 109, 111, 140, 169, 220, 232, 233, 259, 287.
Morey, George, 292.
Morse, Sally, 286.
Morse, Seth, 100, 109, 188, 212, 256, 275, 283, 284.
Mottey, Joseph, 227.
Natalitia, 165, 269, 294.
Nawgawwoomcom, 25.
Needham, 149.
Needham, Thos., 133.
Newel, Rev. 117, 157, 246, 279.
New Connecticut Road, 30.
New Fane, 212.
New Haven, 30, 147, 148.
New Marlboro', 161.
Newton, 149.
Newton, Abner, 20, 45, 120.
Newton, Barnabas, 92, 95, 125, 137, 172, 185, 205, 218.
Newton, Charles, 76, 93.
Newton, John, 274, 289.
Newton, Josiah, 25.
Newton, Paul, 162.
Newton, Stephen, 274.
Northborough, 30, 61, 89, 111, 117, 130, 133, 137, 139, 162, 190, 227, 239, 243, 246, 263, 264, 273.
Northampton, 21.

Nottingham, Mary, 285, 287, 289.
Nourse, B. A., 121, 153.
Nurse, Benj., 121.
Nurse, Eben, 13, 119.
Nurse, Daniel, 121, 130, 136, 139, 152, 167.
Nurse, Lydia, 121, 136, 168.
Nurse, Mary, 121.
Nurse, Moses, 145, 216, 228.
Nurse, Priscilla, 121.
Nurse, Rebecca, 121, 136, 168, 183, 184, 186, 188.
Nurse, Wm., 121.
Old Mill Road, 242.
Old, Town Folks, 170.
Oliver, Alexander, 82.
Otter Creek, 77, 86, 105, 116, 168, 200.
Oxford, 48, 109, 181, 187.
Packard, Winslow, 56.
Paine, Timothy, 232.
Parker, Anna, 183.
Parker, Amos, 121, 125, 128, 152, 169, 216.
Parker, Elisha, 89, 92, 93, 113, 185, 190, 216.
Parker, Ephrm., 106, 107, 109, 117, 128, 135, 146, 149, 155, 182, 184, 185, 203 207, 220, 240.
Parker, Gardner, 286.
Parker, Hannaniah, 59, 80, 107, 197, 237, 252, 268.
Parker, Isaac, 59, 106, 151, 177, 182, 183, 188, 189, 216, 240, 247, 254, 275, 286.
Parker, Joel, 286.
Parker, Margery, 182.
Parker, Timothy, 113, 200.
Parkhurst, Wm., 92.
Parkman, Abigail, 100.
Parkman, Alexander, 110, 163, 213, 264, 266, 268, 280.
Parkman, Anna Sophia, 60, 66, 75, 77, 109, 119, 128, 131, 136, 137, 174, 184, 219, 221, 244, 248, 252, 264, 272.
Parkman, Breck, is mentioned too often to index.
Parkman, Ebenr., Jr., 29, 66, 99, 105, 107, 221, 244, 292, 294.

Parkman, Elias (Brother), 17, 35.
Parkman, Elias (Son), is mentioned too often to index.
Parkman, Elizabeth 10.
Parkman, Eliza S., 103.
Parkman, Francis, 103.
Parkman, Hannah, 100, 247, 292.
Parkman, John, 161, 188, 271.
Parkman, Kezia, 161.
Parkman, Lydia, 161, 175, 228, 229.
Parkman, Neddy, 158.
Parkman, Sally, 86, 100, 123, 124, 128, 149, 172, 242, 271, 273.
Parkman, Sam'l, 100, 117, 123, 126, 187, 219, 234, 243, 248, 271, 273.
Parkman, Sophy, 164.
Parkman, Sukey, 271.
Parkman, Susé (Concord), 175.
Parkman, Thos., 221, 224.
Parkman, Wm. (Boston), 10, 39, 235, 237, 243.
Parkman, Wm. (Son), 109, 134, 159, 164, 218, 228, 229, 271, 273, 279.
Parmenter, Bethiah, 190.
Parsons, Sol., 124.
Perry, Aaron, 177.
Petersham, 91, 163, 168.
Philip's Manor, 292.
Pierce, Francis, 39.
Pierce, Jon'n, 251.
Pigeon, Henry, 155.
Pigeon, John, 147, 148.
Pollard Place, 43.
Pomfret, 89, 105, 191.
Porter, Huntingdon, 249.
Powder Hill, 30.
Potter, Moses, 167.
Potter, Mrs. J. D., 100.
Pratt, Eleazar, 26.
Pratt Eliz., 151.
Pratt, Isaac, 208.

Pratt, John, 36.
Pratt, Molly, 92.
Pratt, Susanna, 93.
Prentice, Henry, 166.
Prentice, Sol., 13, 14, 19, 26, 30, 41.
Prescott, Dr. Jon'n, 9.
Providence, 105.
Puffer, Reuben, 192.
Purpoodock, 145.
Quincy, Dorothy, 58.
Quincy, Edmund, 46, 57, 112, 140, 155, 173, 174, 187, 206, 214, 218, 229, 259, 261, 273, 277, 291.
Quincy, Eunice, 140.
Quincy, Henry, 57, 140, 241.
Quincy, I., 148.
Quincy, Jacob, 58.
Rand, Wm., 165, 167.
Reading, 91.
Remington, John'n, 46.
Revere, Paul, 103.
Rice, Adonijah, 125.
Rice, Dolly, 130, 149, 181, 269.
Rice, Edmund, 83, 263.
Rice, Elias, 13.
Rice, Nahor, 100.
Rice, Noah, 13.
Rice, Moses, 43.
Rice, Seth, 25, 42, 228.
Rice, Solomon, 13.
Rice, Thomas, 20, 37, 45.
Rice, Zebulon, 13, 164, 168, 274.
Rider, Eleazar, 226.
Rider, Sam'l, 242, 263.
Ripley, Rev. David, 161.
Ripley, Rev. Ezra, 71, 109, 134, 241.
Robertson, Beverly, 292.

Rochester, 149.
Rogers, John, 13, 28.
Rogers, Sarah, 103.
Rogers, Wm., Jr., 38.
Ruggles, Isaac, 251.
Rutland, 37, 75.
Salem, 133, 144, 258.
Saltonstall, Rich., 46.
Sanders, Mrs. Lucy, 82.
Sanger, Dave, 84.
Sargent, Henry, 103.
Sargent, John, 223.
Saunders, Charlotte, 137.
Saunders, Jo., 270, 273.
Savage, Ezek., 260.
Sawyer, David, 106.
Schools, 82, 87, 166, 293.
Sewall, Sam'l, 32, 58.
Sharpe, Robert, 10, 18, 35.
Sharpe, Susanna, 10, 18.
Shaw, Coll. R. G., 103.
Shaw, Sam'l, 103.
Shaw, Sarah, 100.
Shaw, Wm., 103.
Shawmut, 25.
Sherman, Nath., 75.
Sherman, Sam'l, 175.
Shrewsbury, 30, 40, 88, 97, 117, 120, 125, 128, 135, 148, 152, 153, 161, 169, 180, 192, 194, 239, 258, 272, 273, 274, 276, 278, 281.
Simon, Daniel, 222.
Singleterry, Squire, 268.
Slave labor, 62.
Small pox, 98.
Smith, Rev. Aaron, 68, 129, 137, 157, 175, 225, 246, 279.
Smith, James, 107, 125.
Smith, Joseph, 123, 233, 253.

Smith, Sarah, 152.
Snow, Ensign, 127, 144, 241.
Snow, Mrs. Susan, 247.
Snow, Thos., 10.
Southborough, 42, 69, 71, 96, 162, 163, 175, 183, 207, 241, 260, 291.
Sparhawk, Ebenezer, 113, 248.
Sprague, John, 232.
Spring, Billy, 77, 135, 211, 219, 231, 261, 266, 267.
Spy, Worc., 85, 144, 178, 184, 192, 215, 295.
Squam, 124.
Stearns, Wm., 203, 232.
Stevens, Chas. E., 31.
Stevens, John, 124.
Stillman, Major, 126.
Stimson, George, 127, 128.
Stimson, Jeremy, 98, 109, 120, 159, 164, 220, 244.
Stimson, Stephen, 267.
Stockbridge, 120, 223.
Stockwell, Daniel, 277.
Stone, Benj., 97.
Stone, N., 41.
Stone, Thomas, 71, 222.
Stone, Rev., 96, 112, 115, 129, 137, 157, 162, 163, 175, 189, 219, 225, 246, 261, 291.
Stoneham, 134, 180.
Stony Point, 148.
Storm, 81, 162, 195, 196.
Stoughtonham, 86, 180.
Stow, 117.
Sturbridge, 164.
Sudbury, 11, 19, 66, 129.
Sumner, Increase, 10, 17.
Sumner, Rev. Jos., 88, 93, 95, 96, 117, 136, 152, 161, 168, 169, 192, 228, 258, 268, 276, 278.
Sutton, 48, 58, 85, 120, 126, 130, 136, 143, 162, 172, 196, 220, 264, 268.
Swamp, Wild Cat, 26, 146.

Tainter, Benj., 154, 162, 176, 244, 246, 274.
Tainter, Simon, 11, 51, 56, 110, 244.
Tainter, Simon, Jr., 14, 43.
Taylor, Betsey, 222.
Taylor, Hezekiah, 212.
Templeton, 113.
Tewksbury, 122, 123.
Thanksgiving, 70, 71, 81, 180, 291.
Thayer, John, 164.
Thomas, Isaiah, 144.
Thompson, Joseph, 189.
Thurston, Sam'l, 246, 251, 262.
Thurston, Sarah, 248, 251.
Thyery, Dr., 14, 15, 19, 22.
Tilestone, Mary, 10.
Tomlin, Isaac, 112.
Townsend, 122.
Townsend, Lieut., 160.
Trowbridge, Lieut., 9.
Tucker, Eph'm, 172.
Tuckerman, Mrs. Edw., 22, 39.
Twitchell, John'n, 177.
Twitchell, Joshua, 254.
Twitchell, Thos., 165.
Upton, 105, 151.
Wait, Thad., 286.
Walcott, Sol., 124.
Wall, Caleb, 31, 44.
Walley Brethren, 118.
Walpole, 194.
Waltham, 135.
Ward, 232, 249.
Ward, Artemas, 95, 175.
Ward, Deborah, 27.
Ward, Increase, 45.
Ward, John'n, 112.

Ware, Beriah, 255, 258, 286.
Warren, Aaron, 125.
Warren, Benj., 143.
Warren, Eunice, 215.
Warren, James, 265.
Warren, John, 178, 256.
Warren, Jonas, 121, 146, 213, 214.
Warren, Levi, 71, 166, 176, 181, 235, 274, 280.
Warren, Moses, 151, 187.
Warren, Thad., 69, 106, 215, 221, 222, 229, 236, 248, 251, 254, 262, 274, 275, 289, 292, 294.
Warren, Thos., 97.
Warren, Tim., 13, 145, 277.
Warwick, 166.
Watertown, 9, 11, 106, 279.
Waters, Cornelius, 288, 290, 291.
Waters, Sam'l, 268.
Webber, James, 145, 147.
Weeks, Coll., 157, 279.
Weston, 109, 134.
Wetmore, Rebecca, 219.
Wheeler, Joseph, 232.
Wheelock, Eleazar, 189.
Wheelock, Eph., 164.
Wheelock, Moses, 172, 186, 217, 278, 286.
Whipple, Squire, 139, 163, 169.
Whiting, Rev. John, 9, 39.
Whitney, Aaron, 91, 163, 168.
Whitney, Eli, 92, 113, 154, 173, 176, 177, 184, 230.
Whitney, Elijah, 154.
Whitney, Hannah, 123, 136, 140.
Whitney, Mrs. Israel, 9.
Whitney, Nath., 136.
Whitney, Peter, 68, 89, 114, 117, 119, 129, 137, 138, 151, 155, 157, 162, 192, 227, 229, 230, 232, 234, 238, 246, 258, 264, 269, 273, 279, 283.
Whitney, Thos., 59, 153, 214, 282.

Whitney, Tim., 59, 154.
Wightman, Rob., 288, 289.
Wigwam Tree, 25, 205
Wilder, Luke, 115.
Willard, Aaron, 145, 163.
Willard, Benj., 145.
Willard, Simon, 145, 151.
Williams, Lucy, 89.
Williams, Sam'l, 119, 224, 230.
Williams Tavern, 25.
Wilson, Benj., Jr., 189.
Wilson, Rob., 59.
Wiman, Sarah, 135.
Winchester, Billy, 189, 192, 211, 212, 220, 222, 224, 229, 230.
Winchester, Jon'n, 212.
Winchester, Thos., 13.
Wit, Sam'l, 157.
Wood, Abr'm, 229, 234, 252.
Wood, Benj., 67, 184, 227, 262, 276, 280, 284, 285, 291.
Wood, Dea. James, 28, 89, 111, 114, 122, 157, 165, 166, 172, 176, 181, 187, 190, 200, 205, 206, 218, 221, 222, 228, 234, 244, 248, 253, 255, 257, 264, 278.
Wood, Capt. John, 112, 122, 127, 170, 172, 182, 222, 231, 251, 276, 280, 283, 284, 291.
Wood, John, 261, 265, 284.
Wood, Joseph, 265.
Wood, Polly, 258.
Wood, Reuben, 184.
Wood, Sam'l, 229.
Wood, Seth, 144.
Wood, Thomas, 265.
Wood, Wm., 204.
Woods Isaac, 292.
Woodstock, 21.
Woodward, Sam'l, 109, 134.
Workhouse, 145, 277.

Worcester, 31, 39, 40, 43, 45, 46, 80, 151, 178, 181, 182, 190, 232, 251.
Wrentham, 55.
Yale College, 113.
Young, Robert, 182.

www.ingramcontent.com/pod-product-compliance
Lightning Source LLC
Chambersburg PA
CBHW030013240426
43672CB00007B/931